Rachael Gurney was born in 1965 in Buckinghamshire, and grew up in West Sussex and The Netherlands. She developed a love of travelling, having been fortunate to go on holidays abroad, from a tender age. After graduating, she worked in the catering industry which funded more foreign trips. The desire to travel, however, proved so strong that she changed career in 1993, to teach English as a foreign language, which provided a route to living abroad. She has visited nearly forty countries and lived in four. Now based in London, she takes any opportunity to travel.

Digging for Australia

Memories of countries lived in

and places visited on the way

Rachael Gurney

authorHOUSE®

AuthorHouse™ UK Ltd.
500 Avebury Boulevard
Central Milton Keynes, MK9 2BE
www.authorhouse.co.uk
Phone: 08001974150

First published by AuthorHouse 6/4/2010

ISBN: 978-1-4520-1716-7 (sc)

This book is printed on acid-free paper.

For my lovely Dad, Alan Gurney

*He lived in different countries, visited many more and instilled
in me my love of other places and cultures. His enthusiasm
for experiencing things different to our own was completely
infectious.
I miss him every day, but when I am somewhere new, enjoy
imagining what he might have felt.*

Acknowledgments

I would like to take this opportunity to thank my family
and friends who I have shared these (on the whole)
wonderful experiences with. Also, to my grandfather, seen
below, telling me about raining frogs in India.

Contents

Part One

A baby explorer

Up a mountain in the Bernese Oberland, Switzerland

Chapter 1

How did I end up here?

Why is it that just when we have everything and are completely settled, that wanderlust suddenly appears and slaps you across the face? For me it was when staggering into an enticing *pâtisserie*, nested in the old walls of St-Malo, very hungover and sleep deprived, thanks to an overnight ferry trip. The hangover was due to the misguided thought that if I drank enough Jack Daniels in the ferry bar even I'd be able to sleep on one of those reclining seats in a ferry lounge. Wrong! And who designed them with metal arms so that each time you are anywhere near dropping off some part of flesh would touch the cold metal and you're wide awake again.

Anyway, despite all this, the *pâtisserie* wove its usual spell and the smell of freshly baked pastries and the look of the chocolate éclairs reminded me that I was back in glorious France. By the time I'd paid and was leaving the shop it was a done deal. I was going to have to move to France. Why now? I'd been to France so many times and despite having longings and vague thoughts about living there, had never done anything about it. Of course, for everyone who has experienced that need to go elsewhere there's very little you can do. Whether it's some divine intervention I have no idea, but the force is so powerful nothing can be done about it.

What's the big deal you might say? Lots of people have left the security of their jobs, family and friends in the UK, or wherever else they come from, for the uncertainty of that "Better Place". Fair enough, but I'd already done that once; left the UK in 1993, having retrained as a TEFL teacher, and moved to the north of Portugal.

So, here I was, seven and a half years later, full of thoughts of fresh bread and red wine - willing to give up all the security of a good, well-paid job running a language school in Porto and leave a centrally-located flat that had become home; not to mention lots of wonderful friends, and one of the most beautiful cities I know. And what for? To start again in France.

However, I knew then that nothing could happen for a while. The new academic year was about to begin so moving would have to wait. The following summer was put aside for a long-dreamed of holiday to Australia, so with finances fairly stretched nothing was going to happen until the following year. So, it was in the summer of 2002, two years after I'd walked into that *pâtisserie* that I moved to France. That makes it sound so easy which of course it wasn't.

Anyway, more of that later. What I am wondering is why there are some of us who are continually on the move. Whether it's having to visit new cities and countries all the time, moving abroad permanently, or moving between countries; it seems that some of us are genetically wired that way. Apart from being exhausting it's also hideously expensive. I wonder how many third world debts I could have paid off if I'd just stayed put! Maybe there is a gene in some of us, maybe it depends how we were brought up and by whom. Maybe a mixture; I'm not sure.

For me, it is possibly a mixture – I certainly know that from an early age I was aware that there was more than the home counties of England. My first vague recollection that there was something out there to explore was probably when my Granddad talked to me about some place where it rained frogs. At the time of course, being a child, I completely believed it - some mysterious place where such things happened. It was only later that I knew that the place was India, and that the only mystery was some bizarre meteorological phenomena.

My second recollection of exotic places was watching Dad's slides projected onto the living room wall. I know that holiday photos can send the best of us to sleep but these were different. Set against glorious red sunsets in Kenya, there were pictures of lions, elephants, rhinos, zebras and many other animals I couldn't identify then.

Bizarrely enough, being the countries that first intrigued me, India and Kenya are two of the places which I haven't visited yet, although India remains at the top of my current "must visit" list. However, the travel seed was sown then, and it was just a case of working out how I was going to do it.

Naturally, it was more then just these two occasions that installed in me my love of travel. I was blessed with having a wonderful father who had travelled throughout the world in the early 1960's and was more than happy to share his tales. What's more he had managed to do it with someone else paying; firstly through his national service in Africa and then with the Merchant Navy to Central America and to the other end of the earth to Australia and New Zealand. I even remember him telling me that he had been to the Pitcairn Islands where the locals had thrown fresh fruit on board for them. My own early memories of travelling were nowhere near as exotic, nevertheless they were very powerful. My first recollections are of eating chocolate crêpes in Brittany aged five and walking up a mountain and eating an Emmental sandwich, followed by a huge slab of chocolate in Switzerland, aged six.

Chapter 2

Cuckoo Clocks

We were camping in Interlaken, in Switzerland. That was before the days of staying in hotels or apartments. However, it was really only pretend camping. All we had to do was find the campsite, and there was our tent. Good old Canvas Holidays. The tent had two separate sleeping areas; one for Mum and Dad and other another for my little sister, Catherine and I. There was also a small kitchen area. No trying to erect a tent, either in the dark, or after too much red wine – especially when you have no idea what you are doing – as in my later camping experiences.

Looking back at the scrapbook, which I had fortunately made at the time, and the millions of slides Dad took, I can also just remember how beautiful it all was: the green valleys, snow topped peaks and chocolate box houses, dominated by the Jungfrau and the Eiger. Being only six at the time though, the most exciting thing was the transport we used - be it the funicular railway to Kolm, the train to Scheindegg or a cable car up to a peak, which were always the highlights of my day. For me, hanging out of a window or swinging in a cable car was always better than the view itself. My mother didn't agree; she turned positively green during these trips, and didn't look at anything apart from the floor.

One day, returning to our splendid tent we found that mice had been tucking into anything they could get their paws on. Having a pet mouse at home, I found this all quite cute, much to the annoyance of my parents. They spent ages concocting some method of hanging the food from the tent poles, only to find that on our return the next day the mice had managed to shin up the pieces of string, and continue their feasting; so, from then on all the food had to be stored in the car. At this point with a general cursing of all things rodent-like, I became very preoccupied with the long-term safety of "Jerry the mouse" back home. One step out of line, and I dreaded what might happen to him!

One other thing that stands out from this holiday is being given my first watch. Since I had recently learnt to tell the time, Dad had promised that for my birthday he would buy me a watch from Zurich. I can remember the awe as we walked into a beautiful Swiss watch shop. I wore said watch proudly for years, until it mysteriously disappeared when in my father's care. I'd badgered him for days as to its whereabouts, after he'd taken it to be mended, but he couldn't remember what had happened to it. I never did find out which black hole swallowed it up. Forgetting things and people was a recurring occurrence with Dad. Once, when living in Holland years later, I was babysitting in The Hague. That evening Dad arrived home (some kilometres outside The Hague) to a very surprised Mum, since he'd forgotten to collect me!

The other truly memorable thing about that holiday was that it was the first time I went to Paris. I guess that was when my love affair with the country started. Immediately, I was overcome by the splendour of the place. It was just so gracious; with wide avenues, beautiful buildings and, of course, the Tour Eiffel. No doubt we drove our parents crazy by asking every thirty seconds when we were going to go up it. Very soon we wore them down and got our wish. In those days there were no nets on the top level which now stops people jumping off, or throwing off ten centime pieces, which apparently could split your scull open if you were unfortunate enough to be underneath.

What an amazing view it was. I hung over the edge for ages, walking all the way round with Dad pointing things out. All this time Mum got greener and greener, and begged us to come away from the edge. She finally got her way and we descended in the rickety old lift. I've visited the Eiffel Tower many times since – once with a boyfriend and we romantically sat in the first floor café, watching the sunset, drinking kir, knowing the bill would probably have bought us dinner. However, nothing can take away that first impression of a six-year-old.

It was some years later, on a visit en-route to somewhere else, that Paris made its second huge impression on me. I remember that by this time my brother had arrived and was about three so I must have been thirteen. We were staying in the same hotel (called the Concortel Hotel or something similar) we'd stayed in before, which I loved for its black and white tiled floor, and curly stairs with iron banisters, and the fact that it was so close to the Champs-Élysées. One evening after dinner Dad wanted to go for a wander and then to sit in a café. Mum was tired so took my brother and sister back to the hotel. I, however, managed to persuade Dad to take me with him. I felt so grown up walking along the wide avenue, and then to my delight we went to one of the pavement cafés with the clear screens so you can see what everybody else is doing. I was allowed to have a glass of red wine mixed with water. It may sound horrible but it's what French children apparently drank, and to me was the height of sophistication. I'm sure it was then that my love affair with red wine started.

My love affair with food, however, started on an early holiday. It was en route to that first holiday in Switzerland. We stopped in Arras in northern France for the night and stayed in a hotel right on the Grand Place. The hotel, the *Grandes Arcades* was typically French, with bedrooms with non-matching furniture, threadbare carpets, those round, excruciatingly uncomfortable pillows, and a dash down the corridor to go to the toilet. The restaurant, however, was completely different. A beautiful black and white checked floor, stone walls and wooden beams on the ceiling. Being considerably older now, and despite my elephant memory for meals eaten, even I have no idea what I ate that night, but I know it was gorgeous and remember being delighted in future holidays when we were able to stop there. The square also sticks in my mind. I think it's probably my favourite one in the whole world. I'm not exactly sure why. It's not that large, hasn't got any spectacular buildings, doesn't have southern European light to set it off but all the same is stunning. Maybe it's because I remember being so happy there.

During the same holiday, on our return from Switzerland we discovered another similar hotel restaurant which was to become a family favourite. It was stuck in the middle of nowhere, next to a road, had the same bedroom decor of the preceding hotel, but had an even more fantastic restaurant. Unfortunately I can't remember what it was called, but I remember the food surpassing that of the *Grandes Arcades* and have a vague recollection that I may have had Fruits de Mer there for the first time.

We definitely weren't your usual British kids abroad, demanding fish fingers or suchlike. I'm sure this played a vital part in developing my love of food. I can still happily sit and read a recipe book with a friend, whose girlfriend thinks we're both very sad! Who cares! I'm definitely one of those who 'lives to eat'. Whether eating river prawns next to a swirling river near Jalapa in Mexico, cooking a Thai dinner in my mad cellar kitchen (with a shower in it!) for friends in Portugal or pouring over food markets in Singapore, it's become a real passion. In fact, my first food memory is probably from the holiday abroad the year before Switzerland. We went to La Baule in Brittany where we camped. I have no recollections at all of this holiday apart from the amazing chocolate crêpes, which I badgered my parents to buy for me every day.

Chapter 3

All things French

But, I'm digressing widely here. After my first taste of camping in Switzerland, we again did camping the easy way, the following year. It was 1973 and we stayed in Royan and then the Dordogne. I can't remember much about Royan but it was probably this holiday when I discovered the delight of steak frites from the campsite café. I'm not sure if they did anything else but it was all I wanted, and was a real treat after Mum's somewhat bizarre camping meals.

At that point I don't think The Dordogne was quite as overrun by Brits as it is now, and was a wonderful place to explore. I remember visiting a variety of châteaux, the beautiful town of Sarlat and various prehistoric sites. These, of course, were nothing compared to the Cougnac caves with their amazing animal drawings. I've always loved caves, especially those with stalactites and stalagmites, and although I probably didn't understand the enormity of these paintings was nonetheless amazed. Now, with similar caves closed, I realise how very fortunate I was.

All this seems very cultural for an eight-year-old, but I also remember a lot of messing around in rivers. The details of the other parts of that holiday are very vague although I do remember it being enjoyable, even more so for the return to the same nameless restaurant we'd discovered the year before, on the way back.

By the following summer of 1974 Dad was working a lot in Paris, so a traditional family holiday wasn't on the cards. However, the next best thing was a trip there to see him. My mother, sister and I had got the ferry to Le Havre, and then the train down to Paris. We stayed in the same hotel, the Concortel, just off the Champs- Élysées. It was where Dad always stayed whilst on business – no restaurant or anything, but a wonderful location. What I remember clearly about my second visit to Paris is that we visited Versailles for the first time. It truly was like visiting a palace from a fairy tale – numerous rooms decorated in opulent materials, over the top furniture, and, of course, those beautiful ceilings. My mother says that from that day I was (and still am) fascinated by them, and spent most of that visit, and countless other ones to castles or cathedrals, walking round looking upwards at the ceilings, continuously careering into anything or anyone in my path. The gardens were equally fantastic, those beautiful terraces that descend as far as the eye could see, each with its own fountain. And, of course, despite being very young, there was a morbid interest in the fact that a certain queen had lived at Versailles and had her head chopped off!!! I was sure as we were walking round I could hear the Red Queen muttering, "Off with her head, off with her head…."

Having been to Paris two years previously I'm sure that some of my memories are mixed up but I do remember the return journey to Le Havre by train. For some reason we couldn't get seats together and I remember having to sit on my own surrounded by Frenchman in suits. These days I'd be fighting to sit next a Frenchman but then it was a terrifying prospect!!

The summer of 1975 and we were off to on another ferry, but this time to The Isle of Wight. Where? What was happening? It wasn't even very far away and definitely not foreign. The reason was a baby brother, Matthew, who had arrived thanks to the allure of romantic Paris. Mum didn't want to travel abroad so there we were, taking the ferry across the Solent. What a comedown from the big cross channel ferries we were used to. I can't remember my reaction to the whole thing but I'm sure there were some annoying questions asked. No doubt we had an excellent holiday but very little sticks in my mind apart from the dinosaurs in Blackgang Chine, and a crooked house somewhere.

Fortunately, it was back to the "proper" holidays the following year. It was again in France and to a tiny village called Arre, close to Le Vigan in the Cévennes. We were staying in my Godparents house. I remember it being tall and thin, built of huge chunks of stone. I think my Godfather had done most of the alterations himself. The one abiding memory I have is of the loo. It was literally a hole in the floor, which you squatted over. And if I'm not wrong, to make it into a shower a duck board was put down and there you were!!! Not really sophisticated enough for an eleven-year-old.

One afternoon, I remember having a walk and stopping on the bridge. My sister and I were casually leaning against the metal rails when we heard a low humming. Then, out of nowhere an enormous swarm of wasps appeared. Apparently unprovoked, they decided they were very pissed off about something and descended on my poor sister, deciding I wasn't of any interest. Well, you have never heard such a noise as the women of the village made. To the screaming of my sister they came running from their houses, all with a different remedy for wasp stings. Fortunately Catherine was ok, but I do remember my repeating over and over "I didn't do anything, it wasn't me!" Guilty conscience or what!

The other main event of that holiday was something which was to help (although that isn't really quite the correct word) shape the direction of my life in twenty-five years time, in ways I could never imagine. It was to nearby Montpellier that we went on a visit one day. I remember the city itself having lots of narrow interesting streets, beautiful buildings and lots of pavement cafés. We also drove south of the city towards the Mediterranean and on the way passed lagoons full of beautiful, pink flamingos. That day was spent on the beach in a place called Carnon. Somehow it must have all made a huge impression on an eleven-year-old, because it was to the same area that I decided to uproot and move to when I had my 'pâtisserie' moment and decided that France was where I had to be.

In the summer of 1977 we set off on another French holiday; this time to the Auvergne. We'd rented a large, holiday villa with some friends in a small mountain village called Picherande, at the foot of the mountains. We spent a lot of the holiday lazing around, and exploring the local countryside. We did, however, have a few trips further afield, and one day travelled to Puy-de-Dôme. We took the cable car up to the Mont-Dore which I remember being very cold for the time of year, but with fantastic views.

Somehow, during that holiday we ended up helping a local farmer with the harvest. On a boiling hot day we found ourselves in a huge sun-baked field with no shade raking the hay which hadn't been made into bails. I'm sure it wasn't what we were supposed to be doing on holiday but was a real experience, and made even better by the lunch of fresh bread, St. Nectaire cheese, and local wine. I can remember in years to come searching for the same cheese and being able to find it in the Food Hall in Harrods – not cheap of course, but worth every penny.

On the return trip we stayed in Bayeux. Obviously famous for its tapestry, the city itself was stunning. The cathedral – a mixture of styles with two Roman spires, a Roman nave, and the Gothic elevation above, dominated it. Naturally, we went to see the tapestry which was housed in what had once been the Dean's house. Despite not being a huge history fan, the tapestry was amazing for its detail and the telling of a story, and that it had been so wonderfully maintained.

A couple of years later, in 1979, we returned again to France. This time the holiday was split between Houlgate in Normandy, and the Loire Valley. All I remember of Houlgate is going to nearby Pont- l'Evêque, where we had a gorgeous meal at "Le Lion d'Or", and where we ate enormous amounts of the ubiquitous cheese. After that, each time Dad went on business to Paris, we'd beg him to bring back some of the smelliest cheese in the world; he would oblige and stink the plane out.

However, despite remembering little of the first part of the holiday it was a different case for the second week. The Loire Valley left a huge impression on me. We wandered round endless châteaux; me, obviously, with my head inclined upwards gazing at the ornate and, frankly, from time-to-time over the top ceilings. However, nothing prepared me for the beauty and splendour of Chenonceau. We walked up a lovely, tree lined road toward the château, which was hidden by the trees until the last bend. There it stood. A beautiful building perched on a number of arches spanning the river. It had some fairytale turrets and an air of magic to it. Apparently it was built in 1513, and by 1559 Catherine de Medici was living there. It is to her that the magnificent gallery is accredited. Sixty-five yards long, it spanned the entire width of the river. It was this gallery with the most beautiful black and white checked floor that rendered me speechless – no mean feat. The other châteaux may have been bigger, grander, but this one just seemed to be so perfect. Even today, when I am supposed to be concentrating on something else, for no reason it will leap into my brain.

It sounds as though all these holidays happened without incident. But of course that wasn't the case. I'm sure that we children drove my parents completely mad with our bickering and, of course, the endless questions. The main one, and no doubt repeated throughout any other family holiday – "are we there yet?" Naturally this wasn't asked any realistic time into the journey but half an hour after leaving and then again every fifteen minutes. Another one was:

"Dad, who are you waving at?"

"No-one, I was just saying thank you."

"Why?"

"Because they were kind."

"About what?" etc, etc.

Unfortunately, unlike my memory for food and beautiful locations I could never remember the reason for Dad often waving at other drivers and continually asked him the same question. However, silly comments weren't just the reserve of the children. My mother had her own favourite.

"Alan, we're going to have to turn back"

"Why?"

"I think I've left the iron /hair tongs/oven on."

Of course we duly turned back to find nothing had been left on. The only things that were regularly left were the sandwiches that Mum had made ions before and put in the freezer (something I never understood!)

A famous family story happened when driving across France. As usual, my sister and I were squabbling about anything and everything. My usually so placid Dad had finally had enough. Whilst driving he manoeuvred himself to give us (a well deserved in my opinion) slap across the knees. As he was driving he timed it somewhat incorrectly and ended up smacking Mum full in the face. Well, you can just imagine the scene. An extremely cross mother, a very apologetic father and two hopelessly giggling kids in the back!!

It was during 1979 when it became apparent that my first prolonged experience of being abroad was coming to fruition. Dad was frequently abroad on business and was spending more and more time in Paris. One day he came back from work with some great news. "How would you like to live in Paris?" Not the normal question you're greeted with when you get back from school!

I was doing somersaults by this point. "I'd love to." All that French food and lovely Paris. Obviously, this had been under discussion for a while as Dad had been wasting so much time travelling, and IBM had decided that it would be more beneficial if we all moved there for two years. Mum and Dad had even already briefly looked at the British School. For the next couple of weeks arrangements started to be made. Then the bad news came one day when Dad got back from work.

"I'm afraid we're not going to Paris anymore."

All my thirteen-year-old dreams were dashed. In fact, I was so wrapped up in my disappointment I almost missed the next sentence.

"But, we're going to Holland instead."

Holland. Wasn't that flat with lots of flowers and flabby cheese with bright red skin? Unfortunately it did little to appease me at the time. I'd been so excited about the prospect of living in Paris but the reality was France was out and Holland was in.

Part Two

Dutch delights

Chapter 4

Clogs and windmills

So, four days after we arrived back in the UK after our holiday to the Loire, we flew to Holland. The removal men had been the day before and packed personal items and four-fifths of the family were ready and excited to go. Despite having been abroad many times I'd never flown so at that point it was more the excitement of flying than moving to Holland that I was thinking about. The same couldn't be said for Mum. She was terrified of flying and showed it. Fortunately, it didn't rub off on any of us and I think we were oblivious to the fact that she was downing G & T's before and during the flight! I'm sure that first flight left me with an enduring love of flying – from the thrill of the take-off, the searching through the meal to find something edible (and always eating everything regardless), the free booze and finally the power of the reverse thrust on landing.

Having arrived at Schipol airport we transferred to the beautiful Marriott hotel in central Amsterdam where we were staying for the first night (courtesy of IBM). Well, I'd never seen anything like it. The reception desk seemed longer than a runway and there were a host of bars and restaurants. And that was before we found the room I was sharing with my sister. It was amazing - two huge double beds, bowls of fruits and bathroom goodies to stock Boots.

The next morning, bags full of said five-star hotel bathroom goodies, we drove down towards The Hague which was where we were to be based. We stayed in a hotel again that night – the Holiday Inn in Leiden. Not quite as glamorous as the Marriott but somewhere which was soon to become a family favourite for the amazing Sunday lunches they did.

And then it was to the reality of Dutch living. We arrived at a typically Dutch house in a small town, called Voorshoten, near Leiden. It was tall and thin, on three levels and with a lounge window that every passer by could look through. Naturally, the first thing that as children we did was to try and bag the best bedroom. Since I was due to start my 'O' levels that year and apparently should be studying more I was allowed to have the large bedroom on the top floor, which had its own washbasin. With Catherine and Matthew in rooms on the middle level I felt so grown up. It has to be said that not much studying was ever really done up there.

The excitement of living in Holland was unfortunately interrupted by the somewhat intrusive necessity of school. Although every weekend was like a holiday as we always went off on a visit somewhere, the reality was getting through the week. I'd never been a fan of school, and despite most people saying that school days are your happiest, I can truthfully say that the evenings, weekends and holidays were great, but that the days were torture. Living in Holland wasn't proving any different, and it was with the same dread that I dragged myself to school every day. At least I really did have something to look forward to at the weekends. One regular occasion was Sunday lunch. We'd meet up with a mixture of ex-pats and locals and then have a long lunch. Our favourite was a restaurant called "*Westbroekpark*". It was situated in the middle of a park in Schevignen, part of The Hague now better known as Milocivic's last residence, and was surrounded by the most amazing roses and gardens.

After a while the waiters were used to one of the dining rooms being completely rearranged by a noisy group of ex-pats and locals, with a number of children running round. The most wonderful lunch for me was a Kinderschotel – veal croquettes, with chips, applesauce and mayonnaise. Sounds disgusting, but was great. It might only have been brought to the majority of the world's population through John Travolta and Samuel L Jackson's conversation in *Pulp Fiction* about the Dutch's love of having mayonnaise with their chip, but we were rejecting ketchup for mayonnaise way back in 1979.

As well as eating out a lot at the weekends, we also did more cultural and touristy things. We visited a variety of museums, some of which were more interesting than others and some which were just plain weird – the national museum of Musical Clocks and Street Organs being one of them. Obviously, being in Holland meant flowers. Where we were living was very close to the famous Keukenhof gardens. Not really high on a fourteen-year-old's agenda, but nevertheless beautiful. I remember being most interested in searching for a black tulip – probably something to do with the rock music I was listening to at the time. I never did find one, but the deep purple!!!! ones came a close second.

Another benefit of loving in Holland was the calibre of the school trips. In the past I'd been to such interesting places as Porchester Castle (only thirty minutes from home) and in the future would go to Harlech and Blaenau Ffestiniog in North Wales on a geography trip. Being on the continent meant that it was so much easier to get to places. It was therefore, that at half-term in the 1980 summer term that I set off with school for Engelberg in Switzerland. Although still firmly disliking school, I'd always loved geography, and therefore left feeling positive. After taking the overnight train, with very little sleep, due to the general messing around that goes with a group of fourteen year-olds, and a huge crash in the middle of the night when my friend Karen fell out off the top bunk, we woke up to the complete opposite of what we were used to and had swapped a flat landscape for mountains.

The first interesting fact was that the nearby mountain peak was called Mount Titless. I mean, who ever came up with that name. You can imagine the giggling about that one – not helped by the fact that the name of one of the teachers at school was Miss Titles. Apart from the mind numbing biological surveys we had to do, it was great to be back in Switzerland after so long, and I remembered with fondness my first visit there. The other recollection I have is of running out of money on the last day when we were supposed to be fending for ourselves. Completely starving, on getting back to the train station in The Hague where Dad was waiting I only had one thought. Despite the fact that I was absolutely knackered having not slept on the train (a recurring nightmare on all my journeys and even when in a comfy bed!), when he asked me what I wanted to do, I said eat. We ended up in another favourite family restaurant – the *Gouden Leeuw*, or Golden Lion in the small town where we lived. It was one of the biggest restaurants I have ever been to - and the nosiest. It was a family game to guess how many minutes it would be until the first crash came from the kitchen. Despite the huge number of meals which were relentlessly produced throughout the day and the general chaos which rained, the food was excellent. Although completely off limits these days for me, they produced the most gorgeous Weiner Schnitzels I have ever had. A huge tasty non-greasy veal escalope, topped with a slice of lemon and one of hard-boiled egg and an anchovy, served with hot chips and green beans. I can still taste it. That particular Sunday was no exception and I ate like a pig and then slept for about twenty hours.

The summer of 1980 arrived and after having spent some time in the UK we went for our summer holiday to Austria. We stayed in a lovely villa in Maurach, close to the Achensee high up in the Tyrol. A ski resort in the winter it was boiling hot that summer and most of the time was spent lazing around in the sun, or messing around in the river. The highlight of the holiday was a trip to Italy. We crossed over the Alps on the Brenner Pass; a fantastic piece of engineering which links the two countries. At times with stunning views and awe inspiring moments because of the drops, we eventually passed through the mountains and dropped down into Bolzano, the closest town. It was probably the hottest I have ever been. I had no idea it could get so hot in the north of Italy. We soon hid under a huge parasol and had a great lunch, sitting outside a restaurant in an enchanting square. Feeling full and mellow towards the end of the meal, Dad somehow managed to knock his beer flying. It landed all over Mum and me and we had to spend the rest of the day wearing sticky clothes; the drive back into Austria was even worse. As you can imagine Dad wasn't the most popular person.

Another day trip was a visit to Innsbruck, the main city of the Tyrol. The centre was cobbled and the arcaded streets were beautiful. Like all tourists we headed for the famous Golden Roof – named due to the two thousand, six hundred and fifty-seven gold-leafed tiles it was made of in 1500. It was amazing and sparkled in the sun – not to put down the rest of the city down which was magnificent and had a large number of buildings built in the Gothic style.

On the same day we jumped forward many centuries and stood beneath the Olympic Ski Jump, just outside the city. What on earth would impel someone to fling themselves down that ramp on two pieces of plastic was completely beyond me. At that point even ski-ing seemed something that no one could possibly enjoy. How it strange it was that twenty-two years later I'd find myself in St. Anton, only kilometres away working as a Chalet Girl. That job must come close to the record for my shortest one, but that is another story!

On the way home we passed through Liechtenstein, a minute country with a tiny capital city, Vaduz. Apart from being extremely picturesque, I can't really remember anything else about it. Much more memorable about the journey home was trying to find somewhere to stay overnight, after we'd travelled through Switzerland. On that particular occasion nothing had been booked – something which was guaranteed to work Mum up into lather and Dad to tell her there was nothing to worry about. Unfortunately, it just wasn't happening and for ages we didn't pass any hotels. We finally came upon a hotel and Dad was duly sent inside but came out soon after to say he didn't think it was the right type of place for a family. Of course we plied him with questions as to what he meant, but he deflected all of them. We finally arrived in Belfort, in France, on the outskirts a fairly non-descript place, but nevertheless with many hotels. By this time, though, it was getting late, and Mum was starting to blame Dad for not having booked anything. Well, who cares when you suddenly come across the *Grand Hotel du Lion*! It might have been huge and modern but most importantly had some vacancies. My sister and I had one room, and Mum and Dad had a room with my brother. It wasn't just any room. It was enormous. The bathroom was big enough to fit two double beds into. Since it was 11pm by then, the restaurant was long-closed. However, the hotel didn't let us down and before long had appeared with a trolley laden down with the most gorgeous French buffet. It obviously did merit being incredibly late that night!

There was something very special at such a tender age to

be staying in lovely hotels. Having moved abroad for work, Dad was definitely benefiting from uprooting the family, and there seemed to be more money around. Not that that was really important, but it did make a change to some of the hovels we'd stayed in whilst on holiday in previous years. That September was no exception. For my birthday treat that year I asked to be able to go to Amsterdam for the weekend, and to visit some of the art museums and diamond factories. So, for my fifteenth birthday we again stayed in the Marriott. This time it was far more of a relaxed stay – no step into the unknown as it had been the previous September when we'd just arrived in Holland. One morning we took one of the boat trips and cruised around the canals, peering into front rooms on the boathouses, and looking upwards at the roof gables. All this was great, but couldn't begin to match the Rijksmuseum. Not only was there an amazing array of art but also the world famous '*Nightwatch*' by Rembrandt. Although by no means one of my favourite artists, it certainly made an impression then, and whenever I'm in a museum now, I always search out anything by Rembrandt.

After the excellent summer and trip to Amsterdam it was back to earth with a bump. It was the start of my 'O' Level year, and for someone who really hated school, no fun at all. Although there were still weekend trips to various places in Holland, in theory I was supposed to being studying more of the time. One ship on my horizon was a Friday evening. I'd been asked to join the local choir at the Anglican Church in The Hague. Although never particularly religious I had sung in a choir back in the UK, and decided it would be something I could enjoy again. I knew from Dad that as well as singing to a high level that the choir comprised friendly people and that choir practice was often extremely funny. I wasn't disappointed. Through the seriousness of practising hard there were many moments of uncontrollable laughter, mainly when trying to record something.

But this wasn't the only ship on my horizon. Although I'd had a 'boyfriend' in the UK, I suddenly realized I had my first teenage crush at the age of fifteen. Was he the same age as me, unattached, someone my mother could approve of? Of course not. I met him at choir practice. He stood behind me, next to Dad, wearing flip-flops and shorts and cracked jokes continually. He was also tall, blond, gorgeous to me, thirty, Australian and attached. I didn't think you could get a much better specimen of a man. Of course, I kept my fantasies to myself, well at least I didn't divulge them to Mum, and spent most of the time at school and when I was supposed to be revising, daydreaming. Things looked up significantly when he started going to the youth group as a leader, and I was able to help out with various activities. Being able to see him three days in a row was a real bonus, and I was always devastated when either he or I didn't make it. Of course, when you're fifteen you think anything is possible – somewhat like my younger dreams when I decided I was going to marry Prince Andrew!!!

Whilst I was happily having my fantasies, I was fairly slow to notice someone else on the scene. He seemed rather straight, shy, was an organ scholar and was no match for my Australian. The exotic thing was that he was half-Dutch, half-American. Another thing that put me off was that my mother thought he was entirely suitable. Despite all this, after furtive glances and embarrassing conversations we finally had our first date. So, one evening in early summer we went to the cinema in The Hague. I can even remember the film, Time Bandits. So there I was sitting in a dark cinema, wondering as millions before have: "Does he like me? Is he getting near? Should I leave my hand in reach on my leg?" Oh, the trauma of it all. Fortunately, I was soon put out of my misery and by the end of the film we were 'going out'.

There was nothing more exciting that having my first proper boyfriend who wasn't English, and being abroad at the time.

Even better was that because Mum approved so much of the image that he was projecting that she didn't have any idea what we were really getting up to. Pete also had a room at the top of his house, and his parents rarely ventured up there. Well, he might have been a classical organ scholar but his room was lined with rock LP's. We spent all our time together listening to very loud rock music, and rolling round on the floor together. Ah, youth!!!

By this time it was the summer of 1981, and our two years of living in Holland as a family was coming to an end. But before we left we had a major holiday to take. IBM had very kindly given Dad a bonus and he decided to spend it on a trip to Scandinavia. By this time Pete had already gone on holiday with his family to France, and I'd received a couple of letters from him, each about fifteen pages long, and with some photos. I knew he'd be away far longer than us and that when we returned to The Hague he wouldn't be there, but somehow the thought of some new countries to add to my list didn't make the separation so bad.

Chapter 5

Scandinavia

So, on the 17th July we set off on our tour of Scandinavia. In one day we drove all the way up through Holland, Germany and into Denmark. The first night we stayed at the Munkebjcrg Hotel, situated in a beautiful forest above the Vejle Fjord. By the next morning it was full-on tourist stuff. We went to Legoland – the original one – and very good it was too. The next day we travelled to Odense, on the island of Fye and visited Hans Christians Andersen's birthplace. I can't really remember very much about it so don't suppose it was that fascinating. That night we stayed at the Hotel Nyborg on the east coast of the island. It was situated right on the water, and was in beautiful grounds, offset by the amazingly blue sky. The evening was even more stunning and the first of many spectacular red sunsets over water which we experienced.

The following morning we drove round to the ferry, which was in sight of the hotel and boarded for the hour-long trip across to Halsskov, on the western coast of Jutland. What was fascinating was the huge number of jellyfish, which surrounded the ferry. You could hardly see the water for them!

Having survived the jellyfish we drove across the rest of the island and arrived in Copenhagen. We stayed in the hotel Hermitage on the outskirts of the city. Fairly unremarkable in most ways, it was there that I managed to excel myself twice in the restaurant, and entertain the waiters for free. For dinner the first evening I choose a Roast Beef Salad. It arrived and included a variety of things I really didn't recognise. The grated cheese seemed a good option! It was only when I'd half-chewed the first mouthful I realised it was grated raw horseradish – very high on my list of food 'no-goes'. In desperation I lunged for the nearest drink to wash it down, and only on glugging a huge mouthful realised it was Mum's gin and tonic. Another pet hate. I spent a good ten minutes coughing and spluttering and vowed to be more careful about what I was eating. Well! That lasted to the next morning. Somewhat distracted because it was first thing in the morning, I poured some milk onto my cereal and tucked into that. Unfortunately, it wasn't milk but soured yoghurt. Why on earth do Danes eat sour yoghurt for breakfast?

Much pleasanter was the centre of Copenhagen itself; spotlessly clean and well looked after. It was full of stunning renaissance palaces, parks and houses. It also reminded me somewhat of Amsterdam as it had a network of canals and waterways. We spent an evening at the famous Tivoli Gardens. As well as housing lovely gardens, which were beautifully illuminated, there was also a very tastefully done amusement park. It was then that I decided that I had to go on a roller coaster. Could I get anyone to go on with me? NO. The only person who volunteered was my brother but he was only six and not allowed. After much pleading I was finally allowed to go on my own. Did I enjoy it? Well, there are definitely better ways to get your kicks!

The next day was far more cultural and we headed to Kronborg Castle in Helsingør. It was a magnificent building which completely dominated the town. Built in the 15th

Century as a fortress it had the antique canons and was also very ornate. However, the interior was less ornate and seemed full of mystery and danger. The worst thing was the dungeon – dark and musty as always. The whole atmosphere was enhanced by the fact that Shakespeare had based his Hamlet on the castle, but called it "Elsinore". Quite how he could have known about the place or visited it, I don't know, but if you shut your eyes you could feel that you were part of it all too well!

After the thrill of the castle, the afternoon was a real letdown. We set off to discover the Little Mermaid. And that is exactly what she is. Little. I had an impression that she would be really awe inspiring, but there she was, curled up on a rock next to a path. A true case of your expectations being dashed.

So, that was Denmark! The next day we took the ferry from Helsingør, from where there was a spectacular view of the castle, to Helsingborg in Sweden. It was only thirty kilometres away and was a very pleasant trip. From there we drove to Jönköping, and stayed in the most beautiful hotel, the Stora, on the shore of Lake Vättern. And that was where all semblance of civilised Sweden stopped. After trailing round quite a lot of the town we ended up in an American style diner – strange in itself considering we were miles from anywhere. Even stranger was what happened much later on when the rest of the family had gone to bed, and Dad and I had gone out for a walk. Despite the fact that it was eleven o'clock it was still incredibly light as we were so far north. All of sudden, coming down the main street were scores of American cars – cruising and disturbing the peace with their horns. It really was a bizarre sight, and we never found out what it was all about!

So, despite all the indications otherwise, we were now in Sweden. The next day we drove the two hundred kilometres north east up to Linköping where we stopped for a couple of nights. That evening we went out for a drive and came across a lovely series of locks that dropped the level of the canal down hundreds of metres. With the sun setting it was magical. The next day we visited the Reijmyre glassworks. I can remember before we arrived feeling rather bored by the whole prospect, but that soon changed once the tour started. The second oldest glassworks in Sweden, it kept the old tradition of hand glass blowing and carving alive. Watching the skilled craftsmen was a treat and some of the pieces on display were incredible. I still have a beautiful frosted owl in my bedroom, which survived being carted around the rest of Scandinavia, taken back to Holland and then the UK, and carted to Portugal and back twice. More amazingly it didn't break when my cat Jack decided to rugby tackle the table it was on not so long ago. After this we continued to the Kolmården Animal Park. Then (and maybe still) it was one of the largest open-air zoos in the world, with a Safari Park, a zoo with different terrains, a tropical house and a dolphinarium, and more importantly for my little bro, polar bears!

The next day we left Linköping and continued northeast towards Stockholm. After the huge expanses of open countryside, Stockholm was somewhat of a contrast. It had been originally built on fourteen islands as a natural fortification against the Danes but was now a vibrant and beautiful city. We stayed at the Park Hotel for three nights and used it as base to explore the city. The most stunning building we saw was the Royal Palace which was situated on the edge of the harbour and dominated the area.

Later that day we set off to see the *Wasa* warship which was raised in 1961. After a very inauspicious start – it sunk in Stockholm harbour twenty minutes into its maiden voyage in 1628 – it had been preserved in mud, and was discovered some three hundred and thirty years later. As well as the ship itself, some 12,000 objects were retrieved. A series of walkways brought you right up to the cannon hatches, the restored interior and a walkway around the ship. Restoration apparently continued throughout the 1980's with a new museum planned, but back in 1981 the exhibition was interesting and somewhat overshadowed Henry VIII's *Mary Rose,* now on show in Portsmouth. Close by to the *Wasa* was Djurgarden – a huge park which afforded great views over the harbour. For the remaining time we spent in Stockholm I don't remember doing much else than enjoying walking round the city, looking at the shops and watching the world go by in the numerous (and very expensive) cafés.

A couple of days later we set off for Finland. This involved taking the aptly named Viking ferry from Stockholm to Turku, on the south-eastern tip of Finland. The trip lasted a full eight hours and provided a stunning view of Stockholm as we left the harbour and then weaved our way through the Archipelagos. Once we could tear ourselves away from enjoying the sun and blue skies, we discovered lunch. Lunch Scandinavian style wasn't a cheese and pickle sandwich, but an enormous Smorgasbord – what we know as a buffet but laden with gorgeous food, including shellfish and smoked salmon. What's more it was a set price for as much as you could eat – so we did.

We finally arrived in Turku, Finland at about 8pm that evening. Unfortunately, the thrill of being in another new country was somewhat overshadowed by the fact that my little brother had decided that he didn't feel very well and we had to keep stopping for him to throw up. Naturally, it was initially blamed on the fact that he eaten too many prawns or had dodgy fish, but in fact he had a bug which laid him up for a couple of days, and meant Mum was hotel bound.

At this point all I could gather about Finland was that it was very flat! The spectacular lakes and forests were obviously yet to come. Helsinki, however, didn't disappoint. Despite arriving late and with a far amount of squabbling going on between everyone, as we progressed slowly toward the centre where we were staying in the hotel Helka, we could appreciate the brilliant architecture. It was only really the following day as we wandered around the city that its true magnificence was apparent though. Helsinki was very different from the other Scandinavian capitals we had visited. It seemed closer to Eastern European cities, which isn't really surprising since for a century it had been an outpost of the Russian empire. Despite that fact that Finland has only been independent since 1917, Helsinki seemed to have a well-developed sense of its own culture, along with a popular culture of street cafés and restaurants. And, of course shops – selling the most beautiful carved glass, local jewellery and wooden toys and art.

One morning we found ourselves in the enormous Stockman Department store – definitely rivalling Selfridges. I'm doubtful, however, if one would really get the service there that we received in Stockman. As we wandered around we noticed that all the shop assistants wore a variety of little flags on their uniforms, indicating which languages they could speak. Most had the Scandinavian languages, English and German, and a huge variety of others. Can you imagine that happening in a department store in the UK? No!!! Maybe a smattering of French, but otherwise the usual talking loudly and slowly in English. Where on earth do we get that from? It's so embarrassing when you hear it happening. The other plus point was that as I was wandering around one of the levels with Dad and my sister we remembered that it was the day of Charles and Diana's wedding. You would have thought that it was us who were royalty considering the treatment we received. As we stood in front of a television set watching and chatting, a shop assistant approached us and asked if we would like to watch properly. We decided that a sit down wouldn't be such a bad idea, so a couple of assistants arranged an enormous roll of carpet (we were in the carpet/electrical department) for us to sit on, and positioned it in front of the biggest television. I can't say that I'm particularly patriotic towards the Royal Family, but it was certainly a more interesting way to have watched the wedding than most people would have managed! This meant that by the time we returned to the hotel to relieve Mum who was looking after my brother, we weren't hugely popular!

Sitting watching the wedding had made me think about my own recent romantic attachment. Before we'd left Holland I'd received two letters from Pete, sent from France where he was on holiday. I'd brought them with me and read them religiously every day. I'd written to him along the way but obviously hadn't received any further ones so continually wondered if it was an on-going romance. Despite the fact that adults did, and still do, belittle teenage love, if you've been there, you know how real it all is. I think this was heightened by the fact that both of us had travelled a lot, experienced different cultures, and had to be fairly independent at times. Well, I didn't have to worry about whether it was still on-going as when we finally returned home to Holland, the front door mat was covered with letters from him. And I mean letters – not just a card or a few lines, but three or four letters a week for three weeks, all of which were about fifteen double-sided A4 size pages!!

On one of our wanders we visited Helsinki cathedral. It was built on a higher level than the rest of the buildings, and dominated the skyline, looking especially majestic from the harbour area. To be honest I can't remember what it was like inside, although I'm sure the domed ceiling was amazing, but I can remember that very close by my endless search for a jade cross came to an end. I'd been looking for one for years, and as we passed by a small jewellery shop I saw it in the window. I wore it on and off for years, always worrying that I would loose it (a regular occurrence with me and jewellery)! However, on this occasion it wasn't me who lost it but an unscrupulous burglar who decided to break into my flat in Porto, Portugal some twenty years later and steal it.

After three nights in Helsinki we continued east and travelled the hundred kilometres to Porvo, where we stayed in the beautiful Haikko Manor, set amidst fir trees and overlooking a stunning inlet. The manor itself is mentioned as early as 1362, when it was owned by a Dominican Monastery, but having been razed to the ground a number of times it was now a famous hotel. In fact, many famous names of world history and royalty have stayed there.

The afternoon was spent lazing around in the grounds – enjoying the outdoor swimming pool and the sauna. The highlight of that day was when Dad and Matthew appeared from the changing room and he charged up to us shouting.

"There are lots of legs hanging up in there!"

"What do you mean 'legs'?"

"You know. Legs."

Completely baffled it turned out that there indeed were legs hanging up, but that they were artificial ones, which belonged to the Finnish Veterans, who were allowed to use the facilities free of charge for the service they had done for their country.

Later that evening we had a meal in the sumptuous hotel restaurant. All starving after a day messing around in the sun, we had a gorgeous meal which included smoked reindeer meat. I wouldn't eat it now, but it was extremely tasty then!

The next day, by then the 1st August, we drove east towards the Russian border. There wasn't any particular reason for this other than Dad decided it would be something different to do - I'm sure that it's not something that many British fifteen-year-olds have done. After a drive of about a hundred and twenty kilometres and a picnic in the woods, we came to a small town close to the border. Here we saw a signpost to Vyvorg, in Russia, and more bizarrely, Leningrad. We continued on for a short while and found ourselves in the middle of nowhere with lots of signs indicating the USSR was close. On one of the later signs there was a picture indicating no photos were to be taken. This was blatantly ignored by Dad who promptly took a picture of the sign and received a stern chastising from Mum. However, with more signs appearing and armed guards, even he saw sense and we turned round.

The next day we left the hotel by the sea and drove inland. We soon encountered the huge forests and lakes, which Finland is so famous for, offset by the almost violet sky. We were heading for Vääksy and the hotel Tallukka. It was situated in the beautiful Finnish landscape on a natural ridge between two lakes. There were amazing views over dozens of square kilometres of lakes, islands, and deep, narrow bays, and each room in the hotel afforded these. I don't think we did much apart from lazing around, swimming and enjoying the views - this was probably a good thing considering the trek we ended up making the next day to get to the overnight ferry from Turku. We set off fairly early in the morning, and since we had lots of time Dad decided that we weren't going to take the main road but follow minor roads so we could enjoy the spectacular views. Well, the minor roads turned into dirt tracks and before too long we were driving round in circles, with every bend wondering if we were going to come face to face with one of the mousses we'd seen on the many signs. By this time, of course, we three kids were squabbling in the back, Dad was in trouble for not taking the main road, and we couldn't see any views, just dust from the dry track we were rallying on! Good thing we had a Volvo Estate really!

Fortunately, we finally found the main road; the rest of the journey was uneventful and we were able to enjoy the fabulous scenery. We reached the ferry and after another gorgeous Scandinavian buffet and spectacular sunset we went to bed and woke up in Stockholm. We then re-traced our steps, although this time staying one night in Linköping, and motored down to Helsingborg where we took the ferry to Denmark. After a night in Copenhagen, we drove to Rødby on the south coast of Denmark and then took another ferry to Travemunde in Germany. We were close to the border at the time and drove through Lübeck, which was actually on the border between West and East Germany; Dad then decided that it was worth trying to see if we could make a little trip into East Germany. After some endless driving round (something we kids had been used to for years but Mum still couldn't come to terms with) we realised that it wasn't going to be possible, and set off for Holland and home.

By this time, returning from a holiday I would normally have started feeling depressed at the thought of the ensuing normality, especially after such a good trip. However, we'd been away since the 17th July and it was now the 7th August, and I couldn't wait to get back. The reason was, of course, a certain boyfriend. At least I hoped he was a boyfriend. I wasn't disappointed. On arriving back at midnight we could hardly get the door open for all the mail on the doormat - a huge amount of it was for me. I settled myself in bed; made sure the letters were in date order and then spent most of the rest of the night reading them. What joy. They were all of the most amazing length, full of detail and descriptions of France and Italy. Quite why he sent so many when he knew

I would be away I don't really know but maybe he felt he was keeping in touch.

The following morning I woke up feeling exhausted but happy, knowing that we would soon be able to see each other. Then of course I remembered that he was still away and wouldn't be returning until the 18th or 19th of August, at the earliest. What was worse was that as a family we were moving back to the UK permanently on the 23rd August – which didn't leave very much time for a blossoming romance. I made sure that any sorting or packing was done during the following week, and visits made, so that I'd have my last weekend in Holland free. Finally, after jumping every time the phone rang, he phoned on the 20th. I can remember waiting on the platform of our local station the following day, a Friday. After the intimacy of so many letters it was back to being shy and embarrassed and circling round each other. That however, soon disappeared and before long we were having a brilliant time. The Saturday was spent in The Hague, hanging out, as teenagers do, but with the added emotion of having discovered each other, but realising that separation wasn't far away. The next day in fact. We said our goodbyes at lunchtime, and then as a family we booked into a local hotel since the removal van had already left.

That evening was a fairly miserable one in various ways. Although Dad was driving back with us to the UK, he would be returning to Holland to work until the following May. So, I was going to be missing my boyfriend, my Dad and friends. The reason for moving back was the start of 'A' Levels for me – not an important one as far as I was then concerned! I mopped round much of the evening, with no desire to move back to the UK. But, that's what we did, and arrived there the following evening.

Thinking back about how disappointed I'd been when Dad told us that we were going to live in Holland rather then

France, I realised that maybe it had been a good thing. I knew Paris already; if we had gone there perhaps I would never have got to know Holland, and certainly wouldn't have had all those experiences.

Part Three

Different Adventures

Chapter 6

Boys, boys

So, back in England after two years of living abroad and having fantastic holidays, it was all rather a culture shock. Another shock was that I'd managed to scrap through enough 'O' Levels to do 'A' Levels. However, I did have to re-take my Maths 'O' Level, as I'd managed to achieve an unclassified grade. That takes some skill! In fact, I hadn't even tried, just looked at the exam paper and decided my time would be better spent revising for something that I might actually pass, and therefore left after about five minutes, causing somewhat of a stir in the examination hall, and sending Mum into orbit when I appeared home.

Anyway, the new school term loomed and wasn't something I was looking forward to, despite the fact that I was returning to the same school. What made me look forward to getting up every day was the constant stream of letters arriving from Holland. Thinking back I'm not sure how a fifteen and sixteen-year-old managed to cope with this type of relationship. We wrote continuously, including the minutest details of our days, and were allowed to take turns phoning each other on a Wednesday. It was strange in a way that Pete still saw Dad on a regular basis in The Hague, and Mum and I were stuck in England. There was, however, light at the end of this particular teenage tunnel, in the form of half term. Toward the end of October, Mum drove the three of us to Dover where we took the familiar ferry to Calais, and then drove up the well-travelled route to Holland.

However, on that occasion we had a far more interesting journey. Despite the fact that Mum had booked a seat for each of us in the club lounge, for some reason we didn't have seats together. She made a fuss, probably because she couldn't work out which of her children it would be less of a liability to leave on their own. Either my 6-year-old brother who had the potential to get up to anything, and was renowned for disappearing and talking himself into places which no-body else would try to get into, or myself who she imagined would be trawling round the duty free or trying to be served in the bar. After a while there was announcement over the tannoy. 'Would Mrs. Gurney and children please come to the Purser's Desk'? What an embarrassment for a sixteen-year-old. We trooped off to find out the reason why, and were told as a result of the mix-up we could spend the journey on the bridge. Oh, joy! My brother might have been over the moon, but all my plans of roaming the ferry were well and truly scuppered. I soon changed my mind – all those men in uniform. Yum! That must have started my 'thing' about men in naval uniforms – I've been there twice!

Thinking back it seems weird, because we had travelled on Townsend Thorensen Ferries numerous times, including the *Herald of Free Enterprise* that time. No doubt, the bridge would have been a terrible place to be that particular night many years later when the ship went down and people died. Arriving in Holland and fate, of course, was playing one of her own little games as it worked out that Pete had had his half-term the week before and was now back at school. However, where there's a will, and all that! We spent as much time together as possible, and our relationship at last seemed to be a proper one. There was lots of hand holding, wistful looks, wandering round The Hague and persuading our parents to let us spend each available minute together. Pete still had the top floor of his house, and his parents, being rather bohemian never dared to ventured up there! Of course, it came to an end all too quickly, and we were soon returning to England. At that time, Holland was more appealing than it had ever been, and I wished I could have stayed there for the rest of my school days.

The next couple of months passed with scant attention paid to schoolwork and as much partying as possible, and with the expectation of Christmas when Pete would be coming to stay for a while. Normally I wanted Christmas and Boxing Day to last as long as possible but on this occasion I was willing them away. Pete arrived on the 29th and we had until the 4th January together. The details of his visit are now very vague, but I remember getting very drunk at a New Year's Eve party, and being vile to him. I can't remember why, but think it might have had something to do with the fact that I felt too young and tied down to deal with a long-distance relationship. In my experience they don't work, as I have tried since.

So, on the morning of the 4th January, after lots of begging on his part and exactly half a year since we had got together, Pete left. He was travelling back with Dad to The Hague, and I discovered afterwards had quizzed him all the way back about me, and what might have happened. I knew then there was no way it was going to work, but didn't really know how to handle the situation. A couple of days later I received the fattest letter yet, which incidentally the customs men had decided to open and if they read it would have known that he was pleading with me to still be his girlfriend. I have recently re-read it and cannot believe how full of raw emotion it was. What was I doing letting him go? I don't know! We had one last telephone conversation where I managed to persuade Pete that we needed to cool things down a little so I could concentrate on my school work (something which I really needed to do as my marks were all terrible), which placated him, and then I think I must have done the dirty deed through a letter. I still wonder today (as you do with some relationships) what would have happened 'if'!

Things continued much as before for the next couple of months. I was sort of resigned to being back in England, and trying to make the most of things by going out as much as possible. It wasn't particularly easy since we were living in a small village, and the only form of entertainment was the local pubs – but they had their uses, and they soon became second homes. That was about the time when I launched myself into another relationship; this one was going to cause me grief for some years to come. I don't know whether having lived abroad, and having already been out with someone who'd had a slightly bohemian upbringing, endeared me to a particular type of person, but before long I was seriously involved with a somewhat unbalanced character, who had lived in Hong Kong, and whom my mother wholeheartedly disapproved of. His name was Doug; often referred to by Mum as 'that rat'. I also regularly heard 'I don't know why you split up with that nice boy Pete' from her.

Chapter 7

Two holidays and a wedding in Holland

By the time the summer came and we were preparing for our annual holiday, I have to say that I wasn't quite as excited about the prospect of going away as usual, as it would mean time apart from Doug. By then I'd turned into a real teenager with attitude (although that was only according to Mum, Dad didn't seem to agree) so wasn't looking forward to the battles that would no doubt ensue on a family holiday. That year we'd rented a wooden chalet in a ski resort called Veysonnez, in the Valais area of Switzerland, high up in the mountains on the other side of the valley to Crans Montana.

It was a fairly uneventful journey, but led to one of my favourite meal experiences. We stopped overnight in the Hotel du Lac, perched high up in the mountains in France near the Swiss border. It was back to one of those hotels with threadbare carpets in the rooms and nothing matching, but had the most magnificent restaurant. It was fairly large, and beautifully decorated with traditional copper pans. However, the Madame was something else. She was a large woman and extremely stern – enough to scare anyone, especially the young waiters whose every move she watched like a hawk. My brother got things off to a good start, by pointing and giggling at a Frenchman who was tucking into a lobster, and had a bib on! That evening I decided to have regional food. I choose snails, followed by a rare steak. When the snails arrived the waiter put them down in front of my father, no doubt thinking that a teenage English girl couldn't possible want them. I felt positively sorry for the poor waiter when the Madame noticed and obviously told him not to jump to conclusions. However, it hadn't sunk in, and later he promptly put my rare steak down in front of Dad. By this point the Madame practically pulled him by his ears towards the kitchen from where we all learnt some new French words. The entertainment added to the whole evening, the food was excellent, no doubt the red wine too, and I went to bed happy and full.

The area of Switzerland we were in was all extremely pretty, although there wasn't an awful amount to do apart from walking. This wasn't really the ideal summer holiday for a sixteen-year-old. However, there were some great days out. One day we took the train up to Zermatt to get a close up view of The Matterhorn. It dominated the skyline and the area, and although beautiful in the summer sun, you could appreciate how foreboding and dangerous it would be if you became stuck on it! Another day we drove up one of the hairpin bend roads that the Alps are so famous for – no mean feat in a Volvo Estate – and went to the source of the Rhône. At this altitude it wasn't even a stream, but a glacier. It was stunning and appeared to be blue, and at one point a tunnel had been cut through a section, into which you could walk.

Of this particular holiday I can't really remember much more, apart from how much I was enjoying sitting in cafés and watching the world go by, preferably (if I could swing it) with a beer. We had one interesting evening in a local restaurant when the young waiter was obviously trying his luck. He brought Dad and me a free second plate of steak for the fondue, and then brought brandy!! The rest of the family weren't afforded any preferential treatment however!

Food played a major part in the trip home, especially in one hotel in northern France where I inadvertently managed to flavour the soup. I was sharing a room with my sister, and before dinner was having a bath in a little sectioned area of the bedroom – yet another one of those French bedrooms. Having a bath is maybe an exaggeration – I was sitting in a tub with my knees up to my chin French style. After I'd managed to untwist myself and get out, there was very shortly afterwards urgent banging coming from the bedroom door. My sister got up to open it and was practically swept aside by a wild-looking Frenchman who seemed to be heading for the bath and me. Hastily trying to cover myself with a towel, well more like a tea towel (another odd French trait), said Frenchman started to wave his arms around a lot, talked extremely high speed French, the only words which I could catch were something about the kitchen and soup, and to put something back in the bath. By this time my sister had summoned Dad, who was somewhat surprised to see his sixteen-year-old daughter in a state of undress with a deranged Frenchman in her bathroom. After everyone had stopped waving his or her arms around, it turned out that there had been on-going plumbing, but it hadn't been finished, and no one had told us not to use the bath. The problem was that the pipe emptied straight into the kitchen, and to be more precise, into the soup. I'm sure it added a certain little "Je ne sais quoi"!

That was the end of the summer and it was soon back to earth with a bang and the second year of 'A' Levels. However, before that there were two pleasant surprises. The first was that amazing fact that I'd passed my 'O' Level Maths retake. I'm sure I wouldn't be able to do the same today, but then I studied every past paper I could get my hands on, and learnt by heart the types of questions. Better even than this was my seventeenth birthday present. My boyfriend excelled himself by actually asking my parents first, and arrived on the doorstep with a cardboard box; inside which was a little black kitten. Talk about love at first sight, and none of the usual relationship complications. He was grandly named Ziggy Stardust and the Spiders from Mars (I hope for obvious reasons, although the vet gave me an extremely odd look when I reeled it off) and managed to live up to his alto-ego by being extremely entertaining. He was often extremely badly behaved (he did all the usual cat things plus a few extras – practically got the Christmas turkey one year, caught squirrels, released a half-dead pigeon in the house which squirted blood all over the beige carpet and up the walls, sat on top of the high sideboard pretending he was an ornament and then leapt into the middle of Mum's coffee mornings, frightening the life out of the older ladies, etc, etc). He was also around to provide comfort and saw me through some of the black teenage days and into my twenties. However, I digress.

The second year of 'A' Levels started with the lethargy which was to continue throughout the year. Having recently re-read my diaries it seems that school and exams were the last thing on my mind. Although I actually physically went to school, in spirit I was miles away, either dreaming about foreign countries or my boyfriend. I should have realised then that I was destined to spend a lot of time abroad. My poker also improved. However, my French suffered as there was very little incentive to go to lessons as they gave a whole new meaning to the word bored. Such a shame since I have always loved the French language and had enjoyed speaking it on holiday. Reading Sixteenth Century plays in French wasn't exactly what I had in mind. After homework done at break neck speed I spent the rest of the time trying to contrive ways – not easy with a suspicious Mother (and rightly so) of seeing my boyfriend on our own. Most of the evenings were spent in one of the village pubs, trying to persuade whoever was working to serve us alcohol. I seem to remember, as with so many before and after me, Malibu and Coke being a favourite for myself and Isabel, my partner in crime at the time.

All this resulted, naturally, in getting twenty-seven percent for my French mock 'A' Level and thirty-something for Geography. Result - not! I was in big trouble by this point and received endless lectures from Mum about the unsuitability of my boyfriend (she was probably right) and that I spent too much time in the pub (definitely right). I tried to appease her by working harder, still managing to see my boyfriend and making regular visits to the pub, but it wasn't really working. At the same time as this was happening, university had to be considered. Obviously with my grades I wasn't going to Oxford or Cambridge, and there was no way I was suddenly going to radically improve, so decided that it had to be a more vocational course for me. The decision wasn't really too difficult when I found out that there were Hotel and Catering Management courses available. Since eating and drinking had always been one of my passions, I decided I couldn't go too far wrong, and having considered various offers, choose to study at Middlesex Polytechnic because it would mean I'd be in London. There was, however, the small matter of attaining one 'A' Level. Not really that difficult a feat for most but at that time, for me, rather an uphill struggle.

None of this was helped by the fact that said boyfriend was starting to behave extremely erratically, had virtually got chucked out of school, and was smoking what was not available over the counter. By the time the summer came and I'd finished school and dragged myself through exams, we'd split up, got back together again and then split up again. It wasn't as easy as this though, and was extremely traumatic for both of us. The saving grace was, and still often is, as in times of stress, the prospect of a holiday. So, in late August 1983 I went on a family holiday to France. We stayed in an old stone house in a small non-touristy town near Avranches in Normandy. It was a low-key holiday, and most days were spent sunbathing on the beautiful beaches, and having great lunches in local restaurants. Since a tender age we were always given a certain amount we could spend on a meal – Dad believed it was up to us to decide what we wanted to eat and made us responsible for our spending. This was always a delight and no different this holiday. In fact one lunchtime we revisited a restaurant we'd been to four years before in a town called Pontabault, and it was one of those rare occasions where second time around it was just as good.

The only cloud in the sky was the prospect of receiving exam results on the return to England. One morning I woke up having had a nightmare that I'd got three 'E's. If only that had been the case. The morning after we arrived back from France, there they were, waiting on the doorstep. I locked myself in my room, along with Ziggy for courage, and opened up the envelope with trepidation. Oh dear! An 'E' for Geography, an 'E' for the spoken component of French, another French 'O' Level and an English one. What a disaster. The worst thing was that I had actually studied hard for English, really enjoyed it, was expected to do well and in fact had had a 'B' predicted. The "well, maybe you could have worked harder" comment from Mum which followed sent me into such a rage that I took myself off to the pub as soon as I could escape, and found solace from a local pub friend who also happened to be my current love interest. We consumed quite a large quantity of cider!

Somehow these results proved not to be such a disaster, and having obtained one 'A' Level I was able to take up my place at Middlesex. However, before all the delights of college, and freedom, I had another brief trip abroad. I went to Holland for a weekend for a wedding and since Mum and Dad were going it meant that I was chauffeured there and back, and able to stay in the Holiday Inn in Leiden. Although looking forward to returning to Holland to see old friends and familiar places I was somewhat nervous about the possibility of seeing Pete again. It wasn't as though there may be a coincidental meeting, the friend who was getting married sang in the same choir as we had both done, and I was attending choir practice on the Friday. However, he wasn't there. Someone who was though was that Australian along with his fiancée, who had flown in for the wedding. It was lovely seeing him again, and remembering that fifteen-year-old crush!

The marriage ceremony, the following day, was full of emotion, and then, on leaving the Church I noticed Pete. I fully expected him to bolt in the opposite direction, or hurl abuse at me. However, he did neither and we chatted away with me promising to go and see him the following afternoon.

The rest of Saturday passed in a very happy, boozy state - we initially had a reception in a restaurant by a canal, and then progressed to a barn dance in the evening. More wounds were healed when Pete and I spent more time together, and even danced. The following day I went over to spend the afternoon and evening with him, and we parted promising to write and remain friends.

Chapter 8

London's Calling!

A few weeks later, and I was installed in Hendon, London in a fairly grotty bed-sit with a batty and deaf (thank goodness) landlady, about to launch into college days. This account is not, however, going to detail those three years, as they are now doubt similar to most other undergraduates, suffice to say there were lots of parties, drinking, late nights, men involved, and not a huge amount of studying. This was compounded by the fact that studying catering meant we had to learn to cook and silver serve properly, which invariably included alcohol, and we even had a separate wine appreciation module. Who ever had decided to include those modules on a college course must have had a screw loose. We of course loved it!

By the Christmas of that year Doug appeared again. He'd been doing something connected with sailing in Portugal, but had decided to return. Despite declarations of love, I didn't succumb to his charms and launched myself back into college life for the new term. However, the resolution didn't last long, and by June we were back together again. We'd probably both grown up a little by then. I was doing work experience at the National Theatre as a Buffet Supervisor (still not sure how I managed to swing that one - some of my colleagues were working in hot kitchens, or hotels with rude guests, and I was feeding arty people, getting free theatre tickets, and hob-nobbing in the Green Room), was earning money and had the responsibility of a job, and he seemed to have benefited for being abroad somewhat!

That summer I also finally managed to meet up with Pete again. He was in the UK for a short while and we spent a day together in London. The clean-cut, organ scholar image was gone, and the bad-boy was emerging. Needless to say we had a great day, but it was all over far too quickly.

That summer, Mum and Dad asked me if I wanted to come on holiday with them, and a quick look at my finances meant that it was the only way I was going to get on foreign soil that year. We returned to the same house in Normandy we'd stayed in the previous year, did the same beach trips, and ate lots of lovely food (including a meal at the wonderful restaurant in Pontabault) but it wasn't quite the party atmosphere I had become accustomed to. I was also missing Doug, and was more than happy when we returned. Apart from a barge holiday on the Thames in September with college friends, the exploits of which I'm sure don't need any describing, the only other foreign trip was a day trip to Boulogne in December. Primarily, a pre-Christmas trip organised by college and a further excuse to drink too much, I was at least able to wander round a French market, have a meal and act as a partial translator for everyone!

And with that 1985 arrived. That year was memorable for various reasons, but unfortunately none of them had anything to do with travelling to foreign shores – well, at least not for me! In February, Doug and I called it a day. It has to be said that I had been becoming increasingly exasperated with him over the previous few months. Partly as a result, I had been spending a lot of time with someone from my course, and was becoming less and less upset by the antics which Doug pulled. I therefore persuaded him that we would be better off apart for the moment and to just wait and see. Oh dear! Another heart broken I fear. By the April he was phoning and writing from Monaco, where he was crewing, and preparing to sail to Antigua and from there on to the States. Alright for some! He told me he still loved me and that if I wanted him when he returned he'd come and "reclaim" me. Of course it was all a little more complicated than that, but I decided I didn't want him. He never returned, apparently married an American to get his Green Card (who was apparently insanely jealous of me), carried a letter I later wrote to him around in his wallet (according to his sister who I bumped into years later) and as far as I know is still there!

After the work experience of my second year – the Travelodge at Scratchwood on the M1, not quite as glamorous as the National Theatres, but great fun nevertheless – I spent my summer holiday partly in London and at home. I had a visitor in London in the form of Pete who stayed for three days, which was fun and almost made up for the fact that I wasn't going away anywhere. Back in Sussex I looked after my cat, kept an eye on the Grandparents as the family were away and generally enjoyed the freedom.

My summer holiday was another barge trip on the Thames with friends from college. Much of the same as the year before but slightly more incidents. After a rather boozy lunch one Sunday in Henley we were reversing out into the middle of the Thames when there was a huge crash. We'd crashed into a smaller boat, and put a hole in it. Fortunately said boat belonged to the same hire company as ours and we were able sort out the problem without too much grief – just the loss of the deposit. Ouch! Soon afterwards we were pulled over by the River Police in Reading for speeding!

Chapter 9

Wine, wine, wine

So that was 1985, and the first year for many that I hadn't been abroad. Fortunately, things improved somewhat in 1986. It was the start of my final two terms at college and despite still trying to fulfil the typical student role, everyone was aware of the impending exams in June and then the need to earn money in the big bad wide world. However, there were two very welcome distractions on their way. The first was in the form of a new boyfriend. He was in the year below me, and we'd been circling around each other for ages. Things had to come to a head at the Annual Dinner and Dance. There was only a term left for me, and he would be on work placement for that term so it was then or never. It was a themed evening, held at Hatfield House in Hertfordshire, and was an Elizabethan Banquet. Tim had been chosen as the Lord of the Manor, or something similar, and then he picked me as one of the serving wenches. That was all the encouragement we needed, and we were together for nearly three years.

The first foreign trip was in April to France. As part of our final year we had to choose an option of Tourism or Gastronomy. Obviously that wasn't a difficult decision for me, and as part of our option we had two weeks in France. The first week was spent in the Champagne region. It is amazing to think that from the gently undulating, barren hills a wine such as Champagne can be produced, but it certainly is. If you like champagne then you can probably imagine what it was like to spend your mornings in a champagne house tasting the cuvées, seated around gorgeous oval tables in opulent rooms, and then doing the same in the afternoon and then again the next day. However, since it was part of our course, and we had to produce a final thesis on it, we had to make detailed tasting notes on everything, easy for the first couple but after a while increasingly more difficult. There was very little time to try to make sense of the numerous, illegible scribbles and write up notes, as the evenings were also filled. Each night we had a sumptuous meal at a first class restaurant hosted by one of the champagne houses and accompanied by a different champagne for each course. The food was lovely, and also needed detailed descriptions, but was Nouvelle Cuisine, and with small portions and a lack of carbohydrates it meant that for a week, along with the lack of sleep we were all as high as kites.

Among the Champagne houses which we visited were Mumm and Veuve-Clicquot, the latter of course being famous as it was Madame Clicquot who enhanced the process of champagne making, by clarifying the wine, which was subsequently adopted by all the Champagne houses. It was the visit to Mumm, however, which was more enjoyable as the house only opens to a certain number of visitors a year, and then only to individuals interested in wine rather than the general public. After our tour we were entertained by a Madame Loilier, who clearly adored her subject, and enthused us with her love of Champagne. She also allowed us to try the Prestige Champagne - René Lalou 1979. Sitting in beautiful surroundings, supping the most divine, quite full-bodied wine, it was a far cry from half-price spirits or Special Brew in the Poly Bar!

However, my favourite Champagne came from the De Venoge House. A smaller house, it had recently added a new Champagne to its repertoire – namely Crémant Rosé Brut. Not normally one for pink Champagne, this particular one was exquisite. It had been based on a crémant rosé, which the house had first developed in 1864, and with the Champagne itself and the beautiful bottle, they were trying to capture the flavour of a bygone era.

This, of course, all sounds extremely civilised, and on the whole during the visits to the Champagne houses and the hosted dinners, we behaved ourselves. I still pity the poor lecturers having to battle with a group of twenty-year-olds who were having alcohol dished out to them continually. They had to correct us continually when we announced that we were having an excellent holiday, in the form of:

"It's not a holiday – it's a Gastronomy Field Trip and the accompanying report will go towards your final grades!"

"Yeah, yeah, yeah," we all thought in unison.

They also had to try and ensure that after our official dinners we would somehow manage to return from whichever bar we were in, having consumed copious amounts of beer, and be bright and breezy at 7am the next morning for more wine tasting.

After a week of the torment of drinking champagne every day, our next stop was Burgundy. I'm not sure our digestive systems knew what had hit them with the sudden influx of rich beef dishes and red wine, and there were certainly withdrawal symptoms from the lack of bubbles. It got so bad that at one point we actually clubbed together and bought a few bottles of champagne – not normally part of a student's budget!

I'd been through and also stayed in Beaune itself previously, and was more than happy to return. It's always been red wine that does it for me, and red wine from this region was no exception. One of our first trips, and somewhere I had been to before was the Hospice de Beaune. A magnificent building, it had been founded as a charitable institution in 1443, and wine was used in medicine for the sick. And why not! The hospice owns acres of vineyards, and thirty-four cuvées are named after different benefactors. The wine is sold at a public auction on the third Sunday of November, and the profits are still used to run the hospital. As interesting as this all was, it was the next part of the tour which we were eagerly anticipating. So, on a wet Sunday morning we found ourselves in the Hospice's musty cellars trying to taste the thirty-four wines – well, maybe a slight exaggeration; the eleven available. It all started sensibly enough, and we took great care noting down the colour, bouquet, and taste of the wines, using the metal *tasse de vins* which had been designed for this purpose. The wines were all freely available and with no lecturers around, and little other supervision it all started to descend in a tasting orgy. I mean, how rude would it have been, having tasted some gorgeous Pouilly-Fuisse, not to have a refill. Some hours later, and barely able to walk, we emerged blinking into the grey daylight. By this time all attempts at being serious gastronomy students had left us, and we settled down to racing our *tasse de vins* in the water which was whooshing along the gutters!

Over the next couple of days we made our way further south, stopping in Beaujolais for a couple of visits. Poor old Beaujolais often gets bad press because of the *Noveau* fiasco every November. It's hardly surprising it often doesn't taste of anything as it's so young. However, we were fortunate enough to taste some of the 'Grand Crûs', and spent some time at the Château de la Chaize in the Brouilly area. We happily drank a number of vintage bottles - our enthusiasm helped by the Estate Manager, who wasn't at all interested in our enquiries about how much it cost, just its quality. However, we finally managed to persuade him that we had enjoyed it so much that we wanted to blow a bit more of our grants, and a number of us wobbled back to the coach clutching our three-bottled boxes.

Although we had some fabulous meals during our two-week stay, it was a visit to Paul Bocuse's three-star Michelin restaurant which was a highlight. Unfortunately we weren't able to eat there, but had an amazing tour of the kitchen, and the wine cellar which stored every alcoholic beverage you could imagine. We even met the man himself. You would think that someone with such a reputation wouldn't need confidence boosters - however, everything possible in the restaurant; serviettes, ashtrays, trays, had a picture of the man himself on them.

After two weeks of behaving ourselves reasonably well, everything came to a head towards the end of the trip when we were in Lyon. Staying in a modern hotel away from the city centre, boarded on one side by the Rhône, and the other by a main road, we adjourned to the hotel bar after a civilised evening out. Before too long we'd drunk the supply of beer, so stumbled out into the cold night (bizarrely it had snowed that day) in the search of alcohol. There were no bars to be found except for a transport café – which to all those who know France well are somewhat different from their British counterparts, and normally serve good food. However, it wasn't food we were after. We happily ensconced ourselves at the bar, and consumed a quantity of local, plastic topped litre bottles of red and white wine. We caused great amusement for the locals as we'd just explained that we were gastronomy students. Eventually we staggered back across the main road – a perilously dangerous feat, and stumbled into the hotel. Well, some of us did. After a few revolutions in the revolving doors, a friend and I unceremoniously fell into a crumpled heap into the reception area, and after a few minutes when we thought we were in an alternate universe, realised we were in the wrong hotel! Quick exit!

By this point the management of the large hotel where we were staying were becoming increasingly irate. Of course it was all highly immature, but hey – we were only twenty! After being told numerous times that we weren't allowed near the pool area, and couldn't throw each other in, and chastised for running round all over the place we were ordered back to our rooms. That's when the real fun started! By now in bed, the fire alarm started ringing. Apparently there was some fracas taking place in one of the rooms, and someone had set fire to something in the bathroom, and then scarpered. One saving grace was that it wasn't coming from the room of anyone from our course, but a different group travelling with us. However, the next morning, the shit had really hit the proverbial fan, and we were all in serious trouble. The lecturers couldn't persuade anyone to own up, the hotel banned the polytechnic from ever using the hotel again, and the atmosphere all day was way below freezing. This, of course, was coupled with enormous hangovers which put a dampener on the whole day.

After two weeks of sleep deprivation and alcohol excess we headed back to the UK. Despite having had an excellent time I was happy to return, not just for the comfort of my own bed, and not having to get up at such ridiculous times, but to see my recently acquired boyfriend, Tim. During the two weeks, he had been working hard on placement and had no sympathy when I moaned about feeling exhausted!

The following couple of months flashed passed, and were filled with the horror of impending finals. For once, however, with regards to education I actually decided to revise. I had also managed to produce a thesis of the trip to France which contained a detailed analysis of everything drunk and eaten, somehow taken from my notes which told me that the wine was 'nice' or 'red', written in an almost indecipherable hand. I therefore graduated from college and was the proud holder of a Hotel and Catering Management Qualification. And what an incredible time I'd had achieving it. I still feel that it really must be one of the dream courses to do.

Part Four

Paying for my own holidays!

Chapter 10

A few trips

The end of all this obviously spelt the start of something else. WORK. A job! I had to get a job. Other people feel the need to disappear for a gap year, either between school and university, or university and working, but having travelled and lived abroad this need wasn't so strong. It was therefore on July 28th 1986 that I started 'proper' work, less than a month after graduating. I think I may have even been successful on my first interview, so there I was, working as Assistant Manager at The Civil Service Club in Whitehall. Doesn't that sound grand? The hours weren't great, working at weekends was a necessary evil every three weeks, but the experience was invaluable. It also meant that I could afford to spend more on eating out, and start saving for a holiday.

It didn't take long, and in October of that year I was jetting off to sunnier climes. Poor old boyfriend had just started his final year so wasn't going anywhere, so a college friend and I packed our suntan lotion, and for the first time I took a package holiday. We went to Majorca and stayed in a small resort – Can Picafort, which was on the north of the island and wasn't too overrun by tourists. There was obviously not going to be any cultural part to our holiday, but we did manage to find a variety of restaurants whose names weren't the Red Lion or which didn't advertise Fish and Chips in English, and chomped our way through platters of gorgeous seafood. We succumbed one day and took one of those boat trips, where you're squeezed on board a fairly dodgy looking vessel with a million other holidaymakers, watered with Sangria, and then presented with trestle tables full of fairly average food, at the destination. This trip however, was worth it for one thing; the amazingly clear, turquoise waters, which graced all the little coves we sailed passed, and lapped up against the huge rocks which rose upwards for hundreds of feet out of the water. There's something so inviting and bewitching about crystal clear water – especially when it's a roasting day and you can immerse yourself in it without the fear of being attacked by slimy seaweed!

One morning we decided that some exercise and exploring was in order so we rented a couple of bikes for the day. As we set off, Elaine announced. "I haven't been on a bike for years, I feel a bit wobbly." That was an understatement, there was a screech, a clank of metal on earth and she was lying ungracefully in the ditch. We'd only ridden a couple of hundred yards by this time, and it looked like our expedition was over. However, she picked herself up, and we spent the day exploring local villages, thankfully devoid of any other tourists, albeit at a snail's pace.

It had been a good break, and energised me for the rest of the year. Before long it was 1987, and in the February I had my first little jaunt of the year. I returned to Holland again and this time it was with my closest school friend from my Dutch days. Karen was due to get married in the June of that year and wanted to have a pre-hen party weekend. Quite why we didn't fly I can't remember, but I do recollect that it was rather a torturous journey. Having fought our way across London in rush hour, we then caught a train which took us to Harwich, and finally boarded an overnight ferry to The

Hook of Holland. Sleeping in bunk beds in the bowels of a ship is never top of my list of favourite ways to travel – and I spent most of the night tossing and turning in rhythm to the ship. I finally fell asleep in the small hours to be rudely awakened by someone over the tannoy announcing that we would shortly be able to disembark. Disembark? We were still in bed, hadn't changed our watches accordingly, and were therefore an hour behind the rest of the ship. So, yet another rush and suddenly we found ourselves, bleary-eyed on Dutch soil. It was then an easy journey on an efficient Dutch train, and before we could settle down for another snooze we were in The Hague. My memory of this weekend is somewhat hazy, but I know that visits to favourite restaurants were involved, and ensuring that Grolsch was still up to standard!

My only other trip abroad that year was again to Holland – and to The Hague with Dad. It was an extended weekend trip, with the main reason for going being the wedding of mutual friends – to be more exact, a friend of Dad's to a friend of mine! Dad and I travelled over by car and ferry, with Dad enjoying his new company Audi. I had previously driven the car but never abroad, so it was with some trepidation that I took over on a stretch of calm motorway outside Antwerp. Dad promised we'd swap back before rush hour struck, but naturally there was nowhere to stop, and suddenly I was faced with mad, Belgian Friday afternoon traffic. I'm sure that in comparison to driving in Portugal where a red light means 'go quicker, so you don't have to stop', it was a walk in the park, but at the time it was quite horrifying.

Belgium. To be honest I think it gets a bad press. They *have* done quite a few important things. They discovered the delight of *Moules Frites,* and that to anybody in their right mind, has got to be the king of entrées. Then, of course, there are Belgium Chocolates – divine. And Antwerp of course.

How can anyone say diamonds are boring? Antwerp itself is stunning – full of pedestrianised, cobbled streets, packed with excellent restaurants. And that's not forgetting cities like Bruges and Brussels. We'd stayed in both whilst living in Holland, and whilst Bruges can be a touch quaint for some, it is full of interesting places to poke round. Brussels itself is spectacular - maybe the little boy pissing is no great shakes, but how could anyone deny the splendour of the Grand Place. And last, but by no means least. Tintin!! What the Belgians can't do, though, is directions. Their signposts appeared to have been designed and placed by someone who has never set foot in the country – and it was on many occasions that we drove round and round in circles, following signposts which took us nowhere. Not surprising, the Dutch tell the same jokes about the Belgians which we do about the Irish!

But back to Holland. The weather was gorgeous that weekend, and when we weren't doing wedding things were able to soak up the relaxing atmosphere. I particularly remember sitting at an outside café early one evening, overlooking the sea. The sky was clear blue, the sea calm, there was a happy Dutch atmosphere, I was with my Dad, and all we had to worry about was where to have dinner. I somehow feel that if we'd been able to transport ourselves over the water to the east coast of the UK, it wouldn't quite have been the same!

It was over all too soon, of course. Back to the daily grind of battling to work on the Northern Line in mid-summer, with no further trips planned. At least the evenings and weekends were jolly, and with my other half having graduated and working, there was money for enjoying ourselves. Life carried on in much the same vein until the following year. I started getting itchy feet – not at that time to physically be somewhere else, but to change jobs. First job and all that, and you think you have to stay in it for a respectable amount of time. I decided distraction tactics were needed, and it had to be something which would tax my brain. Quite why I couldn't have picked something a little easier I don't know, but I decided I'd pick up my music studies. I didn't have an instrument so plumped for music theory. I'd done exams whilst at school but hadn't done anything since. I therefore started studying for my grade 6 Music Theory exam – not too much of a problem when you could work from practice books with answers – but the composition element was a different matter. I didn't have a piano, and couldn't really work out if what I had written was any good, so used to phone Dad, dictate the music, and he'd play it back with the phone in his lap so I could hear it! Not the conventional method I'm sure. All this seemed an excellent idea until the exam itself. I had to go to a local school in North London and sit the exam with lots of school children. Just the smell of the place was almost enough to make me turn tail and flee before even starting the exam, but I forced myself up the steps and into the exam room. For once, I didn't look hopelessly at the questions, as I'd done at school, or leave after five minutes, but tackled the exam. Success! I had passed, and also managed to make it to almost two years in the job. However, by then it really was time to move.

Chapter 11

Tunisia

I landed myself a good job working for BT, as an Area Catering Manager, based at the top of Shaftesbury Avenue. A new job meant more money, and once I had been there for long enough to qualify for some time off, a holiday beckoned. Well, thinking back, apart from a view high points I could have well done without it. My boyfriend and I decided to have a 'proper' holiday together, rather than occasional weekends in the UK.

We booked to go to Tunisia, Hammamet to be exact, in the October. It looked as though it would be a good mixture of some lying on the beach, catching up on sleep, and some cultural stuff in Carthage. Having made the trip there, Carthage was amazing. It was so old but carefully preserved so you could actually see the individual rooms of the old Roman houses. Set against the backdrop of the bright blue sky and sea it was eerily atmospheric. The same day we visited the picture postcard, hilltop village of Sidi Bou Said. Painted white and blue and surrounded by vibrant pink bougainvilleas, the houses provided a stunning contrast to the blues all around them.

This was where the fun stopped though. The holiday had started promisingly enough; the hotel looked pleasant, wasn't high-rise, with the accommodation on the ground floor and a minute from the beach. Maybe beach is being polite. It looked like a rubbish tip at times – scattered with plastic bottles, drink cans, black rubbish sacks and other unmentionable items. They were all being washed onto the sand from the sea. What's more the sea was grey and murky most of the time, and there was no way that I was going in. I am a fair weather swimmer. Always have been, always will. The weather's got to be hot, the sea not the same temperature as a freezer, with clear water, absolutely no 'scary seaweed which is trying to strangle you', (surely there must be a film in that somewhere?), and definitely no waves. The sea in Hammamet didn't fit this bill at all. It was sunny occasionally and we'd rush to the beach. There was never a lack of space – hardly surprising! – and we'd settle down for a good snooze. No chance. I understand about 'personal space' and all that; that Northern Europeans need more than Mediterranean folk. I'm used to it now having lived in Portugal for so long, where 'private space' means 'public space'. But this was something else. At least in Portugal your beach space is yours and no one else's. So, just as I'd be dropping off and starting to dream about crystal clear waters, a Tunisian beach vendor saw another potential target and swooped. He was trying to sell oranges. Oranges! On the beach. I can't cope with peeling them at the best of times, but on the beach! We politely refused. This of course didn't work, and the vendor hung around, most definitely in our space, and then resorted to kicking our feet! Charming!

It was all going from bad to worse. At least I could console myself in enjoying Tunisian cuisine. I'd heard about 'Delhi Belly', in this case 'Tunisian Tummy' and avoided all the usual suspects; peeled fruit, salad, and ice. I'm lucky. I've always been able to eat anything. I really do think I've got a stomach lining of iron. Not on this occasion though. I have no idea what it was but I was in a bad way. Not just a couple of trips to the loo – but lying in a darkened room, hallucinating at one point. A happy holidaymaker I was not. My poor boyfriend tried to help, and even found some digestive biscuits to try and tempt me. They had chocolate on them! Another toilet dash.

I'd like to say the good points out weighed the bad ones, but they just didn't. I know that lots of people return to Tunisia, but I'm not going to be one of them. Despite the problematic holiday, it hadn't caused any problems between myself and my boyfriend. I managed to do that all by myself. I don't know whether it's a trait but when things are going really well in a relationship, I seem to want to throw a hand grenade into the equation. He really was a lovely boyfriend, and I'm sure if I hadn't stuffed things up we'd have got married. The problem was he was too nice, and often let me get away with murder, even though I didn't really want to. I wanted him to say 'no' and tell me to stop being a compete pain in the arse. Unfortunately he didn't, so I kept pushing and pushing. I'd met someone at work, and it was obvious where it could lead. It was just before Christmas 1988 and all-day pub opening had just been legalised. Trouble. Big trouble. Being in catering, we'd finish at 3.30ish, find a bar with *Happy Hour* and proceed to get horribly pissed. Since there were other people from work, and it was a legitimate way to be together, it was all still fairly innocent. I, however, was a real cow. I'd finally get to where I was supposed to meeting my boyfriend, always late, nearly always pissed, and he never tackled me about it. Give me an inch and I'll take the proverbial mile!

Chapter 12

Skiing in Bulgaria

By January he'd finally had enough, I confessed and we went our separate ways. Well, at least until our pre-booked, and paid for, skiing holiday in February. Neither of us wanted to forgo it, so we decided to go, and to avoid messing friends around, shared a room, as planned. Not really the ideal way to experience your first taste of skiing.

We were in Borovets in Bulgaria. Not your first choice for skiing, but as complete beginners it was a good deal. At the turn of the 19th Century, Prince Ferdinand had built a number of villas there for a summer retreat. By 1949 it had been nationalised for the benefit of union and party members, and by the 1960's to try and encourage tourism had been transformed into a winter sports resort. And, for me it was love at first sight. Not with resort – it couldn't in any way be described as pretty, dominated by an enormous, purpose built, ugly hotel, nor with a ski instructor, but with the whole skiing thing – mountains, clear air, blue sky and, naturally, the exhilaration of being completely out of control on a 'Green Run'. It's amazing how you can stumble out of bed early in the morning, with a banging head due to some revolting Bulgarian 'firewater' imbibed the previous night, trudge up to the chair lift with skis which feel as if they weigh of lead, but as soon as you manage to negotiate the chair lift, it all changes. You sit there, gently swinging, surrounded by snow and quiet, with an amazing feeling of peace and serenity, and by the time you fall off the other end, the headache has gone, your legs feel young again, and you've got enough energy to run a marathon.

Naturally, since this was only the first time, the speed we went as though we were snails skiing, and most of the holiday was spent falling over at each turn, falling off a button lift or crashing into a child, your ski instructor, a tree, the drag lift, or anything else that happened to get in the way. Elegant it was not! Huge fun it was! The fact that it wasn't the most picturesque resort in the world, the snow was doing a good impression of grass in some places, the food was interesting, to say the least (and cold) and that one of my ex-boyfriend's friends was distinctly giving me the cold shoulder, didn't matter. I had a ball. And as millions before me, was completely hooked.

One of the few things I regret about having lived in Portugal for so long is the lack of skiing I did. Spain may be great for skiing, but Portugal isn't. This is despite what the Portuguese say. I mean, the one time I saw really snow there, the whole town ground to a halt. Parents didn't even try to persuade their kids to go to school. They bundled them into their cars, and then, in what seemed a never-ending snake, drove up the mountain where the snow had laid. Since, at the time I was living in a house next to the mountain road, we watched with amazement as car after car drove passed with over excited kids in them, and a snowman on the bonnet. It hadn't snowed in eight years, and so for any child under eight and those who hadn't travelled (most of them) it was the first time they'd seen the stuff. It reminded me of when my cat experienced snow for the first time, incredibly curious but unsure at the same time, hesitantly putting a paw into the snow!

There is a high mountain range in Portugal, the Serra de Estrela, and many a Portuguese would tell you that you could ski there. There is a run; that's true, but it's practically horizontal! However, the area is truly awe inspiring, not chocolate box pretty as in Switzerland, but with enormous granite boulders, balanced precariously everywhere, and blanketed with snow.

Portugal was still many years away though, and certainly not Bulgaria. Some of us decided to take a morning off from skiing and travelled to Sofia. It was the first time I'd been to a Communist country, and then it was pre- November 1989. It was a grey day, and this did definitely not help Sofia. Bulgaria had been one of the Soviet Union's most loyal allies, and it showed. Most of the buildings were fairly grey and boring; a few, however, were impressive and clean, including the stunning Aleksander Nevski Church. It was a strange mixture of the Byzantine and Muscovite styles, and eye-catching, but this couldn't lift the general feeling of cold and misery I felt. We ventured inside a department store but that was depressing too. A shelf with one button for sale – well, maybe an exaggeration, but not far off. I'm sure Sofia is a very different place now, and if it is at all similar to other Eastern European cities I have since visited, is vibrant, actually sells things in the shops, and has a café and restaurant culture.

Unfortunately that was the last foreign holiday I had for a while. I did manage a weekend trip to Edinburgh in the May. It was foreign for me though, and the first time I'd been to Scotland. I stayed with my old Malibu and coke friend who had recently moved there with her new husband. I was impressed. Not with the husband I have to say. Isabel soon realised that and is now happily married to a Scotsman – but that is definitely another story! Edinburgh was lovely, the weather was great, the evenings were long and the pubs didn't shut at eleven. Almost like being abroad.

Most of the remainder of the year was spent working. I suppose my choice of boyfriend wasn't really helping matters. Phil was living with someone else (I know. 'Not big and not clever', but I was hooked) so holidays together were out of the question. We did, however, manage some Saturdays and evenings together, and were able to really enjoy the charms of London. After a year of this, though, the novelty was wearing off. I was completely fed-up with the situation, but at the same time not brave enough to ask him to leave his live-in girlfriend (I think I was afraid he might!), and so put a stop to things. Well, I tried to. He was a bit like a drug, and it was proving very difficult to break the habit, not helped by the fact that he was very persistent and wouldn't let me leave without a fight. There must have been something about him, as nearly twenty years later, and after two marriages (both his) we are the best of friends and have helped each other through those dark times in our lives.

Chapter 13

Holidays galore!

Splitting up was made substantially easier, though, by somebody I'd just met. Well, met wasn't exactly the correct term. At this point we were just flirting on the telephone. He was the manager of a team at BT, and when catering was required used to deal with my Functions Manager. One day, however, she wasn't in the office and I answered the phone. Well, some people have got a thing about voices and I'm one of them. He sounded so gorgeous, was interesting and extremely funny. I didn't want to shatter the illusion though and did nothing about it. Curiosity, finally got the better of me, and armed with info from my Functions Manager as to which department he worked in and which desk he worked at, I set off down to an adjoining building to give him a secret once over. Not bad at all, and defiantly worth moving things passed the telephone stage. This didn't prove a problem, and after a first date shortly afterwards, we were an item. One of the best things about him was his love for travel. Once again, I seemed to have been inextricably drawn to someone from one of my two favourite categories – 'have lived abroad', or 'have parents from different countries'. He was half Welsh, and half Swedish, but sounded neither.

His arrival heralded one of the most holiday filled, hedonistic periods ever. From getting together in November that year until December 1989, we had seven foreign holidays. Eight if you count Jersey. I thought I must have found my ideal boyfriend. He was full of ideas, loved reading, eating and drinking, and above all travelling.

Within a month of being together we'd decided to have a weekend break away, and Paris was the destination. My love affair with the French capital has already been documented, but it took on a completely new air going there with a boyfriend, and not my family. We stayed in a cheap, but amazingly centrally located hotel, just behind the Arch de Triomphe, and did what I'm sure all couples do when in Paris. What's more, after the first rainy afternoon, the weather cleared, and we watched the sun set from the Eiffel Tower. Most of the touristy things we did, going on a *Bateaux-Mouches* river trip, visiting Montmartre, I'd done before. However, on this occasion, I didn't have to wistfully hope that we could stop at one of the pavement cafés, as I'd done when on family holidays - we proceeded to spend a whole afternoon in one, near Notre-Dame. I did my best to consume as much Kir as was humanly possible, David likewise with beer and we then staggered off to find the métro. Whoever said that it was an easy system to negotiate obviously hadn't been availing themselves of Parisian cafés. It took a while! We did finally make it, and after a kip, we were back out for oysters and wine.

Three weekends later and we were Venice bound. Neither of us had been before, and decided it would be a perfect time of year to sample the city, minus the smelly canals and tourists. The late afternoon flight left on time, and although we knew there would be very little time that evening to do much, at least we could manage a beer somewhere. Wrong! Approaching the airport, we were informed that due to thick fog it would be impossible to land and that we would have to continue on to Trieste, which was on the border with Yugoslavia. Having arrived there, we were among a number of befuddled tourists who stood outside the airport, in the dark and cold, hoping that a coach might turn up. It did, but then proceeded to scare us all s..tless as it hared towards Venice. Naively hoping that we would be dropped off at our hotel, we then remembered that roads are somewhat lacking in Venice, and we were therefore deposited at the bus station. By this time it was late, and extremely cold, and nobody had a clue where we were, or how to get into the centre. As we were wondering how easy it would be to barter in Italian with a boat taxi – not very I imagine, owing to our Italian being limited to food and drink – I realised that there is sometimes a good reason to book an inclusive package. Out of the mist a lady materialised, waving a 'Magic of Italy' banner, who led us to a water taxi, and before long we were chugging down the Grand Canal. The mist became thicker and thicker, swirling around us, but somehow the driver managed to navigate safely and we arrived at the boat stop in St. Mark's Square. What a way to arrive in the centre of Venice! Well, it would have been if we could have seen anything. You could hardly see a metre in front of you, let alone the other side of the deserted square.

All of a sudden though I could see things - short people in red mackintoshes. If you like films then you'll know what I'm talking about. We'd recently seen *Don't Look Now,* with Donald Sutherland and Julie Christie, in which they pursue someone they think is their dead child, wearing a red Macintosh, through the misty streets of Venice. The film was scary, I was scared. It was all a little too real for me. I didn't want to be in a film that much. The holiday representative seemed blissfully unaware of the demons in my head and having led us over the main square, and down some little alleys (aahhh!!!!) we arrived at the hotel. By this time I could really have done with that drink. Was I going to go back out to search for an open bar? Not a chance in hell!

The next morning I decided I must have imagined the whole episode. What a stunning day. There wasn't a cloud in the sky, no wind, and Venice was picture postcard perfect. I know that when lots of people visit Venice they feel they need to do everything on the tourist trail. We, however, decided that it was beautiful just to observe, so we slowly ambled around, soaking up the atmosphere, stopping at outside cafés for a refuel, and generally poking around the back streets. We didn't even have a ride in a Gondola. Hardly surprising! Why on earth would you pay out a King's Ransom, when you could use a waterbus and get exactly the same views?

I have always been drawn to water, and feel much happier when I'm living near it. Being landlocked can sometimes feel a touch claustrophobic – don't ask me why. I have no idea! I love the vastness of the sea. Venice was no different, and with the sun reflecting off the various colours of the water I was hypnotised. We treated ourselves to a couple of expensive drinks overlooking the water, one at the Grand Hotel, on the terrace, and another in St Mark's Square, but otherwise tried to search out non-touristy places so that we didn't bankrupt ourselves. Heading over the Rialto Bridge into the Rialto area we discovered local food markets and local restaurants which served the most delicious seafood.

We only succumbed on one occasion to the tourist trap, and took a boat to one of the islands, in this case Murano. However, it wasn't busy and we spent a couple of hours wandering around the island and visiting one of the glassworks for which Venice is so renowned. We took the boat back to Venice as the sun was setting over the water, and finished our weekend off by eating Lobster Thermador at an amazing fish restaurant. I loved Venice! But...... how many women were wearing fur coats? At the time in the UK there had been a lot of publicity, and it was very 'Un PC' to have a fox draped round your neck. It was the opposite in

Venice. I have never seen so much fur, and positively felt the poor relation. I also bet that the Venetian women weren't cold!

We managed to survive a bit more of a British winter, with no furs, and then in January decided that some warmth was called for. But where to? We could both swing a week off work, and decided upon Tenerife, as it wasn't too far to travel, but the weather would be good. Despite the fact that it was purpose built, we had a large self-catering apartment overlooking the sea, and an easy stroll to the Lido. Cultural or pretty it wasn't, but it served its purpose, and we lazed around reading, playing backgammon, drinking beer, and eating seafood. I think we even summoned up the energy to play a couple of rounds of crazy golf.

The most exciting thing that happened was the reception we had at Gatwick customs. Obviously the customs men were bored and decided we were worth chatting to. It went something like this:

"Where have you been?"

"To Tenerife."

"Why?"

Why do you bloody well think, we thought. But answered. "For a holiday."

"Have you been indoors all the time? You're not very brown!" one of them ventured. Cheeky mare I thought.

"It wasn't very sunny," we spluttered.

At this point the other customs man joined, in and decided that our passports warranted a look. They must have been a bored custom man's dream. Mine had a Dutch residency stamp and David's a Swedish one, and suddenly two imaginations were working overtime. The stupid questions continued. Unfortunately as sarcastic as you want to be, it's just not worth it. They're the ones who have the power as far as the 'Marigold's are concerned!

"Why have you got a Swedish residency stamp in your passport," they asked David.

"Because I'm half Swedish."

"Why have you got a Dutch residency stamp in your passport?" he persisted with me.

"Because I lived in Holland!" Talk about bloody obvious.

"Why?"

"Because I went to school there," I replied whilst smiling sweetly.

"Why?"

Why bloody what, I thought. Because school is compulsory?

"Because my father was transferred there for work."

"And you don't live there now?"

"NO!"

"When did you last visit Holland?"

Oh, for God sake this was getting ridiculous. "About three years ago."

The stupid questions continued for a while, until they came up with the '*piece de resistance*'.

"What did you do on holiday?"

What the f..k do you normally do on holiday, we muttered to ourselves.

This was all getting too ridiculous and farcical for words. We obviously looked extremely suspect to them, and the passports had added fuel to their fire. However, we finally managed to persuade them that we weren't part of an international drugs ring, and off we went.

The stress of being interrogated like this was all too much, and we decided it was worth the risk of having a further exchange with customs man, and booked another holiday. Although I'd only been skiing once, David went regularly with his sister, brother-in-law, and friends, and so I went with them. We had a chalet booked in the middle of Courmeyer in Italy. It couldn't have been more different from Borovets, the previous year. The town itself was compact and cute with lots of inviting restaurants and bars, and although you had to get a cable car up to the slopes, this didn't prove a problem as it was only a shot walk and there were never any serious queues. There were loads of different runs, lots of mountainside bars, and metres of snow – not a blade of grass in sight.

I had a brilliant week. Ski school in the morning, off skiing with my friends in the afternoon, and by the end of the week even being able to respectably ski and fall down a red run. But of course, all skiing holidays have to involve a little drama, and we had ours. On the last afternoon we were determined to do as much skiing as possible. On the final descent, rather then taking the usual *piste* back we decided to ski down into another valley, get the chair lift back up from there, and then ski down. Bad idea! It started off ok, but we soon came onto a very narrow section, bordered by trees, and very twisty – not good for tired, beginner legs. I then realised that it was leading to a slope which had caused me all manner of problems that morning. By the time we reached it, I'd worked myself up into a nice lather. Although the slope was really wide it was just that it was so steep and icy. I went for the glamorous descent – knew I wouldn't remain standing but was hoping I could go down on my bum. That went all wrong, and I ended up going head first, on my back straight down the mountain, screaming my lungs out. I couldn't see where I was going, couldn't do anything so just had to wait, praying there weren't any trees until I got to the bottom.

Nice beer and sit down. Oh no! We still had to get the chair lift, and then ski back down to the cable car. Thoroughly pissed off by this point I trudged off to the chair lift, and jumped on. A short distance later and my right ski fell off. Fortunately, one of my friends hadn't yet got on, so was able to rescue it for me. A sigh of relief until I realised I had to jump off at the other end, with one ski. I psyched myself up for this, managed to manoeuvre myself off the chair lift, but then fell over, and the chair lift hit me on the back of the head. Oh good!!! Pissed off doesn't start to explain how I was feeling. By this time the light was fading rapidly and we set off down the final run. All my confidence had gone by this point, and every turn was a major accomplishment. I was taking it very slowly which enabled me to stay upright, when out of nowhere came the mountain 'sweepers', making sure that all skiers were off the mountain. At that point I could have easily killed one of them. They kept swooping in between us, shouting that we should be off the mountain, and to hurry up. Did that help? No. By this point I was turning green with rage, and was ready to deck anyone that came anywhere near me. I decided that venting my anger might help me get down.

"Why don't you just f..k off and leave me alone. Can't you see I'm f..king trying to get off this f..king mountain! You are f...king me off!" I don't suppose they understood a lot, but probably got the general impression that I wasn't a happy bunny, and I'm sure didn't appreciate the imperative, adjective, determiner, and verb forms of said expletive that I'd used. They continued to swoop close to us for the rest of descent, with me continuing to mutter away, doing my best Mutley impression. I can't describe how relieved I was to be off the piste, sitting down with boots off, and a drink in my hand. Despite the last afternoon's antics I was even more hooked than the previous year, and by the time we flew home was already looking forward to the following year's holiday.

Where all the money was coming for all these holidays, I don't know. We both earnt well, but seemed to be continually spending. Maybe it was just priorities. I was still sharing a flat, as was David; we didn't have cars, and apart from buying books and CD's didn't spend money on much else. Apart from food of course. We still had money for that. We regularly ate out, and I'm not talking fast food joints. We tried many different restaurants in central London, but continually returned to one, Saigon in Frith Street. I haven't eaten there for years now and it's probably closed down. The prices would probably have given me a heart attack, when I was earning Escudos in Portugal. But it was good. So good. The most exquisite Vietnamese food appeared every time we went there, and was washed down with a generous amount of Sake. We often took friends there for them to experience it and before long the waitresses recognised us. I'm sure if you're rich and famous being found a table is nothing special, but when you aren't, and the waitresses are rearranging the restaurant to fit you in on a busy evening before Christmas, you feel special. I think they appreciated that fact that we loved the food so much, and were always polite and friendly to them. What a difference it makes. To this day I can't stand it when people are condescending or rude, for no reason, to waiters. It makes me want to tip beer all over them. Of course we weren't always well-behaved diners, and one evening, the following year, excelled ourselves – well, David did. I had just got a new job, and we'd gone out to celebrate. We drank more Sake than usual and by the end of the meal we definitely weren't the quietest table there. For some unknown reason David decided to throw his hot wet towel at me. I reacted with cat-like reflexes; moved my head, it sailed passed me and hit the man behind me straight in the face. Oops! Silence. We apologised profusely, but I doubt the man really believed us as we were both hysterical with laughter by that point.

It was May now, and I hadn't been abroad for two months. We decided to have a weekend away over the bank holiday, and for some reason choose Jersey. I have no idea why, but neither of us had been before and it was close. For a change it decided not to rain, and in fact the weather was beautiful. We hired a car, and drove (I did to be precise – boyfriend hadn't quite mastered the art) around the island, stopping whenever we fancied it. Jersey was strange. The scenery, weather and gorgeous beaches were like those of Brittany, but the island was full of cafés selling pie and chips, and Brits on holiday.

Next, was our third holiday, and we decided not to have a summer holiday together but to save it for the autumn, when I knew the effects of the weather would be kicking in. That's not to say we didn't squeeze in a few weekends away. One of them was at Sandbanks, near Poole, in a lovely hotel with a Jacuzzi, and jellyfish all over the beach. We did our own thing on the next break – David went to Sweden with his Swedish cousin, and I went back to Edinburgh to see the same friend I'd visited the previous year. Unimpressive husband was no longer on the scene, lovely new boyfriend was, and we had a great weekend. What's more we went to Glasgow for a day, played baseball in the park and then had an amazing curry. I liked Glasgow, although I was only there for a day, and haven't been back since. I'd like to go again. All the accounts I hear and read is that it is now a thriving and vibrant place.

Having not had an official summer holiday, we decided that we should treat ourselves to that autumn break. We didn't really care where to, just wanted some 'R & R', and so found ourselves on the way to Santorini, a small island in the Cyclades, in Greece. Oh, wow! You know sometimes your expectations of a place are so high, and that almost invariably you are let down; well, this was the opposite. We knew nothing at all about Santorini, and it just kept getting better and better. We were staying out of the centre, in a small place called Kamari. We had a fairly bog-standard apartment, but it was on the ground floor and was only a couple of minutes from the beach - which was black! The island must be volcanic then. The sand certainly felt like lava as it was boiling. There was a lovely relaxed feeling to the place; the water was clear, there were some gorgeous little bars which overlooked the sea, lined by some feathery bushes which ran the length of the beach. It would have been all too easy to have just stayed there – beach in the morning, grilled cheese for lunch, beach in the afternoon, and then dinner and lots of cold beer. However, we decided that we really ought to make a trip to the tiny capital, Thira and took a local bus, which bumped and groaned and took us steadily uphill to the other side of the island.

The town consisted of beautiful white and blue houses, swathed in bougainvillea and other plants of whose names I have not a clue. We strolled round the narrow streets, working our way in the direction of the sea, but with no idea what was in store. It was truly a heart-stopping view. The edge of the city clung onto a cliff, which dropped down hundreds of feet into the clear blue sea. It overlooked the dormant volcano, which rose out of the water in the bay. We discovered later that this was one of the fabled locations of Atlantis. It had my vote! Standing on the edge of the cliff, looking around, you could see both ends of the island, making it look like a *croissant* with its ends folding into the volcano. Somehow, from that height, I could almost swear that you could see the curve of the earth. What a truly spectacular sight it was. And that was in the daytime – the sunset was magical. We sat quietly on a low stone wall, watching the sun change from yellow to orange, then pink, and finally sink into the sea. It was almost a mystical feeling - we were after all in Greece.

That wasn't the only incredible experience of that day. Having scrambled down the cliff, taken a boat over to the volcano, which we climbed, peered worryingly into little crevices from where there was steam emanating, we decided to stay in Thira for dinner, and worry about finding a taxi home later. After watching the spectacular sunset we found a little bar for some pre-dinner oúzo, and thought about food. Neither of wanted a run-of-the-mill experience after the day we had had, and so walked straight passed any restaurants which had signs in English selling Chicken and Chips (although I would never have gone in them anyway), in search of something which at least appeared more authentic and different. Oh boy did we find it.

Walking down one of the narrow cobbled streets we came across a restaurant, set in a tiny stone house, with beautiful arches for doorways. However, there was no menu! After dithering for a while we decided that we were in the right mood for the unknown, and stepped into it. The moment we crossed the threshold a tall, arm-waving Greek rushed up to us, beaming from ear to ear; he also bore an uncanny resemblance to a certain rock star.

"Why is Freddie Mercury working in a Greek restaurant?" I

whispered to David. It obviously wasn't him, but if he'd had a twin brother......

"Good evening! How are you this wonderful evening? I am so glad you are here. You will have a great time. Sit down there!" We did as we were told. The owner, as we discovered he was, then proceeded to explain to us the lack of menu.

"I don't want people in here who won't take a risk, so I have no menu, and wait to see who will come in. I will show you a variety of cold starters, you choose what you want, you then do the same for the main course and the chef will cook them." At this point he waved over 'Swedish Chef' from the Muppets. This was getting more surreal by the minute.

"Hi! I'm Wayne from New Zealand." He just happened to be the spitting image of the Muppet. We settled down to our meal, having been presented with an *ouzo*, soaking up the jovial atmosphere. I had the most delicious octopus marinated in *ouzo*, and whilst eating this watched 'Chef' who was busy cooking our main course in the corner of the restaurant – no kitchen here. During the main course – also delicious – we enjoyed watching other bemused customers hovering at the entrance of the restaurant, picking out those who would scarper and those who would be entranced in. After a while 'Freddie' came over and plonked himself down next to us. We talked about all manner of subjects, starting with those who do and don't take risks. The owner admitted to us that he had another business – the jumper shop next door. Not just any jumper shop though. They were all hand made from natural fibres and were for the rich American tourist market. It was this that provided his main income; the restaurant was what he did for fun. And it showed!

At the end of the meal I asked 'Chef', who by this time had also joined us, if he could recommend a local *digestive*. At this point he lowered his voice and told us that he did indeed have something. It came from a neighbouring island, and was obviously not exactly legal. We were told that as you drank it, it would appear to dissolve in your mouth and at the same time be fiercely hot. "What's more", 'Freddie' added, "You'll have the most amazing dreams, and in the morning you'll have completely clear heads." I had the first swig – fire didn't even begin to describe the sensation. I got told off for making a fuss by David, which he soon took back after his first swig. By the time we left the restaurant we really were rolling around. Somehow we managed to fall into a taxi, get driven to the other side of the island, and make it into bed. The dreams certainly were amazing, and in the morning we were hangover free.

We returned once again that week to the same restaurant, and even recommended it to friends who visited the island the following year, and had a similarly bizarre but hugely enjoyable experience. As far as meal experiences go it definitely has to be in my top five!

Although the glow of a hot, autumn holiday unfortunately soon wore off, at least we had a weekend in Paris planned for December. However, even the timeless romance of Paris couldn't really salvage that weekend. By this point David was very unhappy at work and had developed all manner of stress related symptoms, including being argumentative. At one point when he wanted to stay in the hotel on his own, I just had to amuse myself in Paris. I remember that, although I was sad that all was not a hundred percent between us, I did appreciate being able to do exactly what I wanted that afternoon. I wandered around the Opéra district of Paris, stopping wherever I fancied, drooling over the gorgeous Delicatessens which were everywhere, and generally soaked up the pre-Christmas atmosphere of Paris. I think it might have been from that afternoon that I have always been able to enjoy somewhere on my own, and in fact, sometimes, quite selfishly to prefer it. You can just do exactly what you want, when you want, without having to explain why. If you want to spend an hour in the Matisse room at the MOMA in New York, have spicy potato somethings for breakfast in Singapore or talk to anyone you fancy, then you can.

1991 arrived, and proved to be, in some ways the starting point of my doubts about living in the UK – not that they were in any way tangible that early on. In the meantime we had a ski-ing holiday booked to look forward to. We went to Livigno in Italy. Not the prettiest resort in the world, and quite a trek from our chalet to the chair lift up to the slopes. I'd always wondered why is it that most people can apparently effortlessly march toward the lift with their skis slung over a shoulder, or can cleverly carry them with their poles? Try as I might I have never mastered it, ending up either covered in bruises, always lagging behind everybody begging for them to wait, or worse still, knocking myself or some poor unsuspecting skier round the head!

The skiing and partying was fairly full on this holiday, but unfortunately was memorable for another reason. Being somewhat overconfident one afternoon, no doubt egged on by lunchtime beer, one off our party jumped and landed with a crack. Fifteen minutes later and we were loading her onto a helicopter – how she kept so cheerful I don't know. Maybe something to do with the fact that she and most of our group were doctors! It turned out that a dislocated hip was the problem and that was the end of skiing that year for Sandra. The rest of us rather tentatively wobbled down the rest of the slope, and no one was too upset when all the slopes were closed the next day because of blizzards. Lazing around by a pool, ice skating and playing silly games was much safer.

That, unfortunately, was the only holiday that year. Towards summer things had become somewhat difficult between

David and me, but the reasons and the way it manifested itself were certainly not the usual ones. He was increasingly more disillusioned by the world of business and consumerism, and was continually having internal battles about it all. Practically, it meant that holidays were not on the agenda as they were far too hedonistic. I'd just started a new job which I was quickly realising was a one-way ticket to an unhappy me, and coupled with the prospect of no holidays made it all worse. At least though, I'd finally escaped from the 'trauma' of the Northern Line every day and was now able to drive to work in a company car. It also meant that with David now living in Buckinghamshire we were at least easily able to escape into the countryside at the weekend. The other plus point was that his flat was in a small village, and located between a lovely country pub and a fabulous Indian restaurant.

However, pretending everything was all right couldn't last and during the summer we split up. That didn't last long either, and after a weekend away in Woodstock David had decided to chuck in the job which he hated so much, and to write full-time. He moved into my flat in London, and we were on new territory yet again. This arrangement meant that there was even less likelihood of a holiday together. I was determined, though, that skiing wouldn't suffer, and when the time came to book I did and he didn't. In retrospect it was probably for the best.

Everything was about to change again. I had come to really hate my job, had already handed my notice in, and was due to finish at the end of January. This was done without another job to go to but I'd didn't care. By just after New Year and the start of 1992 it wasn't the only thing which I was without. David and I split up again.

Chapter 14

1992 - Planning my escape

Life had been rather traumatic, and the skiing holiday that year really saved me. We went to Verbier in Switzerland. The weather was great, the skiing excellent and we had a wonderful week. In fact it was so wonderful, that I came up with another of my mad schemes. Being without a job and a boyfriend and enjoying being abroad so much, I decided that being a chalet girl was the answer to my problems. Quite where I got that idea from I don't know but at the time it all seemed very sane. It was therefore, that a couple of weeks later, I left a cold, grey England and flew to St Anton in Austria. Of course doing this wasn't without its traumas. David and I were still in contact by phone, and he had started to give me a hard time about moving abroad!! Bloody hell! Not that he was offering an alternative; he just didn't want me to go. Selfish? Men? Never!

From the start it was doomed to disaster, and the whole episode lasted barely three weeks. I was sharing a room the size of a rabbit hutch with a chain-smoker, and said rabbit hutch was next to the central heating boiler so it was constantly sauna temperature. The chalet, which I was responsible for, was at the other end of the resort, located on the third floor, and without a lift. This meant that after I'd done the weekly shop on a budget of about 50p per guest per week, I then had to lug it up the stairs. All this teamed with the fact that the holiday rep manager was a *prima donna* who had clearly never managed anyone in her life, and drank so much that one night she ended up in hospital having her stomach pumped!

My reaction to all this, plus the split up with David, and being career less, meant that I went somewhat off the rails myself. Burning the candle at both ends didn't begin to describe it. Every evening, after mountains of washing up were done I'd head for a local bar with the other chalet girls, and more often than not, the guests. Jeigermeister was the favourite tipple as a shot, washed down by whatever was to hand. I basically spent every night doing this, nursing enormous hangovers in the mornings, not helped by the lack of sleep or the bedroom from hell. I really wasn't interested in doing my best in the job, or representing the company particularly, and did the big 'no, no' by getting too friendly with one of the guests! By this time I was also completely run down, and going down with something (that something turned out to be bronchitis). It wasn't really surprising then when the powers that be decided that maybe my days as a chalet girl were numbered. Thank God for that really!

Of course there were a few high points. One of them was on an afternoon off, when I and some of the chalet girls decided to go to Innsbruck. We didn't have much money so opted to hitchhike, and managed to flag down two cars at roughly the same time so we arrived together. I think I must have blocked out some of that little Austrian experience, because I can't remember very much of that afternoon, apart from my need to go and look at the Golden Roof again. It was still golden, and still stunning, and took me back to when I'd last seen it as a fourteen-year-old, when life wasn't half as complicated and I didn't get myself into such ridiculous situations.

The other memorable experience was tobogganing – not exactly a surprise given that I was in a ski resort – but this wasn't your normal tobogganing. Located half way up a *piste* from the main resort was a famous bar – the Krazy Kangaroo – where a variety of antics regularly occurred. One evening we discovered that in the past people had tobogganed from the bar down to the resort when it was dark. However, the local council had unfortunately decided that it was too dangerous, and had banned it. But, hey, as we all know rules are made to be broken. It was therefore, that the following evening I liberated some large bin liners from the chalet and along with that week's guests we made our way to the bar. After an evening of beer consumption we staggered and slid to the top of the slope. Was it enjoyable? Not sure that's quite how I'd describe it, but I've rarely experienced the adrenalin rush I got from that or laughed so much through sheer hysteria. Basically, after only a few metres we all became separated from our bin liners, had no way to steer or slow down, and hurtled down the slope, often colliding with each other until we arrived at the bottom of the slope in a large ungracious heap. The beer had naturally softened the blows, but the next day every single part of my body ached, and I was bruised all over. How immature but what fun!

So. Back to the UK, tucked up in bed with bronchitis, and generally feeling sorry for myself. It did give me time to think though, and I decided that I'd have to give the catering industry another shot. I started working for someone who had an idea about setting up a club through a newspaper, giving discounts at various restaurants. Now of course, this seems commonplace. At the time though it was all very new. My part was to cold-call restaurants in central London to see if any owners were interested in the idea. Well, I've had some jobs in the past, but this was horrible. It even made a part-time job I had whilst at school at a beauty parlour seem bearable – one of the less glamorous tasks was to heat up used leg wax, then strain it through a sieve, getting rid of the hairs so it could be used again!! Anyway, after only a couple of hours of cold calling I knew it wasn't for me, gave up walking up and down the side roads off Oxford Street, went into John Lewis and bought a new duvet – as you do! So, I was back at square one deciding what to do with my life.

I had previously discussed the possibility with David of us both going abroad and teaching English. This was a somewhat strange proposal, given how much I had hated school and learning. Nothing happened at the time, and I had all but forgotten it. With vague thought about this, before long I managed to get a job working for a contract caterer, based in Oxfordshire, as a Sales Manager. I didn't want to give up my flat until I was sure, so stayed with friends of my Godparents. (I couldn't stay with them, because they rented out their house for six months of the year, to spend the time in their house in the Cévennes Mountains in France of which I've already written.) This lasted about two weeks, until one morning I woke up and it had all become incredibly clear. I was going to train to teach English as a foreign language, and move abroad as soon as I could.

The relief was immense – having actually made a decision about the future, and feeling good about it. I left my job, gave notice on my flat in London, and set about looking for a course. With no income, Mum and Dad offered to give me shelter, so along with nine years of accumulated junk I moved back down to Sussex. It also meant that I was reunited with my lovely Ziggy cat. I successfully passed an interview and reserved a place for a month-long course starting that October. Meanwhile, I was living in Sussex, with a couple of months to fill, and not a huge deal of money. Fortunately, I managed to have a holiday abroad due to my parents' generosity. Mum and Dad, and my brother were booked to stay with friends of my Godparents in the

Cévennes. It wouldn't cost any extra if I went along and Dad kindly told me I was welcome if I didn't mind having a holiday with them. As if!

So, that August we headed down through France towards Montpellier, stopping an hour north of the Med in the tiny village of Molières, which, since my last visit to the region, my Godparents had moved to. We didn't stay with them but with another family in the same village who had a self-contained apartment for rent. It was a great low-key holiday. My parents and brother had already visited the village, and together we revisited old haunts. Although the village was perched on the hillside overlooking a valley and was stunningly beautiful, unfortunately there was no bar. When you're in the South of France in the summer you need a bar!

On a trip to the other side of the valley one morning, my brother and I decided to stay in the local café and reacquaint ourselves with the very civilised pastime of drinking *Pastis*. Unfortunately, it didn't stay that way and after a couple of hours we discovered that we were fairly drunk, and had no easy way of getting back. We ended up walking down to the main road and along the valley, all in the mid-day sun. The worst was still to come when we had to walk up the hill the other side. It was a good forty-five minute walk and with every step I melted a bit more. Note to self; if you are going to drink a lot in the middle of the day, make sure you don't have to walk anywhere in the boiling heat.

As well as the lovely French beverages there was also all that great food. We had many enjoyable meals; some eaten under umbrellas in traditional, sunny squares where I had my regular lunch of *escargots* and rare *steak frites*. There were also the simple meals of French bread and cheese and fresh apricots which we ate sitting in the garden with the stunning view. It was so pleasant that at the age of twenty-six, and having travelled a fair bit with friends and boyfriends that I could so happily have such a good holiday with my parents and my brother.

Unfortunately, it all came to a close too quickly, and it was back to the UK, and a month of thumb twiddling whilst I waited for my course to start. A slight diversion came midway through September when I met a naval officer at a party in Portsmouth. During my course we kept in touch, and one weekend met up for our first date and took it from there. As for the course, as anyone who has done it knows, it's one of the maddest four weeks you can have – basically studying from dusk till dawn. By the end of October, however, it was all over, and I was a newly qualified Teacher of English as a foreign language. Unfortunately, it was smack in the middle of the academic term and no chance of getting a job until January. I put all my efforts in to finding a job for then, concentrating on France mainly, and in December when funds were running low got a part-time job working in WH Smith's.

It was fairly dire but I obviously I showed some sense and quickly was allowed to do the book window display, and following that be in charge of the pens and electronic typewriters. Since I had no idea how to use an electric typewriter and much less to demonstrate how they worked, it was an interesting month! Fortunately, I had the distraction of a certain Naval Officer and we had some good nights out.

Christmas approached quickly and on Christmas Eve I went out for a couple of drinks with some friends and met an interesting guy. We talked about books and films, and I very much enjoyed his company. This made Christmas Eve special, and although it turned out to be interesting in its way, it was New Year's Eve which led to far more fruitful and long-term changes. It was at a party held by one of my skiing buddies, Kathy - because it was in London I had stayed overnight. The next morning my friend's brother phoned up to wish her Happy New Year. He worked at a language school in the north of Portugal and just happened to mention that the school was looking for a full-time teacher, due to unforeseen circumstances, and that if his sister knew anybody who may be interested to let him know. So, nursing a hangover, I was talking to someone in Portugal who knew there was a teaching vacancy.

A couple of days later I had a telephone interview with the Director who offered me the job, and before I knew it was packing my cases for Portugal. This however, happened at the same time I received another phone call. Ever since then I'm sure that bad timing has followed me wherever I go, as it hasn't happened just the once! The rather gorgeous guy from Christmas Eve phoned up. He'd been away over Christmas, returned to the UK and tracked me down. We had a lovely evening together, talked and talked about books and films, our love of skiing and being by the sea. We went to see *Blade Runner: The Director's Cut* another evening, and as well as now being my favourite film, it reminds me so much of Bill and what could have been. By this point I was head over heels, (which I hadn't felt since things were going well between David and myself) and wondering if it was really a good idea to move to another country where I knew no one, or stay and see what happened. However, that was never really going to happen since it had been a dream for so long so we said goodbye, promised to keep in touch, and I left. Of course I have no idea what would have happened if I had stayed. Bill and I kept in touch throughout my first six months in Portugal, and I'd get interesting postcards from wherever he happened to be testing windsurfers. We even met up in the summer a couple of times, but by then he'd met someone who he was to get married to, and as I know, since after all this time we met up in the summer of 2003 for lunch, is very happy.

Favourite Starters

Vietnamese Spring Rolls

~

Soup de Poisson

~

Grilled Goats Cheese Salad

Moules Marinière

'Grandes Arcades' restaurant, Arras, France

Part Five

Escape to Portugal

Chapter 15

Blue skies

Portugal. I'd never been there, never really thought about going there, didn't know anything much about it apart from the ubiquitous port and didn't know a word of the language. And here I was, moving to a country, which not only did I not know, but also knew nobody there, and was embarking on a new career. Fortunately I didn't really have time for the jitters and was soon on board a plane heading for Porto in the north of the country. What I couldn't work out was why there were so many people speaking what I imagined Hungarian would sound like – I decided they must have been going to a conference. The horror hit me when, on landing, I realised that everyone around me was speaking the same language and that therefore it must be Portuguese. It was like nothing I'd ever heard before, and I couldn't understand a word.

To counteract the horror of this, the upside was that I was met at the airport by one of the teachers so I didn't have to try and communicate with the locals. Tim then drove me northeast towards Guimarães, the town where I was to be living and working, which was up in the hills. It was a beautiful January day – the sun was shining and the sky was so clear and deep it was almost violet. The countryside was covered with pines and eucalyptus, and I was full of positive thoughts as we made our way. Just to put a damper on this, Tim, the teacher who had collected me and the brother of the friend I'd been with on New Year's Eve, explained the reason why there had been a sudden vacancy. Two weeks previously on New Year's Day morning one of the teachers had been found dead in his Land Rover. He had gassed himself. What was I letting myself into? Were the job and the place so bad? However, Tim explained that the man had suffered from depression, and very sadly hadn't coped. What's more the first person I met when I arrived was his widow.

On arriving at the school I was given the option of two places to stay; one was in a little flat overlooking the main square, and a minute's walk from work. The other was in a shared flat a fair bus ride away on the side of a *Penha* (translated as cliff, but in reality a pyramidal shaped hill), which overlooked the town. Despite the fact that I hadn't seen either I opted for the shared flat, as I didn't know anyone and thought it would be more fun. This turned out to be the right decision. As we drove up the steep road towards the house I was stunned by the beauty of the surrounding countryside – not pretty Alpine style peaks, but rugged peaks formed from granite. What also made an impact was the preponderance of greenery. Because so many of the trees were either fir trees or eucalyptus, it was hard to believe it was only the start of January. However, the best was yet to come. After we'd negotiated a steep hairpin bend drive I was faced with a huge plot and in the middle of it a large whitewashed villa. As we carted my belongings up the outdoor stairs, and across the huge balcony, which ran the whole way round the upstairs flat, and I was enjoying the fantastic view, I looked down to see a swimming pool!! I felt as though I'd escaped from the grey cold of Britain to the colourful, fantasy world of *Oz*.

This initial feeling didn't last long unfortunately. I met one of the girls who I was to be sharing with. She made me feel welcome by making cups of tea and sharing treasured chocolate digestives. We chatted for a while and I found out about her situation. She was living in the flat with her boyfriend, and was four months pregnant. Clare then told me that the man who had committed suicide had been her partner's stepfather. They hadn't been particularly close but that didn't stop me feeling that the only reason I was now in Portugal was that someone had died. And not only that; I was sharing a flat with his stepson!

That was the least of my worries. Having arrived on a Thursday I presumed I wouldn't start teaching until the following Monday. But no – I was definitely thrown in at the proverbial deep end. And what a first class I had to contend with. To call them monsters would be unkind to monsters. They were aged thirteen, about twenty of them and mainly hormonal boys. The course I'd done had prepared me to teach English to adults, but I had no idea what to do with children. They led me a merry dance the first lesson, and I seriously wondered how I was going to cope. The likelihood of them sitting still and concentrating on anything was never going to happen, so from then on I used a mixture of activities and games, and I hate to admit, bribery, to try and help them with their English and maintain my sanity. They loved the games, but unfortunately the noise level resembled what I imagined it would be like standing next to the engine of a Jumbo. The secretaries were forever coming upstairs and asking us to keep the noise level down. Amazingly, the little sh…s did seem to be learning and frequently surprised me with intelligible sentences. Of course, they still took any opportunity to disrupt the lessons, and one week decided that using animals was the way. The first lesson that week, and a puppy arrived in class. I don't even need to describe the chaos which ensued. Finally, I persuaded the perpetrator that the puppy had to wait on the balcony for the duration of the lesson – which was finally agreed on, but as long as the puppy could be continually checked on. The second lesson one of the kids brought in a matchbox with a spider in it. The expectation on their faces was indescribable – they could hardly contain themselves as I was made to look inside. Fortunately, for me, spiders have never proved a problem, and I confounded them by asking questions about it! The last lesson of the week, and they'd obviously had a council of war as to the next attack. A larger box arrived, and one of the kids told me he had brought his pet along. He took whatever it was out, opened his hands and no doubt the whole class expected me to jump on a table. It wasn't even a mouse, but a pet hamster. As their jaws hit the floor I asked if I could hold it, and as I did told them I used to have a pet mouse. The begrudging respect started from then. In fact, at the end of the summer term they were the most appreciative classes that I had, and I received a huge amount of melted chocolates. Of course they were a few relapses. One boy obviously had some kind of behavioural problems. One week he went through a stage of drawing green willies all over his exercise book, and occasionally he would suddenly show them to me! And of course as a fairly naïve teacher I fell for the classic schoolboy trick. By the end of June it was unbearably hot, and it was all I could do to wear anything in class. So it was a strappy dress I had on one afternoon. It took me a fair while to realise that they hadn't suddenly become dedicated students when continually asking me to come over and check what they were doing, but that as I was bending over they were looking down my front!!!

However, I am seriously digressing, and if I related all the stories about students and their antics it would be another book. Having survived the first day of teaching I had the weekend ahead of me. That gave me time to get to know Guimarães. I went out for dinner on the Friday night to a typical Portuguese restaurant, and then proceeded to be given a tour of the local bars. On the Saturday evening I was invited over to Gabrielle's for dinner. It was with some trepidation I went, as she was the lady who had recently been widowed. However, I had no reason to feel nervous. Along with her son and his girlfriend, Clare who I was living with, and Tim who had met me from the airport, we had a lovely evening. What an amazing lady to have made dinner for us so soon after the tragedy, and to be so welcoming to me. She was truly an inspiration.

On the Sunday lunchtime I was invited over to Tim's for lunch, preceded by an aperitif sitting outside a café in the sun. By the end of the sunny, sociable weekend I was smitten with Portugal, and knew I'd be there for a while.

So, a bit of history. Guimarães itself is famous for being the 'cradle of Portugal' – namely the birthplace of the current Portugal. It was in 1128 that Afonso Henriques, son of Count Henry of Burgundy and his wife, the illegitimate daughter of the king of Castile, seized power from his regent mother and her lover, Fernando Peres and dispatched then to exile in Galicia. So much for appreciating what your mother gives to you. This took place in São Mamede, close to the castle, which he used as a stronghold. Despite being small in comparison with many other castles, and virtually a ruin, the castle still maintains the square keep and the seven towers. It is an eerie place, and in true Portuguese fashion has no safety measures in place, so you can clamber up the steep steps, walk around the castle ramparts with nothing to stop you falling off the edge. Many visits were made with friends' children with hearts in mouths! Having dispatched his Mum, Afonso was duly acclaimed King of Portugal in 1143, and Portugal was born.

From then Portugal's history was as colourful as any other European county, but it was an episode that occurred a hundred or so years later, which I was told about my first weekend that fascinated me in a gruesome way. It's a story that every Portuguese schoolchild knows. Alfonso IV's son Pedro married into Castile yet found true love with Inês de Castro, a Galician lady in his wife's court. He wasn't very popular for this and Inês was brutally murdered by three advisers of Afonso IV. Dom Pedro saw red, and took his revenge on two of the murderers he eventually captured by drawing their hearts from their bodies, one from the chest and one from the back. He then had Inês's long-dead corpse exhumed, place on a chair next to his, and had her crowned. Nice!!! Anyway, enough history.

Guimarães itself is bathed in it. The small centre is concentrated around two squares, which are beautifully preserved and evoke memories of time past. It is a mixture of styles – with Romanesque and Renaissance styles vying for attention. It is one of the most beautiful places to be on a warm summer's evening when the square is crowded with people, the various café tables and chairs are spread over the cobbles, the buildings are floodlit and traditional music is performed from one end.

Within two weeks I also had the pleasure of another amazing city. I spent the weekend in Porto. As Portugal's second city, it is situated on the mouth of the Douro River, spectacularly perched on the rocky bank. At that time I hadn't been to any other Portuguese cities but had heard the local saying that goes. "Coimbra studies; Braga prays; Lisbon shows off; and Porto works." It was certainly bustling, with people rushing through the cramped streets. The area close to the river has been designated a UNESCO World Heritage Site and I decided it was completely justified. Within this area, called Ribeira (riverbank) there was a small square right on the edge of the river, the Praça de Ribeira. It wasn't a particularly beautiful square, daily life very much went on as usual and there was a strange tiny Post Modern cube as a fountain to add to the ambiance. I was immediately smitten with the place and it is still one of my favourite places in the world to sit and have a beer and watch the world go by. I felt the same about the rest of Porto that I saw. However, at that time in my life I was more than happy to be living halfway up a mountain, in the fresh air, especially as I had just escaped from London after nine years; I did feel, though, that at some time I'd be living in Porto.

For the next few weeks I was busy getting the hang of teaching, settling into the lifestyle, and trying to figure out what everybody was saying to me. Portuguese was still sounding like Hungarian, and even the smallest chore such as buying a stamp was a monumental task. However, the language problem didn't stop the pure enjoyment of being in Portugal. The weather was brilliant – each day the sun shone and the sky was deep blue. The job was going well, and consisted of a four-day week, with lots of time off during the day to sit in the sun and read or simply gaze at the stunning view. Everybody worked in the evening, and as we all finished work at the same time we'd troop across the medieval square to our local. It was a small family run business, not trendy in any way but was perfect for our needs. What's more we could run a tab toward the end of the month if need be; if we were going out late leave our school bags behind the bar for safekeeping, and our shopping in their fridge, and three of the four fairly gorgeous sons took turns behind the bar. What more could a girl want?

All my concerns about the reason that I was living and working there were quickly dispelled. Clare and Russell were quickly turning into good friends, and one of the other teachers who was sharing the flat with us completed the foursome. Most of the time I didn't know what Adrian was talking about because of his strong Stoke accent, and because of the amount of booze he knocked back. Russell and he were like naughty schoolboys. They'd be dispatched off to walk down the hill to get some supplies, and because we had no bars in the immediate area where we lived, stop off for a quick one and turn up four hours later. Usual stuff!!

Another regular party trick of Adrian's was to arrive home late, mid-week and drunk. That wasn't the problem though. The pain was that if he had the slightest suspicion that anyone was awake he would want to have a heart to heart. It went something like this.

"Rache, Rache. Can I come in and talk to you?"

No reply. "I know you're awake, I saw the light."

"Go away Adey."

"I'll make you a cup of tea."

"I don't want a cup of tea. Go away!"

This would go on for ages, by which time he would have come in anyway with said cup of tea, sit on the end of the bed and talk the biggest pile of s..t you have ever heard. We got very used to hearing taxis slowing down to come up the steep drive, the lights would go out on cue, and sometimes when we'd stayed up late we'd dive into bed fully clothed! The piece de résistance was when Adey rolled in one night when Clare was incredibly pregnant, asked her to get out of bed as he wanted to get in and have a chat to Russell about something "really important." It always was.

Getting up the morning after a visitation and we knew what would greet us – crumbs and jam all over the work surface where Adey had made himself a 'Scooby snack' the night before. One morning there were screams from the kitchen from Clare, and then 'yuks' as we followed a trail of blood from the bread knife, over the kitchen table and across the floor to the fridge. Having opened the door, we were faced with a hunk of cheese in a plastic wrapper, swimming in a pool of blood. Nice!!

My second weekend trip was up into Spain. It was the beginning of the *Carnaval* holiday and Spain was the place to be. The weather was still gorgeous, and spring was well on its way. Friend Tim and I drove northwards towards Spain, but rather than driving straight up the coast went inland and over the mountains. As the sun was setting we found ourselves in Monção. The town itself is small and with an attractive old centre, but the highlight was catching the minute car ferry over the river Minho and into Spain, with an amazing backdrop of a brilliant red sky. From there we motored on to Pontevedra where we decided to stop for the night. The joy of this kind of travelling is that are no schedules to keep, nothing booked, so you can do what you want, when you want. Once we had arrived and parked we wandered round the town until we found somewhere to stay – another mad conversation took place to try and explain what we wanted; this time, of course, in Spanish. Once that was out of the way, we set off for the most important thing; *tapas*. It has to be the most civilised thing in the world. I had never been to mainland Spain before, and was desperate to find out what all the fuss was about. I wasn't disappointed, and being so near the coast there was fish everywhere. Rather than ordering a main meal we just ordered a selection of *tapas*, drank a lot of something, and staggered home.

The next morning we headed towards the coast, and slowly made our way north but kept to the coastal roads and followed all the inlets. I was in for yet another pleasant surprise – the beaches. There were miles and miles of beautiful, pale, sandy beaches, and hidden coves, with the most startling turquoise sea lapping them. I thought I'd been uprooted to the Caribbean. I certainly hadn't expected this from the Atlantic coast. We stopped for lunch in a little out of the way restaurant where we ate well, and interested the locals! London was a million years away.

Eventually, we made our way inland and arrived in Santiago de Compostela, in Galicia. The city stands on a hill, and completely dominates the surrounding countryside. It is famous for two things, its cathedral and the amount it rains. Luckily for us, it was still beautifully warm and sunny – the rain would come on later visits. The other thing it is famous for is being the supposed resting place for the remains of St. James. Quite how he ended up there I don't know. The story goes that in the year 813, his tomb was discovered. According to legend, a hermit saw strange lights in the form of stars over the hill of Libredón, an old Roman fortress. This unusual sighting was reported to the Bishop, who discovered on the site a funeral monument in which he believed were the bodies of the apostle and two of his disciples. It is said that in AD44, after preaching in Spain, James was martyred and his head cut off in Palestine by Jews. His followers decided to put his mortal remains on a ship and head for Galicia. On landing, they took the body of Saint James to the site on which his city now stands.

Whether it's true, who knows, but the resulting cathedral, which was started in 1075, is magnificent. It completely dominates the main square and is awe-inspiring. It is a mixture of various architectural styles including baroque, Renaissance and neoclassical but it was the Gothic façade with its intricate detail which fascinated me. However, it wasn't the only stunning building. On the opposite side of the square is the Raxoi Palace built in the neoclassical style and on the north side the Hostal de los Reyes Católolicos that was built between 1501 and 1511 to provide accommodation for the pilgrims. It was now been transformed into a sumptuous *parador*, one of the five-star state-run hotels, which are found throughout Spain. Unfortunately, our budget only ran to a cheap B & B (however, even that was only a minute's walk from the main square) but we able to walk round the reception area, and into the beautiful courtyard garden where we dreamt what it would be like to afford it.

All this culture soon made us thirsty and we set off in search of a bar. It didn't take long. The centre of Santiago is pedestrianised and is lined with bars and restaurants. Having had our first glass of red wine, and complementary *tapas* we decided to see how many different types we could try. This of course meant going from bar to bar, having a glass of red wine in each. Basically, it was a pub-crawl with a difference! After sampling a fair number I decided that my favourite was a mussel topped with a chilli vinaigrette. Delicious. There weren't just *tapas* to eat though. Being so close to the sea there was a preponderance of seafood dishes. What's more it was fresh, very fresh. In fact, in all the windows of the restaurants dinner would be on show. There were amazing displays of crayfish, mussels and other delights, and huge tanks full of lobsters, trout and eels. Another dish which was on offer was octopus; they were huge, whole and came complete with tentacle and suckers. Yuk!! Fortunately they tasted much better than they looked. One of the other local specialities was a particular type of cheese. Wandering passed all the restaurants I suddenly noticed what looked remarkably like a severed boob sitting on a plate in the windows. Once I had stopped giggling I was informed that in fact it was cheese, but happened to be formed in the shape of a *tetilla*, a teat. I think the kid in me then took over because I couldn't walk passed the restaurant windows without a titter! Unfortunately I never found out why they were so shaped.

Another spectacle was the *Carnaval* parade. In the UK

it seems to me that these types of traditions have been forgotten, and even parades that do take place are somewhat half-hearted with reluctant children forced to take part. But this was Spain, and it was completely different. It seemed that the whole town was involved – both children and adults alike dressed up in fantastic costumes, and those who weren't in costume lining the ancient streets for a good view. My favourite costume was someone dressed up as a table; compete with table cloth, crockery, cutlery and wine glasses stuck to it. Excellent!

Feeling decidedly fatter after the weekend we dragged ourselves away on the Monday morning, and headed back to Portugal. However, I knew that I'd be back in Santiago. In fact I think I must have spent *Carnaval* there a further three times.

Crossing back into Portugal on the coast road we made our way to Viana do Castelo. The province it is in is the Minho which is considered by many to be the most beautiful part of Portugal. I was rapidly coming to the same conclusion, and although Guimarães where I lived was in the southern Minho, this was the first time I had been to the north. There are amazing river valleys, wooded hills, trailing vines and the coastline is barely developed. The area is also very traditional in many aspects and I wasn't surprised to see oxen being used to plough fields. By then I was used to seeing chickens running all over the place.

Although we enjoyed wandering around the historic old centre and its Renaissance buildings, it was for the *Carnaval* atmosphere that we were really there. Having had a good dinner in one of the many restaurants, we set off to discover where all the locals would be celebrating. However, something weird seemed to have happened since we crossed over the border from Spain. *Carnaval* had been forgotten. A lot of the bars were shut (maybe because it was Monday) and the ones which were open were ghostlike. We trailed round from bar to bar, asking locals where they thought the action might be happening but to no avail. There was nothing happening. We went to bed!

Towards the end of March I returned to the northern Minho, but this time it was to the much wilder national park of Gerês. The countryside changes dramatically from the wooded hills of the east, and gives way to mountains, waterfalls, river gorges, reservoirs and forests. It is truly stunning, and you can't help be filled with an enormous sense of insignificance when surrounded by it all. The focal point of the park is the spa town of Caldas do Gerês. The town became popular in the early years of the last century, and along the sedate old street there is a row of grand Victorian hotels. Unfortunately many of them were either boarded up or run down. Bearing in mind the huge number of visitors the town attracts I still can't believe that nothing has been done to renovate these hotels, and market them to holidaymakers. Everywhere we looked people were hiking, cycling or canoeing down the fast running river – surely they needed somewhere to stay. Having stopped for a pleasant lunch we left the town and took a narrow road which led further up into the hills. Well! I have done my fair share of mountain roads, but at least in Switzerland the roads have a proper surface on them. Not only did we have to defy the sheer drops down to the bottom of the valley, with no walls or metal railings, but also there were potholes a foot deep littering the road. It was not a pleasant trip. We finally arrived at the plateau, to relief all round. Once the joy of still being alive had worn off a little, we were struck by the quietness of the place. It was like being back in time; there were no shops, few cars, in fact hardly any sign that this was the 20th Century. As we got to a tiny village and made our way towards a little bed and breakfast one of my friends knew, our way was blocked by a herd of goats. There were loads of them, the kids running around bleating for their Mums. Roast baby kid is a speciality in this part of Portugal. I didn't eat it, and have refused to since.

In the afternoon we set off, armed with bottles of Portuguese bubbly and mountain cheese to find somewhere peaceful to enjoy our feast. After a short while, though, we had to abandon the car as the potholes had turned into craters by this point. We scrambled down a path and came to some mountain pools. We sat on an enormous granite boulder and gazed at the stunning blue colour of the water, whilst basking in the sun and enjoying our bubbles. One of my friends, Guy, decided that the temptation was too strong and went for a dip. We looked on in amazement as he gingerly got into the water. It was obviously freezing but he put on a brave face and did a few circles of the pool.

By this point I had fallen for this stunning National Park, and took any opportunity to return to Gerês. For the rest of the weekend we did very little but soak up the scenery and take it easy.

Up until this point I hadn't seen a day's rain, and decided that it was a superb place to live. But, there was a reason for the greenness of the countryside; that was the rain. The Easter holidays arrived and I was looking forward to two friends coming out for a break. In turn, they were looking forward to a mixture of sitting in the sun and doing some sightseeing. I had been telling them how marvellous it all was and was sure we were all going to have a great holiday together. And then the rain started; continuing without stopping for most of the week. As anyone who knows the north of Portugal, it is seriously miserable when it rains. None of the houses have central heating, and the gas heaters make very little difference apart from smelling strange and adding to the damp problems. This was compounded by the fact that living in a summer holiday villa halfway up a mountain, it was even colder and damper, and the clouds came down so low they came in through the windows. We tried to have a good time, went to restaurants in the evenings but we were basically house bound and the stunning scenery I'd been going on about was completely hidden by the clouds.

However, there was a brief respite and that was when we went to Porto for a couple of days. It stopped raining and as the sun came out, we headed down to Foz. It is on the coast, a couple of kilometres from the centre of Porto and is a wonderful escape from the intensity of the city. What's more, you can forgo the bright orange buses, and take one of the creaky, wooden trams which wind their way along the edge of the river, passed the palm trees and on to the sea. Heading down the Avenida do Brasil there is a row of beachfront cafés and bars, next to the sea. I had already been there once but it was great to be able to show it to other people. The bars are situated right in front of the beach, and you can either sit behind huge glass windows or in deckchairs on the wooden decking. What's more, rugs are provided so on a bright cold day in winter you can still sit outside. That particular day however, it was warm and sunny and my friends started to believe me that Portugal could be gorgeous.

The following day was again bright and sunny and to make the most of it we headed off to the port cellars early so we'd have the rest of the day outside. As you walk down the steep cobbled roads of Porto and look across the river Douro the view is dominated by the names of the port lodges, spelt out in huge white letters across their roofs. The port houses are actually in Vila Nova de Gaia, which is a city in itself. We walked across the bridge's lower level to reach the houses, as my friend Lisa has no head for heights. However, whenever I had the opportunity I walked across the upper level some sixty metres above the river. It's fairly scary as the railings are hip height, the pavements are very narrow and traffic hares passed in either direction. What's more when a bus goes passed the whole bridge shakes! Not for the faint hearted.

We made our way to Sandeman's for the first tour and tasting of the day. Back then you didn't have to pay, which made it even more of a bargain. Apart from the five of us, (Clare and Russ had come to Porto for the weekend as well) there were only about four other people on the tour. We learnt the basics about Port making, and were then given a tasting. One of the guides took us to the large tasting room, full of port memorabilia, and an enormous wooden table which we sat round. He brought two full bottles of port and poured us each a glass of tawny and a glass of white port. I'd never had white port before and was instantly hooked. They were both delicious. What was better was that the other visitors left and the bottles had been left behind. Even though it was only about eleven o'clock it seemed rude not to drink it – so we did. It seemed a good idea at the time. Afterwards we attempted to get back to our hotel, but unfortunately it meant climbing up the steep street. We decided to use the steps, and at one point Clare (who by then was very pregnant) and myself were practically crawling up, giggling hysterically whilst being scowled out by the old ladies washing their part of the steps. One quirk of the Portuguese seems to be their love of washing pavements. I never did figure this it out as it seems a complete waste of time, but it makes them happy so who am I to comment! Anyhow, having finally made it back up the hill we all had a little lie down, and tried to get up the strength for lunch. Later on the same day we delivered my friends to the airport who left, feeling positive having had two rainless days and at least had seen Porto in the sunshine. They unfortunately still had no idea what the stunning countryside around Guimarães looked like!

Things didn't improve much when, some years later I was

actually living in Porto; Lisa (this time on her own) came for another visit at Easter. The weather was beautiful, and for the first few days we enjoyed being outside and sitting in the sun. This didn't last either. Not because of the weather. On the third day Lisa had been to a café for lunch when I was at work, and by the time I got home she was in bed with food poisoning. It was obviously a bad bout because she spent the rest of the week in bed, and didn't see any more of Porto in the sun!

After a couple more free days, summer term started, and Portugal started to heat up. There were, however, a few wet and windy interludes – one was particularly memorable. One evening it was pouring down, the four of us flatmates were huddled up together on the sofa trying to keep warm whilst watching the minute back and white telly which came with the villa. We were watching John Carpenter's *The Fog*. It was all very atmospheric, especially with our own fog swirling around outside. Just as it had got scary the wind really picked up outside, the shutters started rattling and the patio furniture was blown from one end of the balcony to the other. And then Clare (who is never at her best watching horror films) jumped and screamed at the same time, which set us all off! Who needs a horror film when you have reality!

In May I had another weekend away. This time it was to Coimbra, a hundred kilometres south from Porto, on the coast. It is a beautiful old city, and is perched on top of a hill above the wide River Mondego. The small centre is a moody place, full of ancient alleys and lanes. Fittingly, it is Portugal's oldest University City, and in fact it had the only university in Portugal until the beginning of the 20th Century. It was for this reason that I spent the weekend there with a friend. In May, each year, there is a huge party to celebrate the end of the academic year. When we arrived the city centre was full of students wearing their black robes, wandering around from bar to bar, party to party. Unlike in the UK where most of us hire gowns for a day when we graduate, in Portugal students have their own gowns and often wear them during their student years. We joined the throngs of people and made our way up the steep streets to the old city centre and through the Arco de Almedina, an arch cut through the old wall. Walking passed gorgeous hidden courtyards and pretty balconies; we came to the Sé Velha, the old cathedral. It is apparently one of the most important Romanesque buildings in Portugal, and since it was started in 1162, has been little altered. It was definitely worth the climb. We wandered round the university buildings close by, and felt transported back in time. Having done the culture bit we then turned to the other pursuit of the day; namely sitting in a bar or restaurant.

For me, that was practically the last memory of the weekend. I do remember having a good cheap meal in one of the numerous restaurants, and then making our way to a huge cordoned off area near the river for a live concert. Being Portugal there was no silly alcohol ban, and therefore there were booze outlets everywhere. It started off fairly sensibly with a few beers but for some reason it turned into one of those Tequila nights. As anyone who's been there knows, those nights are forgotten nights. I had one of those and woke up with one of my all time nightmare hangovers. There was nothing I could do. I had all the bells from all the churches in Coimbra crashing in my head, and as for my stomach. None of the usual remedies worked and I couldn't stay in bed all day as we were staying in a hotel. Despite the fact that we had the whole of Sunday to continue exploring I knew that I wasn't going to make any progress; the only thing I wanted to do was to be at home in bed. Very disappointed with me, my friend, however, could see the state I was in and we drove home. Well we drove for a while and then I had to scream to stop whilst I threw up yet again. Nice!

I liked Coimbra, but for a good few years later couldn't think about it without feeling unwell. About three weeks later my friend gave me the opportunity to redeem myself as a weekend away pal, and we again went south, but this time only as far as Aveiro. Although mainly known for its beautiful beaches north and south of the town, Aveiro itself is well worth a visit. Until 1570 it was apparently a thriving port but then the mouth of the river silted up. In 1802 a canal was cut through to the sea and the port reopened. Today the main economy is the saltpans which surround the town. The town itself isn't full of stunning buildings as many other towns in Portugal are, but it is extremely cute in its own way. A sort of mini Venice in a faded rundown way. The town is built around a network of canals, which are lined with pastel coloured houses. There were lots of interesting, narrow alleys to explore and most of them had the most amazing seafood restaurants. The weather was lovely and we spent a very pleasant weekend wandering around in the sunshine, stopping off in the numerous cafés. Although we ended up in a club way into the early hours, I steered clear of the Tequila and didn't waste another Sunday.

By then we were at the end of May, and excitement was mounting about the arrival of Clare and Russell's baby. To be honest, it was a mixture of excitement and terror at the thought of a Portuguese hospital for Clare, who, before she was even admitted was figuring out a way to leave as early as possible. I can't say I blame her, once I had been inside - talk about outdated facilities, equipment, and even worse, attitudes! On the 2nd June Rosie arrived safely and the following day I went to visit them. That was after I'd queued up at the outside ticket office where you were barked at by an officious attendant, told that only two people could visit at one time and then asked for money for the privilege. Once Gabrielle and I had fought our way passed the red tape, we then had to get passed the security man. He was practically frisking people as they went up to the wards, and was confiscating any food he found. We had come laden with fresh fruit and chocolate, as the hospital food apparently took institutional catering to a new low level and Clare was desperate. However, the guard was having none of it. There was no point trying to explain that Clare wasn't ill but had just had a baby, rules were rules and we couldn't break them. Not until the next day that was, after we'd briefed Russ and he smuggled in contraband Kit Kats. What a palaver!

All this didn't take away the joy of seeing Clare, and being able to have a cuddle with her new baby. It was the first time I'd been in close contact with a newborn baby and I was completely bowled over. After a couple of days Clare demanded to be discharged, and she and Rosie came home; which was a good thing as the effects of fatherhood were rendering Russ hopeless. If I hadn't cooked for him I think he would have starved. Opening the fridge one evening I found a supermarket bag with nappies and cigarettes in it! At that time we were all still sharing the same flat but suddenly there was a baby, which was strange for all of us. I spent the first few days cooking for Clare and Russ whilst they got used to the idea of being parents, and we quickly had to learn about looking after a baby. It brought a new meaning to the phrase 'induction by fire'. Miriam Stoppard's book was invaluable and got us through many minor crises.

During the boiling hot afternoons, Clare would make the most of some free time and sunbathe on the balcony just outside my bedroom, where Rosie and I were both having a siesta. This was a regular occurrence on afternoons I wasn't teaching. One day, however, we were both slightly concerned that Rosie seemed very cold, and had a distinct blue tinge about her. After we had panicked for a while, and considered the terrible prospect of the casualty department at the local hospital (to be avoided at all costs as I discovered some years later) sense prevailed and as Clare cuddled Rosie, I turned to Miriam.

"You might feel hot but this does not mean that your baby does," I read. "Have you been in a hot place whilst your baby is in a cooler place?"

"Err, yes" replied Clare. "It's boiling outside but in here; (being a tiled floored summer villa) it's really cool. What does it say I should do?"

"Take her outside where it's warmer, I suppose." Guess what! It worked, and Rosie turned from blue to pink! This might seem completely logical to anyone else but at that time the pair of us knew next to nothing about babies and it really was trial and error. There was no-one in the immediate vicinity to help, Clare's Mum was in England, and they didn't have midwives as we know it. At least Russ's Mum, Gabrielle was living on the other side of the valley and was very practical and down to earth about the whole thing.

This was in sharp contrast to all the interfering, middle-aged and older Portuguese women who had some strange ideas about what was best for a baby. Talk about old fishwife tales. We'd never heard so much nonsense. "Your baby's too cold (when it was 35 degrees); hungry (having just had a feed); you should do this and not that!" It was winding me up and Rosie wasn't even my baby – you can imagine how Clare was feeling. Everything came to a head one extremely hot, humid day; Clare and I had decided to go to a nearby town, Braga, for a market trip. This was before any of us had a car so we took the hot, smelly, forty-five minute bus. We had a good wander round and ignored all the old crones giving us the usual "advice". So Clare could have a good rummage at a clothes stall, I held Rosie and stood underneath an awning to keep out of the sun. At which point the stall owner decided to prod the awning to get rid off the collected rainwater –

all over my head. There is nothing I hate more that getting my head and face wet, and I was soaked. How I didn't drop Rosie with the shock, I'll never know. She, of course, started wailing, which was exactly what I felt like doing. Before Clare had realised what was happening, the 'crones' starting putting their oars in.

"That baby's wet and it will get sick. It's very bad for it. Why did you do it?" etc, etc.

That was the last straw. Clare gathered Rosie and I up, and we strode off to the continued wailing of the crones. Almost in unison they got their comeuppance.

"Why don't you just f..k off and leave us alone. We know the baby's wet. Do you think we f..king did it on purpose, it was one of those bloody stall holders." As we continued screaming at anyone who mentioned water and babies, the stallholder came charging after us, accusing us of stealing. In all the kafuffle Clare was still holding some clothes she'd picked up from the stall. By this point half the market had joined in, and before anything else could happen, Clare threw the clothes back at the woman, and we stalked off. The journey home was disgusting – Rosie and I both soaked through and not happy bunnies!

The end of term was rapidly approaching, and with that, all the summer entertainment. At the weekends there were live bands playing in the square. We'd set off for an evening out, bringing baby and all the paraphernalia with us, and head for a good spot in the square close to our local bar. As well as providing beer they also provided a babysitting service and Rosie would spend the evening on the owner's bed! How many bars in England could you do that?

Another event we had was a football match between the teachers and our local bar. The Portuguese take their football very seriously, and this was no different. A local sports hall had been booked, and on a roasting Saturday afternoon we all made our way there for the local derby. On one side were the fit, tanned sons and their mates from the bar who were very easy on the eye. The same could not be of their opposition, the teachers. You have never seen such a mishmash of a team; all ages, shapes, sizes and very few who actually knew what they were doing. Even the loan of some of the bar team didn't help and the teachers were well and truly thrashed. It was great fun though, but fortunately didn't end there. Back in the centre of Guimarães we made our way to "Bessa's" (the family name for our local, although sometimes known as Rick's Bar from *Casablanca* as the owner's first name was Ricardo!) for a post match beer and discussion. It wasn't just beer which was on offer though. A huge spread had been put on – cheese, cold meats, huge prawns and even a cake in the shape of a football pitch. All this was washed down with Portuguese bubbles. Delicious!

Everybody was definitely feeling in holiday mode by then, helped by the fact that there was only a week of term left. Most of that week was taken up by invigilating tests, and marking. Furthermore, one of the days was a national holiday, so we were basically already on holiday. We spent the time off during the days sitting in the sun marking tests, then leaping in the pool to cool off; the evenings having dinner on the balcony or in a local restaurant, and then we'd make our way into the centre of the old town to soak up the atmosphere. Sometimes I had to pinch myself to make sure it wasn't all a lovely dream; this was what most people saved up to do for two weeks a year. However, I decided not to spend the summer in Portugal but to return to England. I'd already re-signed my contract for the following academic year so knew I'd be back. What's more, I'd also sorted out a little flat for myself to move into, downstairs from where I had been living.

Although I had thoroughly enjoyed myself for those six months, I was really looking forward to going back to England. I spent most of the time at Mum and Dad's place and from there went on trips to stay with friends, and even spent some evenings with the naval officer I'd been seeing before I'd left for Portugal. I also had a pleasant summer diversion with a young man who he happened to be a friend of my brothers. I'd known him for a couple of years but just as someone my 'baby' brother knew. That summer, though, everything was to change. Said 'boy' happened to be living in his parents house which was just over the road from Mum and Dad's. One morning Mum said to me that Richard's Mum and Dad were going on holiday and had offered their house to some friends. This meant that Richard and his brother were homeless, and could they possibly come and stay with me whilst my parents were away. Er, yes! Richard's brother decided to stay elsewhere, so we had the run of the place. I don't really need to go into details but suffice to say that on the second evening when I got home after being out with a friend, and I found Richard sprawled out on the coach with my lovely cat Ziggy lying on him, I decided there was only one way it could go. We settled down to watch a film together, demolished my brother's bottle of Pastis, and then staggered upstairs! What's more, my brother even forgave us for drinking it all, saying he couldn't think of two people he'd rather drink it than us. Bless!

The other major event of that summer was my sister's wedding on the first weekend in September. However, that cheerful occasion was overshadowed but something else. A couple of days before my beloved Ziggy Stardust, who I'd had for eleven years, was run over and died instantly. I was beside myself – in fact the whole family were really sad, and it was one of the few times that I'd seen my Dad cry. It had been amazing how much a cat could become part of a family.

Obviously, since it was my sister's wedding a couple of days after, I had to pull myself together and be happy for her. To be honest I really wasn't in the mood. I wasn't particularly close to my sister, and certainly couldn't figure out what made her tick. The wedding itself was held in a registry office in north London, not exactly salubrious, and then a lunchtime reception at a central London hotel. The reception certainly wasn't like any of the ones I'd been to before when friends had got married. There weren't that many guests – those who were there were mainly all my parents' generation (not saying that they didn't know how to party, but some of their vintage definitely didn't) or were the bridegroom's family who were Nigerian, and that meant no booze. Despite the fact I was at opposite ends of the head table from my brother, we managed to have a good time, and I was very glad to have had some say in getting a decent wine. At the end of the afternoon, Matthew and I wobbled our way to the tube station. I put him on a tube south to Waterloo, and I made my way into the centre of town to meet someone who at one moment I thought I might have someday married. It was David. I'd only seen him once since the start of the previous year, and that had been a disaster. You know, sometimes neither of you are ready and it's all too horrible. By then we'd both had time, and had different experiences. We spent a good evening in one of our old local haunts in Covent Garden, and in even more of a state I made my way back to the hotel where I was staying with Mum and Dad.

Unfortunately I hadn't quite recalled that I wasn't sharing with my sister anymore, and literally fell through the door of Mum and Dad's room, crashed into the metal put me up, shushing myself as I went, and then fell into giggling into a heap on the bed. "Had a good time then?" Dad asked. That'll be a yes!

Chapter 16

A new flat

A week later and on the 14th September I was packing my bags and heading back to Portugal. It was great to return and the moment I arrived I knew I'd made the right decision. What's more, I didn't even have to go straight back to work. I spent the time moving into my new flat, lazing around the pool, and revisiting favourite bars. Even when work did restart we only had to do some testing of new students, and not much else, and carried on in this fashion until the 6th October. What a life! And we'd been paid for the summer, and still had a four-day working week.

Life very quickly settled down into the familiar routine. Although my close friends Clare and Russ, and baby Rosie had moved to a village the other side of the valley, we still spent a lot of time together and I was able to really experience every change in Rosie. The whole thing felt so much more real then living in England – not seeing friends from time-to-time but regularly spending proper quality time with them.

Having my own place was great and at any opportunity I'd cook for any willing victims. Hopefully the meals themselves made for good evenings, but I know that simply coming to my flat was an event. You walked straight into the tiny living room, which was only divided from my 'bedroom' by a huge wooden wardrobe. The sleeping area was completely dominated by the heavy wooden double bed, and this in turn was dominated by the headboard. It was no ordinary headboard I can tell you. The Portuguese seem to have a penchance for solid, dark, elaborately worked wooden furniture. Most of it is terrible. Possibly, one piece in an enormous room would look ok, but in Portugal pieces were crammed into the smallest homes and looked so out of place. I had my own special example. I used to wake up having had bad dreams about gargoyles and monsters, and then realise that the reason was the carved, imposing headboard that menacingly loomed over me. To get to the kitchen you had to go through an 'Alice in Wonderland' size door and down the stairs, trying to avoid smashing your head on the concrete ceiling as you went down. I can't remember the number of times I'd remind people but by then they'd already have knocked themselves half senseless. To add to this, the fridge was wedged in a space underneath the stairs, and I lost count of the times I leant down to get something from it and then smashed the back of my head getting up! However, the *piece de résistance* was that in one of the corners of the kitchen there was a shower. Bizarre, to say the least.

Despite living in an extremely strange flat, I was very happy with my lot. I recognised that I was fortunate the job was working out, that I'd made lots of friends and the scenery was beautiful. However, I'd got a little fed up with people saying to me over the summer how lucky I was and how much they wished they could move abroad. Lucky! I'd retrained at huge expense, left all my friends and family, moved house – not to say country and career – and gone somewhere, on my own, where I'd never been before, didn't know anyone and didn't speak the language. It's said you're not supposed to make major life changes at the same time – nonsense! I did it and survived. When I'd say to people that if they wanted to live abroad then they could do, I'd be met with exclamations of "Oh no, I couldn't possible actually do that" and then continue with a list of the reasons why – a house to sell, kids at school, bla, bla. In fact, that September somebody I'd met the previous March, namely Guy, the friend who had swum in the freezing cold mountain pool in Gêres, moved to Portugal with his wife and their two boys. They managed it. What's more they are still there, run their own business, and have bought a house. Enough said. Except, fast forward to 2003 and now being back in the UK I can't believe the number of TV shows with people relocating abroad. They're all such rubbish – on the whole they go to safe places dominated by British tourists, they have money in order to buy a property and are wrapped in cotton wool by the programmes' producers. Nonsense!

The most interesting event of that term was a local tradition called *Pinheiro*. It is held every year at the end of November and, quite frankly, I had never seen anything like it. It involved drumming. Lots of drumming! All day and most of the night. And that wasn't all. At the end of the evening all the drummers congregated at the castle, and then started to process into town. At the head of the parade were a couple of enormous oxen, who looked as though they were ready to charge. What's more they were pulling a huge pine tree behind them to be erected. It was all very pagan and atmospheric.

December passed quickly and suddenly it was Christmas. Due to a lack of funds I'd decided to spend the holiday in Portugal. It turned out to be one of the strangest Christmases I'd ever had, and all the traditions I was so used to were completely thrown out of the window. To begin with, I suddenly had a guest for the duration of the holiday. My friend Tim had his sister staying – she being the friend I'd been staying with the previous New Year when I had found out about the job, and I was looking forward to seeing her again. Unfortunately, Tim was taken ill and ended up in hospital, so rather than being on her own Kathy came and stayed with me. On Christmas Eve we hoped to meet up with other friends and have a few drinks in a local bar. No! Every single bar was shut. On Christmas morning I'd envisaged sitting on the balcony in the sun, sipping champagne before contemplating cooking. No chance! The weather had changed. For the whole holiday it rained and was cold and damp. On Christmas morning we went to the hospital (my second experience which hardened my reserve never to need to go for myself) to visit Tim. On our way through town I noticed that lots of the bars and cafés were now open. What was going on?

Having done our hospital visit, we guiltily left Tim to have Christmas Day on his own. We drove back passed all the open bars and up into our personal cloud which had settled around the house for the day. I'd volunteered to make lunch but soon started to regret it. We wandered up the hill to where we were going to spend Christmas Day with friend Cath, her daughter and Adrian. Cath's kitchen was basically the size of a shoebox with a tiny portable oven, and a two-ringed gas hob. The first problem was to try and figure out how I was going to fit a turkey, spuds and stuffing in the oven, and do the veg and gravy on the hob. Talk about juggling. All this wasn't helped by the normal, but extreme mother and daughter squabbling going on between Cath and Caitlin, and the arrival of Adrian who was determined to get as pissed as possible, and then every five minutes to either ask how long lunch was going to be, or to squeeze into the kitchen to see if he could help. No!!

Somehow, the food was finally ready, and we all settled down to do what you should do on Christmas Day wherever you are – eat too much turkey, drink too much red wine and watch *The Wizard of Oz* – excellent!

New Year's Eve was similarly weird. There was nowhere really to go, so we decided to have a curry feast in my flat - Guy and Ros left the kids upstairs, groped though the mist and appeared laden with curry and red wine. Lots of Jalfrezzi, Dhal and wine later, we staggered outside at midnight, and squelched around in the mud singing (if you could all it that) Auld Lang Sine.

1994 began and bought a mixture of incredible highs, and terrible lows. The start of the year, though, was very pleasant, mainly centred on lots of good meals with friends. One memorable evening started at my friend Fran's house. I'd been invited round for dinner as her brother was over for the *Carnaval* holiday, but had said that I had to get up early the next morning to get three buses to get to the airport in Porto to meet a friend, so wasn't up for a big night. Why do I ever say that? Talk about waving a red flag at a bull. Many hours later I ended up in a bar with Fran's gorgeous brother (think mid-nineties Hugo Boss advert man), and many hours later than that woke up at home, a) next to him, and b) remembering that I was supposed to be on a coach. I can't really remember ever feeling worse – and to this day cannot even look at a bottle of tequila, let alone drink a Margarita - and the hot shower made no difference! What's more I could hardly talk, let alone in Portuguese, so phoned Cath up to ask her to call me a taxi. As she squawked down the phone at me, I had to try and explain how I hadn't managed to get up on time, and why Fran had just arrived to pick up a similarly sorry for himself brother!

I had the most horrible ride to the airport, with a taxi driver who drove like a lunatic, and whilst waiting at arrivals instead of being excited that I had a good friend coming to stay for a week, was figuring out how long it would take me to career to the loo. Amanda took it as any good friend would, and when we finally got home didn't complain when

I sat her in the sun with a book and a beer, and I slopped back to bed. Fortunately all was well in the morning and we had an excellent time during the week. The crowning point came when we went to Porto for the following weekend.

On the Friday night we made our way down to Ribeira, and the little square overlooking the river with the Port lodges on the opposite side, so I could show Amanda one of my fav spots. Having had a few beers we went to one of the many restaurants lining the river, and settled ourselves down. As soon as we arrived, there seemed to be a certain buzz to the atmosphere, and having ear wigged as much as I could, it seemed as though Bobby Robson was upstairs. At that time I wasn't that interested in national football, but had certainly followed the World Cup four years earlier when Bobby had taken us so close to glory. I asked the waitress if he was indeed upstairs, and she confirmed he was. After we had finished dinner, and quite a bit of booze, I checked if it was ok to go upstairs, and we wobbled over to where Bobby was sitting.

"I'm really sorry", I spluttered, "but I realised you were up here and just wanted to stay hello, and how much I admire you." Bobby was completely ok with all this. In fact, he announced that it was his birthday, and as they were just about to have some cake asked if we would like to join them. Since he was there with both his wife and some friends, we didn't think we would be imposing too much. So we sat down and proceeded to spend the next hour or so with them. Bobby, of course, had just moved up from Benefica in Lisbon to join FC Porto as coach, which was why he happened to be in Porto. As Amanda chatted away to his friends, having discovered they knew the same horsy people in Dorset, I talked football with Bobby, and where to go shopping with his wife. We were then invited to stay for port, and very happily glugged our way through a bottle of vintage, and then another one. I'd heard that Bobby was a really nice man, and this was certainly the image he projected on the TV – in reality he was exactly the same. What a lovely evening. What's more he very readily agreed to sign a few restaurant cards for me to give to friends, and of course a personal one for me. Amanda and I finally left, and began the slow struggle to get back up the slope to our hotel. The next morning I woke up with a horrible headache, but remembered a strange dream I had.

"I dreamt we met Bobby Robson last night," I said to Amanda.

"I had the same dream," she replied. "I think it was real. Oh, and you were sleep

talking last night about monsters in the wardrobe!" That'll be the booze then!

On returning to Guimarães that afternoon, news of our encounter soon spread, and blokes I didn't even know would come up to me in the café and ask me about Bobby Robson. From then on I always checked to see how FC Porto were doing, and was delighted when they were the national champions three time in a row from 1994/95 to 1996/7, two of them when Bobby was coach. I have followed them ever since, and upon moving to Porto in 1997 felt like a real fan. I even managed to see them playing a couple of European Champions league matches at home. That was all to be much later on, and one of the games was another story!

It might seem to someone used to the city life, that my existence at the time wasn't that exciting. All I did was eat and drink, and sit in the sun as much as possible. There wasn't much else of a stimulus, but I was completely happy. Every morning I'd wake up, and look at the fantastic view over the hills and mountains in the distance, before making my way into town for work. I suppose the only thing I really missed was the variety of films to see. At least there was one cinema – if it could be called that. It really was a 'flea pit' – worn, red, velvety seats, the floors incrusted with years of dust and dirt, and only one screen. What's more the same film was shown for about two or three weeks. But! There was a real plus point. There was a tiny bar which sold cold bottles of Super Bock – the local beer. We'd have a few beforehand, dash out at the interval (even today they still have intervals at some cinemas in Portugal), and then smuggle a few in past the scary usherette who was on the door trying to stop contraband from being taken in. She wasn't very good at it – and on hearing the clinking of bottles would get her torch out to try and find who the perpetrators were. It was like being back at school! Of course from time to time it all went wrong. On one occasion, going back in after the interval, as Ros opened her bag to try and get her ticket out, she managed to tip her beer into her handbag! Sticky!

Portuguese TV was a real non-starter – sometimes we see a good film scheduled and get ready to watch it. More often than not it would start at least half an hour late, would have adverts of at least fifteen minutes, and sometimes wouldn't even be shown to the end. Once, it took three days and three different channels for a whole film to be shown. After a while we didn't either bother to start watching.

One morning, after way too many beers, I woke up with a pounding head, something digging into my back and feet that felt like lead. On pulling back the duvet I revealed the especially sexy look of being naked, apart from having my bra and my long lace up boots on. Obviously hooks and laces had been a step too far. Classy!

Easter approached very rapidly, and I tried to prepare my flat to accommodate Mum, Dad and my brother Matthew, as they were coming for a holiday. A bit of a squeeze to say the least. The day they arrived was an advert for Portugal at its worst. It was pissing down, and you could hardly see in front of you. In vain I attempted to dry off sheets and duvet covers. At least I didn't have to try and make it to the airport. They'd decided to take the long ferry crossing from Portsmouth to Santander and drive down. At that point I could only imagine how Mum was feeling, as she'd never had sea legs. The plan was that I'd hang balloons round the gatepost so they could find the house. During the afternoon I was lazing around with a friend trying to keep warm to avoid the damp from completely taking over when the phone rang. Woops. They'd somehow arrived in the area much earlier than expected – had been lost for the last hour, and had even driven passed the entrance. To say they were pissed off was an understatement – all arguing with each other. I tried to establish where they were, but they'd all just rant about being in a café next to the main road. Helpful! I finally got enough sense out of Matthew to figure out which café they were at, and gave them directions. Not a good start and we couldn't even sit out in the sun. Things thankfully improved, although the weather, in its own special Portuguese way was appalling for most of the holiday.

However, we had lots of café visits, and lots of good meals and on the whole fun. Mum and Dad marvelled at the religious parades, and Matthew and I sat in bars and waited for them. Easter Sunday was a spectacle in itself. I felt like we'd woken up in the middle of a war zone, but it was just the firework nutters letting off their spectacularly uninteresting to look at but eardrum shattering bangers in every field around us. This happened every Sunday to a lesser degree but poor Matthew experienced it for the first time and with a monumental hangover, having been inflicted to a night out with Adrian. At least he had the Easter egg hunt to look forward to. The previous evening Guy and Ros had written their somewhat pissed cryptic clues, and then had staggered round the area trying to put the clues in the right places and in the right order. The kids coped with it all fine, but poor Matthew could be seen going in completely different directions to everyone else.

Once the hangovers had abated and fireworks stopped, we made our way to Porto for a couple of days. What's more, exactly what had happened the previous Easter occurred and the sun came out. We did the normal Porto routine – a tour of the port houses, then some port tasting, and then went along the river to the coast. We sat outside one of the cafés overlooking the sea. I remember feeling so contented, sitting there sipping a beer in the sun with Mum, Dad and my bro. Dad was also really enjoying himself, and I realised that I was so completely his daughter, and motivated and made happy by the same things. Enjoying ourselves there that afternoon, none of us knew what was in store for us as a family and me personally, and that so much happiness would be wiped out. Whenever I have since been to that café, and it's a fair few times, I have happy memories because of what a good time we had there; but it's always tinged with sadness. Saying that, many years later I went there on a chilly November evening on a first date, which turned into a full on relationship with a sexy Scot.

The Easter holiday came to an end, and the family set off for Santander. Summer term was much the same as it had been the previous year, and sometimes I really couldn't believe what a great time I was having. And just as I thought that, and despite that fact that there was the amazing high of my trip to America, Canada and Mexico that summer, things started to come crashing down. After the end of term I stayed on in Portugal to make the most of having time off in the sun, and in the middle of July returned to England. Although I had a good time there seeing friends, it was the beginning of August which I was looking forward to. I had saved up some money and decided to have a 'real' holiday. I'd never met my cousins, well Dad's cousin and his family to be exact, and had always wanted to go to Vancouver where they lived, so that's what I did.

Prior to that, though, the first blow came. I'd spent a couple of days in London visiting Phil and when I returned home to Mum and Dad's I was greeted with the news that my ninety year-old grandmother had died. I know about all the clichés – she had a good innings, had an interesting life etc – but none of that really matters when it's your own flesh and blood. This was especially as it was so sudden and there had been no time to say goodbye. Because it was so sudden it meant that there had to be a post mortem, and by the time everything had been sorted granny's funeral was the day before I was due to leave for Canada. Because it was such an early flight I was staying overnight at the airport and had to go almost straight from the funeral to the airport. I can remember having so many mixed emotions – on the one hand being so excited about the prospect of going to countries I'd never visited before, and seeing family I'd never met before, and then dealing with grief and sad occasions which I am absolutely hopeless at. In fact. Dad even announced that he wasn't going to stand next to me because he knew I'd cry so much – which I did.

Then, before I knew it, I was struggling onto the train up to Heathrow with a rucksack on my back. Although I wasn't really back packing it seemed to be the most sensible option as I had lots of getting from one place to another to do, and all on my own. I quickly decided that it was a bloody terrible idea as I thought my back was going to break after the first five minutes. However, I made it to the luxury of the Forte hotel where I was spending the night, and began my next little adventure.

Favourite Travelling Songs

The Passenger by Iggy Pop

~

Ramble on by Led Zeppelin

~

Free Fallin' by Tom Petty

~

Four Seasons in One Day by Crowded House

Choosing my boat, in Dinan, Brittany

Part Six

North American nosh

Chapter 17

Vancouver

Walking through customs in Vancouver, after I have no idea how many hours travelling and completely exhausted, having not slept at all on the flight over to Seattle and then on to Vancouver, I wearily scanned round the arrival area for someone I'd only met when I was a little girl, and had otherwise only seen a few pictures of. Suddenly, though, it was like seeing Dad with dark hair and a beard, and there was Peter, his cousin. We were soon heading southwards away from the airport and towards Tsawwassen. It was my first real look at North America and I was struck by the space – the roads were so wide, there were huge open expanses and fields with barns in them, and houses made of wood with porches and rocking chairs just like I'd seen in films.

Before long we arrived at my cousins' house and my uncle and myself settled ourselves down in the garden to relax. All I wanted to do was go to bed but to combat jet lag that was strictly forbidden. What's more, there was no way I could refuse a glass of homemade wine. Together with the jet lag and wine, it seemed all rather surreal. I had flown halfway round the world, and had previously only spent holidays in non-English speaking countries. But here I was, miles from home, surrounded by complete Englishness – even down to the antique chair that was the twin of one Dad had.

Before not too long my aunt and their son, my third cousin or something like that, arrived home. We had a lovely first evening together over a good meal, which included blueberries, which to me were quintessentially Canadian. What was also most definitely North American was the fridge. It was enormous, and for anyone who loves food and drink was a dream. It had sections for everything and was so large you could have lived in it. Somehow, one day I will definitely have a fridge like that. Having had dinner, we walked down to the beach which was all of three minutes away; suddenly my uncle told me to stop as I had just walked across the border into America. Apparently I'd just walked over the 49th Parallel! I didn't think it was supposed to be that easy. Somehow I'm sure it can't be the case now!

I then begged to be allowed to sleep, and finally crawled into bed. I was staying in the large, guest bedroom and felt very happy and relaxed. I also had time to reflect for the first time that day, or days, or whatever it was, on the events of the journey. One of the reasons I felt so good and that I hadn't slept on the flight was that I had been sitting next to a gorgeous, green-eyed man. From the moment I set eyes on him when checking in, to realising by some amazing chance we were sitting next to each other, and finally, when at Seattle he took me to the desk where I boarded the short flight to Vancouver, it was one of those romantic situations where the attraction is so strong that you just talk and talk. We swapped numbers, with him promising to phone as soon as I got back to the UK almost a month later. What's more he did; on the day I returned and we met up a few days later.

But that was in the future. The following day was a Saturday, and despite having been wide awake at five that morning, I got up with loads of energy for the day ahead. My aunt and uncle weren't working and had decided to take me to Vancouver Island for the day, on the ferry. It was a beautiful day and the crossing was spectacular – such a sense of openness. We drove north of Victoria itself and were quickly surrounded by enormous pine trees. However, even the scenery wasn't enough to keep me awake and the jet lag got the better of me. I revived in time to appreciate Victoria. It was rather quaint and touristy in parts but that didn't really matter – especially when we found a little, Italian restaurant to have an early dinner in. This was rounded off by the return ferry crossing, and despite all the amazing fresh air and jet lag I managed to stay awake for the whole evening.

My stay in British Columbia was excellent and I spent a packed week there. Vancouver itself was stunning. I've always been a fan of hills meeting water, and this surely was the best example. Cradled between the ocean and snow-capped mountains, the mirror-fronted downtown skyscrapers formed a dramatic contrast to the surrounding nature. What's more, in the middle of the city you could easily get to the beach, and there was a huge area of parkland surrounding part of the city.

I spent a day in the centre discovering some of the things the city had to offer; visited the Art Gallery where I went to a Georgina O'Keefe exhibition; looked at the Totem poles in Stanley Park, and went into countless shops which sold local jade. I have always been attracted by the stone and the shops were my idea of heaven. I finally decided to buy some individual beads so I could make some jewellery, and even discovered that you could buy red jade.

Not only did I have a companion during the day in the form of my aunt, but in the evenings my cousin Robert was around. It was very strange meeting someone for the first time who was almost exactly the same age as me, but also had the same name – R Gurney! We went to watch local baseball; saw films; hired videos and one evening went out for dinner with some of his friends, in the centre of

Vancouver. It was the after dinner entertainment that made the evening, though. On the waterfront, the crowds were gathering for a firework display. It was the accumulation of a week's competition, and the finale was an incredible display of fireworks over the bay, released in time to Handel's music which was played through a series of speakers. It was the most memorable display of fireworks I have ever seen.

One day I had to entertain myself so borrowed a bike and went out for a ride. I set off down the coastal paths and again was struck by the space around me. Not only were there endless fields, estuaries, salt marshes, but also the sea itself, in the form of Boundary Bay, and in the distance just appearing through the haze was the top of Mount Baker, looking as though it was suspended in mid-air. I remember feeling an incredible sense of freedom – I saw hardly any people, heard few cars, saw lots of birds, some of which I think were birds of prey (but not being any kind of ornithologist wasn't really sure), and enjoyed the light breeze coming off the sea. It was only after I'd visited that I discovered that it was a globally significant bird area.

Chapter 18

San Francisco

Before long, the week was up, and I was heading towards the airport for my next destination; San Francisco. I had always wanted to go, and being on the West Coast anyway and heading down to Mexico, it seemed ridiculous not to go, even if it meant being there on my own. It was one of the few American cities I was interested in - I'm not really sure why. Perhaps it was to do with The Beat writers of the fifties or the music in the sixties, or maybe always being entranced by the car chases up and down the steep, straight roads in films and in particular from *The Streets of San Francisco*, which I was addicted to when growing up. It was also somewhere Dad had been to and liked, so that was always a good bet.

Although I arrived there in the second week of August, I knew that the weather could be changeable to say the least, and that I might have a week enclosed in the famous fog which hung over the bay. The weather god was smiling on me though. We had an amazing descent; the plane followed the coastline, flew over the top of the famous Golden Gate Bridge, and then did a huge loop back towards the airport. What I hadn't realised was that the runway was built on the edge of the bay. I was convinced we were going to land in the water, but nobody else seemed the slightest bit worried and with what seemed like a couple of feet left we landed.

Since I was arriving mid-evening and didn't really feeling like traipsing the streets I had already booked a central hotel. It was right in the centre of downtown San Francisco, just off Union Square. Having been dropped off by the airport bus somewhere central, I crawled at a snail's pace towards the hotel – not only due to my increasingly annoying rucksack (why the hell hadn't I bought a suitcase with wheels?) but also by being distracted by everything so American surrounding me. There were beautiful, old architectural delights mixed with dozens of cheap looking electronic shops, then a few palm trees in the centre of Union Square, and suddenly designer stores everywhere. Having successfully checked into the hotel - something that I am always slightly anxious about when I have booked months before and, especially in this case from Portugal - I decided it was the right choice to have booked a decent one. Having dumped my hated rucksack, I went out in search for dinner, and being so close to Chinatown decided that Chinese it had to be. I wandered around for a while soaking up the atmosphere and the warm evening air, until I came upon a small restaurant which looked inviting, and was full of locals. I had the most delicious meal, very cheaply, and with a full tummy rolled down the hill (thank goodness) and back to my comfortable hotel. So far America was just fine!

Unfortunately, my budget didn't extend to staying at the King George for a week, so having eaten as much breakfast as I could and cleaned the bathroom of little bottles of shampoo, shower gel and shower caps (I never use shower caps but it would be rude to leave them), I made my way back up the steep roads to a slightly less salubrious hotel in the Nob Hill area. Having said that, it was cheap, the room was enormous and clean, and there was an old-fashioned en-suite bathroom. The telly might have been out of the ark, and there was no plug for the bath (the benefit of being a girly who has lots of bottles in her wash bag is that one of them will always fit in the plug hole) but it was comfortable, quiet, safe, brilliantly located, and home for the next week.

Having got my hotel sorted out, the first thing I wanted to do was catch a glimpse of the famous bridge and bay area. However, before that I decided to go and purchase my Bart bus pass, which I could use anywhere and travel on the cable cars. I'm not quite sure why they are called that; they look like trams to me. I walked back down the hill, already soaking up the atmosphere when the Hyde and Powell cable car trundled past me. All I really wanted to do was jump on there and then, and hang off the side as I seen so many people do in films. I managed to resist the temptation and went and found the Bart office to buy my pass. I then got distracted for the first of many times during my stay. I noticed an enormous building in the same area and went to discover what it was. A shopping centre. It sounds terrible to say that that was what distracted me when I had San Francisco to discover, but it wasn't going anywhere. As for this building, it wasn't really the shopping I was interested, but the amazing interior. The San Francisco Centre, as it was imaginatively called, had the most incredible escalator system I have ever seen. They surrounded the open interior of the building, and spiralled up seven storeys to the top – probably not for the vertiginous of us, but I thoroughly enjoyed going up and down. I even had a sneaky look in an enormous music store and realised that even earning Portuguese Escudos I would be able to afford some CDs at the end of my trip.

Dragging myself away from the escalators, I bought my travel pass and joined the queue for the Powell cable car. On any other occasion I wouldn't have bothered and got the less exciting bus, but it was my first time in San Francisco and I knew that it was the only way I could really get my first glimpse of the city. The cable car wound its way up the steep streets, affording a view of many of the famous sights, and then suddenly, such a familiar one; the sight of Alcatraz at the end of Powell Street far out in the bay. What's more it was a clear blue day, and there was only the narrowest band of fog hanging over it.

Although we'd only gone a few blocks, there already seemed to be so many different neighbourhoods, and they were all so close to each other. Some had a real European feel to them, especially as we passed close to North Beach. Finally, what all tourists must surely want to see the most – the Golden Gate Bridge. All the superlatives start tumbling out, but rightly so. It spanned the Bay so gracefully, and in the sunlight shone bright red against the blues of the sea and the sky. Spectacular. Arriving at Fisherman's Wharf I spent a while just gazing at the view over the Bay and then back up to the city. It has to be said that this view was far pleasanter than the one directly around me. I know it was a Saturday in mid-August but there were so many people – and lots of them were incredibly fat and dressed in pink and purple shell suits. Yuk. Obviously this was prime tourist ground, but, even so, it couldn't explain the amazing array of tourist tat shops, and high price ice-cream parlours, cafés and restaurants, people were trying to squeeze themselves into. I found myself in an area with lots of seafood stalls which seemed to be the most authentic thing about the area. I bought myself a half-pound of prawns and a lump of sour dough, found a quietish spot on one of the piers, and sat down to enjoy my mid-morning 'Scooby Snack', whilst watching the sea lions basking in the sun, and the boats coming and going.

After a bit more wandering, and trying to avoid being squashed by the hordes of pink and purple people, I decided it was time for lunch. Normally I would just choose somewhere which looked interesting, but on this occasion I had found somewhere in my guidebook which I thought merited a look. Fifteen years earlier the whole restaurant had been uprooted from its former location, a number of blocks away, and plonked down onto Pier 39. As the guide indeed said, it was authentically rustic and not pricey. Having queued up and ordered my lunch, I then picked a spot on one of the trestle tables and went over to the bar to get a well-earned beer. I thought the waiter was being incredibly rude when he asked me how old I was – I thought you weren't supposed to ask a lady her age! After some spluttering, I realised that he was checking I was old enough to drink. I was nearly twenty-nine at the time, and having told him this decided that he was a very nice waiter and not rude at all. After a quick chat with him and another man at the bar, I skittishly walked back to where my lunch had been delivered. I sat gazing out through the window enjoying the splendid view, and incredibly tasty tuna and Brie melt topped with Jalapenos, and lovely chips, or French Fries as I had to call them, otherwise I'd end up with a packet of Walkers!

Another quick beer and I then walked back through Fisherman's Wharf, still packed with the pink and purple people, and headed towards the Municipal Pier. It was shaped like an enormous apostrophe and surrounded an area of water which had a narrow but sandy beach. I sat there for a while reading and contemplating, and then succumbed to the lunchtime beers with a quick nap. I then walked to the far end of the pier, watching the fisherman with their catches, and from a different angle got breathtaking views of the bridge and the city. Directly behind me was a steep area of grass, and overlooking it an array of the most beautiful Art Deco houses. I'm sure I'd seen them in films and I can't begin to imagine how much they cost. What a view to wake up to if you were lucky enough to live there.

Dragging myself out of dream world, I wandered a little

further towards Fort Mason and poked around little shops and stalls in the warehouses on the piers. As it was such a beautiful day and I wasn't sure whether I would be lucky for the rest of my trip I decided I had to see the sunset from a really good position. I jumped on a bus going up Columbus, and headed towards Coit Tower. Walking up the steep hill towards the Tower, I decided it looked like a fire nozzle and then discovered it was built to commemorate the city's volunteer firefighters. That wasn't all it looked like!

The decision to come at sunset was a stroke of genius. There weren't many people around, the view over the Bay area was stunning and it was the end of a perfect first day. Having returned to my hotel to recover for a while, I found a local Mexican restaurant, stuffed my face and then spent the rest of the evening lazing around in my hotel room listening to music and watching telly.

Most of my days had the same pattern. I tended to get up early, do whatever was on that particular day's agenda, have a mid-day meal and some booze, have a kip in a park, some more sightseeing, then back to the hotel. Being on my own, this suited me fine. For my second day, I planned to go down to the area around Clement Street which was in the middle of the Richmond District. The reason was the number of bookshops and Asian shops which were located there. The area itself was a really quiet residential one with nothing much to see, but it was inside the buildings where the treasures lay. The Green Apple Bookstore was a delight. It was the most incredible, ramshackle place I have ever been to – there was a mixture of old and new books, piled up all over the place on either side of a labyrinth of aisles and small twisting staircases. It was truly a booklovers paradise. Having poked around for a while and made a few purchases, I then ventured into an Asian foodstore. I've always had a love of cooking so it was great to find somewhere where you could buy all the ingredients you might need. Reading this you might think it's strange to be so excited by books and food shops, but at the time I was, of course, living in a small town (although the Portuguese deem it a city) in the north of Portugal, and interesting shops didn't exist. There was nowhere to buy CDs or books, no shopping centre and certainly nowhere to buy ingredients for Oriental cookery. The most exciting purchase we'd recently been able to make was when our little supermarket started to sell Baked Beans! When word got out we cleared the shelves in a couple of minutes – obviously the manager didn't understand supply and demand as there were no more beans for months!

All the shopping had made me hungry so I found a little local Vietnamese restaurant. I hadn't had a Vietnamese meal since I'd lived in London and used to go to my favourite place in Soho. The decor was sparse, and there were only a few tables but the meal was fantastic and about a quarter of the price I used to pay. Feeling somewhat fat, I walked the couple of blocks to Golden Gate Park to get a little exercise. I had no idea it was that enormous (the park that is) – stretching over a thousand acres right down to the Ocean – and consisting of many different areas, such as woodlands, huge expanses of grass, themed gardens and wide paths for the energetic roller bladders who whizzed passed. I made for the Japanese Tea Garden and enjoyed the serenity of the place, the exotic plants and not least the 18th Century Buddha. It soon all got too much and finding a sunny, quiet spot on the grass I had a well-earned snooze. Feeling revived I headed for the Shakespeare Garden, which featured all the types of plants that are mentioned in his works. Not only plants, but benches engraved with quotations in bronze made it the place perfect for contemplation. Wandering slowly back toward the main road, I skirted around one of the wooded areas to come face-to-face with an enormous pair of dark eyes looking at me from the undergrowth. As it ventured out I realised it was a racoon. Not only was it incredibly cute but also much larger than I had thought racoons were.

I could have spent the rest of the day in the park, but was feeling drawn to the sea. The park is four miles in length, and my feet were starting to get the better of me, so I hopped on a bus, and before long was staring out at the Pacific Ocean, some 1,500 kilometres south from when I'd seen it the week before. The beach was home to all the normal activities, and I enjoyed walking on the sand with the ubiquitous ice cream. It was only when the beach ended and I started to walk up towards Cliff House, perched unsurprisingly enough on a cliff, that I realised how beautiful the area really was. There was a large green, almost wild chunk of land where the ocean and bay met. My guidebook described the area as being able 'to induce a rapture that will last for days.' It was right. After soaking up the atmosphere for a while I wandered off and eventually found a bus stop. Up until then I'd marvelled at how efficient the system was. Of course, it was late Sunday afternoon and we weren't exactly in the centre of the city. However, there was somewhere to sit and wait and I soon got chatting to a local who had visited London, and we happily passed half an hour talking about travelling. When the bus came it took ages to get in the centre but that wasn't a problem as I was able to see different parts of the city.

The following day I set off on foot to poke around the district I was staying in, and headed up the extremely steep hill towards Nob Hill. From the top the views of the city were again amazing. It was all very grand and my first stop was to have a look inside the Fairmont Hotel. There was no way I could have afforded to stay there but had read that it was worth a visit to look at the enormous lobby – it was! I then headed down California Street towards Grace Cathedral which although is made of concrete is a replica of a Gothic structure and only took fifty-three years to build. I have always had a weakness for Gothic architecture and this was no exception.

By this time my stomach was starting to rumble and I continued down California Street in search of a restaurant I'd read about. I found it easily enough, but getting somewhere to sit was a different matter. The Swan Oyster Depot was tiny with only a couple of tables and counter seating. Not only was it a restaurant but also a fishmonger, and the place had the reputation as being the best for seafood in the city. I spotted a stool and hopped up to be met with an array of fresh seafood and friendly staff. I had a huge 'prawn cocktail' for lack of a better name; although it bore little resemblance to what you might me served in the UK, some crackers and a cold beer. I chatted away for ages to some of the staff, one of whom bought me a beer, and some businessmen who were sitting next to me. When they left the waiter very cheekily asked them if they could leave without paying for my drinks, as I'd been such good company. What's more they did. Having had a lovely lunch and feeling that there are lots of good, friendly people around who don't have hidden agendas and more importantly buy me beers, I started the long walk back up the hill. I was heading for Russian Hill, which although originally the burial ground for Russian seal hunters now had a combination of old Victorian houses and some of the city's most elite addresses. It was certainly a strenuous stroll around the area and feeling in need of a break I happened upon what turned out to be the original Swensen's ice-cream parlour. Having chosen a chocolate concoction, I stated to count my money out when the assistant said that a red star had shown up on my receipt meaning it was free. I was certainly having a cheap day food wise. The ice cream was especially delicious.

A couple of blocks later and I arrived at Lombard Street, better known as the "crookedest street in America." – the one you often see in films. It was ridiculously steep and because of this had steps for the pedestrians – but it also had cars that were snaking their way down the hill. I felt the urge frequently to check behind me for cars that looked like they might have any kind of problem with their breaks. Fortunately I survived, and having stood on the corner and chatted to an elderly local for a while, I walked a fair distance to North Beach. My legs were giving out by then so as soon as I reached Washington Square I crashed out for a while. I woke up remembering I was in the heart of the legendary Italian area where the Beat movement was born. The square was bordered by an array of bakeries and coffee shops, and there still seemed to be a lingering aura of the alternative culture that existed here during the fifties. I made my way to the City Lights Bookstore which Lawrence Ferlinghetti founded, and which still published and sold works by little-known, alternative authors. The literary atmosphere was palpable and I spent a long while poking around this bookshop and others, soaking it all up. As it was so interesting I decided to stay in the area for an early dinner and looked around for something appropriate. It had to be Italian, so I choose a restaurant on Columbus where I could watch the world go by. Although the restaurant wasn't busy, I was ushered to a table back from the window, tucked away. Asking if I could have a window seat I was told no, they weren't for single diners. Charming. After the menu, bread and water had arrived I decided I really didn't like it at all, and stomped out. I found something much smaller and pleasanter on the other side of the road where I could sit wherever I wanted.

The following morning, Tuesday, I decided to book a trip for my last full day in San Francisco, the Wednesday, to visit Muir Woods in Marin County. That would leave the best part of the Thursday before my night flight for Dallas.

But that was later, and I spent the morning on a trip to Alcatraz. I've never really been one for organised trips, but I'd heard good things about the tour of the island, and there was so much history that it seemed churlish not to go. During the short trip out to the island I read about the history, and discovered that the island had served a variety of purposes including its original use as a military fort, and then during the beginning of the 20th Century as a military prison as well. It was used as a federal penitentiary from 1934 which gained 'The Rock' its notoriety. Disembarking from the ferry the change in temperature was very noticeable and it started to add a feeling of chill to the place. I opted for the tape tour of the prison as it meant you could go at your own speed, and it came highly recommended. It was indeed excellent, aided by comments from former rangers and some inmates themselves. It was so strange walking around this cold, chilling place, listening to real accounts, when in my head I could see the many Hollywood films that had been set here. After a while though, these images disappeared when the gruesome reality of being incarcerated on the island became apparent. I remember two things which particularly shocked me. The first was seeing the wall in the kitchen where the knives were stored. There were outlines painted on the wall of all the different sizes so if one had been taken it would be immediately obvious. Apparently, even knives and forks were carefully counted at the end of each meal. The other area was "D" Block – otherwise known as solitary confinement. It was a really depressing place with a slot in the door through which meals were served. The cells themselves had solid doors and were windowless. Although it was incredibly interesting, it was a stark, soulless place, which I suppose is hardly surprising as it was used to lock up America's public enemy number ones. They weren't sent there for rehabilitation, but because nowhere else could hold them. Among the most famous inmates were Al Capone, Robert Shroud ("The Birdman of Alcatraz") and Machine

Gun Kelley, who were "honoured" on a huge display on the wall.

Although the Rock managed to secure most of it prisoners, there were numerous escape attempts and all but five prisoners were recaptured or died trying. It was presumed that the five drowned. By 1961 San Francisco was starting to become twitchy about having the prison on its doorstep, and combined with the cost of repairing the rapidly deteriorating building, Robert Kennedy announced the prison would close. By March 1963 the last inmate left. Bizarrely, the only other inhabitants of the island arrived, voluntarily, seven years later in the form of Native Americans who landed there and claimed it as Indian land, trying to establish an educational and spiritual centre for themselves. However, the dream couldn't last, and after a couple of years with dwindling recourses they too left. And quite thankfully, so did I. It was fairly harrowing, and I was more than happy to board the ferry and head back towards the city.

It must have been such a torment for the inmates who were able to see the landmarks and shape of the city so well. Returning that day, the ferry certainly afforded the most amazing view. You could see the straight roads running parallel to each other as they headed up to Nob Hill. What a sight! Disembarking, I decided I needed something more pleasing to the eye than bare cells so headed off to find the Museum of Modern Art. Although not particularly large it has a significant collection and contains painting and sculptures that represent the major modernist and post-modernist movements. There were a few Matisse pictures which kept me happy for a long time, but apart from that the main attraction was a vast collection of contemporary photographs.

After that I was in a modern mood and spent the rest of the afternoon wandering around the Embarcadero and the Financial District, gazing up the various architectural landmarks, especially the distinguishing pointy top of the Transamerica Pyramid, which dominated the skyline wherever you went.

Arriving back at my hotel I decided to give my friend Cath a ring, just to confirm she'd be at the bus station when I arrived in Jalapa, Mexico. We chatted for a brief while and just before ringing off Cath said something like.

"OK, I'll see you on Thursday evening then."

"What?" I squeaked. "I'm arriving on Friday. I don't leave San Francisco until

Thursday night. That's why I've booked my trip to Marin County for tomorrow."

"But you told me you were arriving on the 18th," Cath replied.

"I am…." I started, as Cath interrupted.

"Rachael: The 18th is Thursday!"

Oh God. How on earth had I managed to mix my dates up? I was convinced that Friday was the 18th. I think maybe it has something to do with a terrible habit I have of not checking tickets once I have got them. I tend to have a vague idea of the time of the flight but never look until the evening before. However, I'd never nearly messed up and practically missed a flight by a whole day.

So, suddenly I only had a day left and most of that was going to be spent outside San Francisco. I started to worry that perhaps I'd get stranded somehow, or the bus would break down and I'd never make it back to the hotel on time to get my stuff and leave for the airport. However, I'd already paid for the trip and didn't want to waste the money.

Of course everything went fine and there were no unforeseen events which stopped me from catching my flight. I found the pick-up point for the tour and climbed onto the small mini-bus. We drove through the city and finally onto the bridge which I'd been looking at all week. The view back over the city was fantastic and being so high over the bay was also exhilarating. Having crossed the bridge we then made our way up towards Muir Woods. Although only twelve miles from San Francisco the roads were steep and winding, so it took a fair while. The area was designated a national monument in 1908 by President Roosevelt, after the land was donated by congressman Kent who had bought the land as it contained one of the last areas of old-growth redwood.

On arrival, the parking area was crowded and there was yet another tacky tourist shop. Fortunately, this was soon overshadowed, literally, by the amazing trees. There were beautiful, quiet groves full of redwoods which seemed to go up to the sky, some over two hundred feet tall, and most aged between five hundred and eight hundred years old. It was awe inspiring just to be there but also to think of how much had happened in the years that the trees had been there. It was a very reflective place, so I ignored the guided tours and took a self-guided one. This meant I could have time on my own away from all the purple and pink people.

There was lots of useful information about the cycle of a tree's life but I decided it was a bit too much like a biology lesson at school, which I hadn't understood then. I contented myself by looking at all the different types of flora and fauna – whatever they were –and soaked up the peaceful surroundings. I even saw a deer which seemed as surprised to see me, as me him.

The spell was broken after an hour or so when we had to get back on the coach. At least I had my Walkman so could block out the wittering going on around me and enjoy the descent back down to sea level in relative peace. We arrived at Sausalito, a resort town overlooking the bay. During the 1880's and 90's it had flourished as a whale town, infamous for gambling dens and bordellos. There was little evidence of this, and the town seemed to serve only as a tourist attraction and playground for the rich of San Francisco. I wandered around the shops – at least there was lots of interesting delis – bought myself a sandwich and sat on the water's edge enjoying the view. As lovely as it was, this view was about to be spectacularly surpassed. Heading back towards the city, as we approached the Golden Gate Bridge the driver took a right turn and told us we were going to stop on the edge of a cliff. It was the first time the famous San Francisco fog had done its stuff. It was drifting in from the Pacific and hanging over the whole bay area. It wasn't thick enough to completely block out the view, and on the opposite side of the bay you could see the tips of some of the tallest buildings, eerily appearing through the mist. I had been blessed with the bluest of skies and hot sun for my entire stay, but it seemed fitting that as my time in San Francisco was coming to an end, the mist was descending. It was just as eerie crossing back over the bridge, being shrouded in the mist, and not really being able to see where we were going. I'm very glad I wasn't driving!

We made it back safely to the centre, the bus hadn't broken down and I still had a couple of hours left before I needed to leave for the airport. After a last wander round, by which time the sun had come out again, I prepared myself for the next stage of my holiday. San Francisco had been a great success, and to this day I feel that I could quite happily live there.

Chapter 19

Mexico

Feeling very contented, I got a late airport shuttle bus to take a night flight to Dallas, and then on to Mexico City. Sounds easy. It most certainly wasn't. I was knackered before the flight even left, as I had to hang around the airport for ages until the 2 am departure. The first leg was painless enough. The plane was half-empty, so there was ample room to spread out across three seats and I even managed to sleep for a bit. We arrived at Fort Worth airport in Dallas at 7am, and having finally got to the terminal – I thought the plane was going to taxi forever – the fun and games started. There was a new metro loop system which was supposed to make it easy to get to the different parts of the airport. In true Belgian style, though, there was a distinct lack of signage and it took me ages to find the check-in desk. Having received my boarding card, my favourite, battered, old leather handbag decided to call it a day with spectacular results. The strap broke and the entire contents spewed out onto the highly polished floor, scattering in all directions, including a placket of tampons! Oh good!

The connecting flight to Mexico left soon after and I started dreaming about finally getting there. As the plane started to descend I could see the huge flat valley, surrounded by mountains on all sides, many of them topped with snow. Before long the enormous scale of Mexico City became apparent – it is the oldest metropolis in North America, and now was the most populous city in the world. However, in contrast to the excitement of arriving was the rising dread of getting through immigration and finding my way to the bus station. My friend Cath had warned me about the system. Apparently, in order to try and catch smugglers, and to make it fair, a system of lights had been introduced. Having finally managed to properly fill in the landing card for foreigners, and retrieved my rucksack, I headed towards the customs gate and the button that everybody had to press. If it was red then they could search you as much as they wanted, and if it was green couldn't touch you, even if you were a suspected trafficker. Feeling very tired I'd worked myself up into a right state and was convinced I'd get red. Luckily I didn't. That was just the first test though. I had strict instructions from Cath about how to get a taxi to the bus station. I had to buy a voucher from a particular booth inside the airport, and make sure that it was properly zoned; and at the same time deal with pesos, speak Spanish and make sure my luggage wasn't nicked. I managed this and clutching my voucher I made my way outside and looked for the white and green taxis which I could use it. Apparently these days tourists are advised not to use them, but I didn't have any choice. With some trepidation I clambered into a taxi, having managed to avoid hundreds of other taxi drivers who were desperate for me to get into theirs. I have certainly never seen taxis like them. They were nearly all VW beetles, with the passenger seat removed, leaving a gap through which said passenger had to struggle. That was nothing compared to the drive across the city to the bus station – it was nerve racking to say the least!

I finally made it at about 12 noon, and had four hours to wait for my bus – well three after the next saga. The bus station was enormous, and of course I had been set down miles from where I needed to be. Having heaved my rucksack onto my back, and visibly melting by the minute in the sweltering August heat, I set off to find the office I needed. Not only were there different areas for the various bus companies, but also a division depending on the class. Cath had already booked me a ticket by fax from Jalapa, and I was to be travelling in premier class. This basically meant that I wouldn't be travelling with chickens, and might get a film and a cup of coffee.

I might not have been travelling with chickens, but it seemed that they were going on somebody else's bus – they were running round all over the place. This, together with masses of people all swarming in different directions, some who appeared as bemused as me, and all talking at the tops of their voices, it was the perfect picture of abject chaos. I found myself in one large area with more chickens, and people queuing up at a counter. Since I couldn't find anywhere else which looked like it was the place I was supposed to be, and there was a sign bearing the name of the bus company I was using, I joined the throng. When it was finally my turn, I remembered that I couldn't speak Spanish, and had only acquired the rudiments of Portuguese. After much confusion, (heaven forbid that this might happen at a British bus station), a very patient attendant pointed me in the direction of the office I was looking for. After a bit more wandering I found it. I have rarely been so struck by such a contrast in surroundings within a few feet. As I walked through the automatic doors I was greeted by the most gorgeous whoosh of air-conditioning, quietness and no chickens. My joy lasted all of a minute! I approached the desk, which was manned by a beautiful Mexican girl in a scarlet uniform, and tried to explain I had a seat booked for the 4 o'clock bus to Jalapa. Except I didn't. There was absolutely no record of me, or of someone booking me a seat by fax from Jalapa. I was convinced Cath had made the booking, so after some pleading was finally allowed to see the seat allocation. Definitely no Rachael there – however, there was a vacant seat. I persuaded the girl it must be mine, and maybe she could phone the bus station in Jalapa. Sounds easy, but that alone took me an age to explain.

The panic was rising rapidly and I decided that I wanted my Dad. What he could have done I have no idea, but it was a comforting thought for a millisecond. I really couldn't understand what the girl was saying on the phone, but she seemed quite smiley, so I was feeling positive again when she hung up. Yes, the seat was mine. It had been booked and paid for in Jalapa, but the fax hadn't arrived, so there was no reservation in my name. What a relief! I still didn't have a ticket, and for reasons known to them the bus company couldn't issue me one.

"How will I be allowed on the bus then?" I asked. To be honest it was probably more

like, "How much is that pizza?"

"Just show them your passport, tell them what has happened, and they will let you on. If you have any problems ask them to come and talk to me." She made it sound so easy!

I still had two and a half hours ahead of me, before the bus was due to leave, and that is a lot of time for one's imagination to start running wild. I tried to doze for a while but Mother Nature decided it was her time to add to my woes and my tummy started hurting, which meant no chance of any sleep. I eventually got talking, well, arm waving, to a Mexican guy, who assured me he'd help me get on the correct bus. The waiting room was rapidly filling up, and since I knew the bus was only a thirty-seater, wondered how on earth I was going to be able to get the last seat. Everybody else could speak

Spanish so what chance did I stand! By then I'd lost most of my sense of reason, and it didn't occur that there might be other buses leaving from the same office. Finally the coach pulled up. No point in rushing, so I waited patiently (which felt like another age), put my rucksack onto the conveyer belt and watched it disappear through a large flap.

It was my turn. I duly showed the inspector my passport and mumbled something to him. He wasn't having any of it. No ticket, no bus. I pleaded with him to go and talk to the girl at the check-in desk. Guess what? She'd gone home. A bit more persuading and he found someone else to phone the bus station. I was finally allowed on the bus, and a huge wave of relief swept over me. Do you think that lasted for the five-hour journey? Oh no! I started to panic about whether my rucksack had actually been put on in all the confusion. I even wondered if I was actually on the right bus myself. Madness! I tried to put it out of my head, and enjoy the view outside. Even that didn't help. After only an hour or so it got dark, and I couldn't see anything. I tried to concentrate on the film, but had seen it too many times before. I finally fell asleep, exhausted, as it was now Thursday early evening, and I hadn't slept properly since Tuesday night. The sleeping was cut short by one of the most incredible thunderstorms I have ever experienced. We were now driving on fairly hairy roads, close to the mountains, and the rain was coming down in sheets, interspersed with the most amazing claps of thunder and lightening which lit up the whole sky. I couldn't bear to think if the driver could see where he was going.

To my huge relief, as we reached straighter roads, and the odd sign of civilization, I noticed a sign pointing to Jalapa in the direction we were going. Now all I had to worry about was my rucksack. We made our way into Jalapa, which unfortunately I couldn't see much of, as it was dark and still raining, and soon arrived at the bus station. I don't think I have ever been so relieved to see anybody. The driver drew back the curtain which separated him from the passengers and there, in front of the bus, was my friend Cath and her daughter Caitlin. What's more, as I was starting to get my sanity back, amid hugs, my rucksack was unloaded!

My first evening in Mexico was a complete blur, and having not written anything down, I have no recollection of what we did at all. Fortunately, my memory of the rest of my visit is still very clear. The following morning we set off for a wander around Jalapa. It was a hilly city with narrow winding alleys, and appeared to be rather haphazardly built. But it was the first sight of the city in daylight and I was completely smitten. I had never been anywhere like it in the world, and was amazed by all the different smells and sounds, and the incredibly vibrant colours everywhere. Just the trees themselves were mesmerising, not green-leaved but covered in a riot of oranges, reds and pinks. They weren't the only spectacular sight. Looming over the city, which itself was at four thousand feet above sea level, was the snow-capped Pico de Orizaba, the highest mountain in Mexico, itself at over twenty thousand feet.

As amazed as I was by the scenery, and everything going on around me, the thought of 'real' Mexican food was starting to call. Cath had frequently told me about its delights back in Portugal, and there were a couple of dishes I particularly wanted to try. The first was a pre-lunch appetizer, which could be sampled in special fish bars. They were only open for a few hours before lunch and sold a variety of seafood. The seafood, be it Ceviche, which was raw white fish 'cooked' in citric juices, lobster, crab or prawns, was then mixed with more lime juice, onion, chilli and coriander, served with crackers and beer. It had always sounded divine and I choose a prawn one which didn't disappoint.

My first afternoon in Jalapa, and I was lucky enough to be

invited into someone's house. It was Caitlin's birthday party and was being held in one of Cath's friend's large, colonial style houses. After the tradition of the cake, whereby the person whose birthday it was had their face pushed into it – very strange but hilarious – it was then the tradition of the *piñata*. Traditionally a clay pot filled with mandarin oranges, sugar cane and sweets, this one was made of *papier maché and* had sweets in it. Suspended from the ceiling, the kids, who were blindfolded, took turns whacking at it with a stick, until the contents were scattered all over the room. They may be fairly commonplace now, but back then I'd never seen anything like it.

That evening's entertainment was slightly more cultural, and Cath and I went to the cathedral where we saw a performance of Beethoven's 9th Symphony; the Ode to Joy. It was a truly magical setting for such a wonderful piece of music, and I don't think I will ever hear it performed in such a way again. What's more we heard it twice that week as Cath had invitations to attend a cocktail party at the town hall (one of the orchestra was a old friend), followed by a performance. We were duly introduced to various dignitaries, who seemed bemused as to who we were!

By the end of my first evening I was completely enamoured with Jalapa, and couldn't believe that I hadn't seen any other tourists enjoying it. Apparently, this beautiful state capital of Veracruz, and the rest of the state itself are largely ignored by holidaymakers as they rush through on coaches to Yucatan. More fool them in their compounds in Cancun, eating international food. Veracruz itself was, of course, where Cortes landed in 1519, when the Aztecs were in charge, and the state played a pivotal role in Corté's march to Mexico City where he defeated the Aztec rulers.

At the time, Jalapa was a Totonac ceremonial centre, and wanting to know more about the history of the city, we paid a visit to the Anthropology Museum, on the outskirts. It is second only in importance to the anthropology museum in Mexico City, and it showed. The amazing collection was displayed in spacious, marble halls and open-air patios, and the exhibits were on show, chronologically, in a descending series of halls. The first thing I saw was a huge Olmec head, carved from basalt. The first Olmec civilization was established around 1500 BC, and somehow seven such heads had survived the enormous space of time. As stunning as there were it was the exquisite jade figurines which grabbed my attention. I know that jade isn't all sparkly like so many gems are, and has connections with death, but I feel that this makes it all the more interesting. Dragging myself away from the figurines, I headed to the rest of the exhibits from the Olmec culture, and the other two main pre-Hispanic cultures of Veracruz, the Huasteca and Totonac. These sections were filled with, amongst others, cremation urns in the forms of bats and monkeys; terra-cotta jaguars; amazing Totonac murals; life-size sculptures of women who died in childbirth and highly stylised smiling figures.

Going round museums always makes me hungry and the anthropology one in Jalapa was no exception. We headed back into the centre of Jalapa towards the local market. Not only were there stalls selling beautifully bright scarves, clothes and silver jewellery, but the most important thing, lunch. We choose turkey served with mole, which is a rich sauce made from a variety of ingredients, including chillies and some bitter chocolate. To mop the sauce up we bought a selection of tortillas; some beige, some green (flavoured with spinach) and some black (flavoured with squid ink) and took our cheap, but amazing take-away home to eat. Delicious. There is nothing worse than going to a pseudo-Mexican restaurant where you are given two tortillas if you are lucky. We had a bag full!

The local food was rapidly becoming one of the highlights of my stay, and every meal just kept getting better and better. I can honestly say I have never been such a pig as I was that week – I was so desperate to taste as many of the dishes as I could. One day, the friend of Cath's who we were staying with, offered to drive us to a local river resort, Carrizal. Many of the local rivers were used by white waiter rafters, but this one had three swimming pools surrounded by lots of palm trees to shelter under. The best bit by far though was that, overlooking the swirling river was a wide veranda attached to a restaurant. It was there that I had the most delicious river prawns. They were straight from the river, and incredibly fresh. Called Chileatole, the pawns were cooked in a gorgeously hot tomato based sauce, served with mountains of soured cream, proper guacamole, refried beans, mounds of grated local cheese, and tortillas. It was the real thing and of course, the sauce was flavoured with the famous local chillies – Jalapa being the home of the jalapeño. Who needs fancy restaurants? I was wearing my swimming costume, barefoot and sitting on a plastic chair but eating one of the most memorable Sunday lunches I had ever had!

After lunch we headed for the edge of the river where there was a natural sulphur spring walled off from the river itself. Despite the fact that it was supposed to be incredibly good for your skin, trying to get in was almost impossible – it smelt like a truckload of rotten eggs being poached! Having finally, very gingerly, slid in to the warm water, we started to try and enjoy the benefits. It wasn't just the smell which was off putting though – there were, what I can only describe as what looked like a mixture of huge, slimy bogeys and furry seaweed floating around. Before I could do anything about it, Cath had scoped up a huge handful and slapped it on me. Thankfully, it felt like a huge dollop of exfoliating cream, and if you didn't look too closely at it whilst rubbing in, was an amazing sensation.

As we relaxed, soaking up the benefits and incredible scenery, I realised that tourists on masse, wherever they come from, are often ridiculous. From out of nowhere, about forty Mexicans appeared. There wasn't a bathing suit in sight, in fact they seemed to have their Sunday best on, shoes and all, and proceeded to walk precariously around the pool, balancing on the narrow, concrete wall which divided it from the swirling river. This was amusing enough but it was when they got to the final stretch, near to where we were sitting, which had a slope down into the pool that the fun really started. The wall must have been slippery because a woman starting sliding into the water. She couldn't get any grip on the slope as it was covered with algae so grabbed on to somebody, who in turn grabbed another person, and before too long, about ten, fully clothed Mexicans were enjoying an unscheduled dip. It has too be one of the funniest things I have ever seen, aided by the fact the soaked ones didn't seem that bothered and there was lots of screaming and giggling.

One of the other things that Mexicans are extremely good at are indigenous, roadside markets. We stopped off at one after we'd had enough of the eggy smell, and I marvelled at all the natural produce which was for sale. There was endless bags of chilli paste hanging from the stall roofs, jars of locally made honey, bundles of sugar cane, exotic fruits, and things whose names I can't remember. We had a green coconut each, with the top lopped off with a huge knife, and sucked the milk through a straw. Delicious!

During my whole stay in Mexico I didn't see any trouble, or feel in any danger, but one day during my stay there was a definite feeling of twitchiness. All around the town I'd seen campaign billboards and signs for the various political parties. Earlier that year the leader of the PRI party, Colosio, had been assassinated, and his mantle had been taken over by Zidillio (who should have been a football player with a name like that). There was a general feeling that there could potentially be trouble at the outcome of the general election. This was highlighted by the mass-buying going on at the supermarket. By the time we got there the shelves were almost bare. It was frightening to think that people could be so worried about an election result, that they would fear leaving the house to go shopping. Fortunately, there was no major trouble following the re-election of The PRI. Years later, they stunningly managed to land the country's economy in crisis though!

One evening I did something very untouristy and went to the cinema. It was quite an experience. The cinema was a real old fleapit, but sold Dos Equis beer, and lime and chilli crisps. The film was fairly bad, *Wolf,* but the experience excellent. People came and went throughout the entire length of the film, talked about every aspect of it, and anything else they fancied, and made noises to accompany the film. At the end, lots of people stayed to watch the start and the parts they'd missed. Mad!

My time was rapidly running out, but I managed to squeeze in a few last meals. One was at a lovely, rustic restaurant, covered in old pictures of Jalapa. In one corner there was a fairly elderly lady, whose sole job was to make tortillas. Piles and piles of them. My meal that night was gorgeous. I had a butterflied chicken breast with layers of avocado on top, a tortilla covering it, and surrounded by a creamy, yet fiercely hot, jalapeno chilli sauce. Despite the fact that my waistline was starting to resemble that of a five-month pregnant woman, I still managed to find the space for one last dinner. I tried to squeeze in a little of all the dishes I still hadn't eaten. One of them was tamale, wrapped in a banana leaf, and the other, which sounded disgusting but was delicious, was an *empanada,* a little pastry filled with mould from the husk of a corn!

Chapter 20

New York, New York

And that was the end of my trip to Mexico. I said goodbye to Cath and Caitlin, who I'd see back in Portugal in a couple of weeks, and was dropped off at the bus station. The return journey was far less eventful – I got to Mexico City having been able to enjoy the scenery the whole way, as it was a morning departure. Unfortunately, I had to take two flights back to San Francisco to get my next connection. Having booked the Vancouver and San Francisco trips together I was given a free stopover so decided to go to New York on my home. The flight was an early morning one and as it didn't seem worth going back into San Francisco for the night the airport it was. Initially it wasn't a problem. I found a quiet area, close to one of the gates which had closed for the night and tried to get comfortable. A helpful porter brought me over a blanket and I managed a couple of hours sleep. However, in the early hours airport security closed all the gate seating areas, including the one where I was, and I was herded back through the secure area. Now what to do? I was in the main entrance of the airport and there didn't appear to be anywhere particularly safe or quiet to try and sleep. Eventually, I choose some seats with no arms, put my luggage on the floor as close as possible to me, and wound my handbag round my arms. Surprisingly, I fell asleep. I woke up the next morning to my alarm going off at 6. No wonder I'd slept well. I must have known that even if anybody had wanted to nick my bags they would have had to scramble over half the airport to get to me. All around me, on the seats, and on the floor there were about a hundred people asleep!

I gingerly picked my way over the sleeping beauties, had a wash and change in the toilets and made my way to the departure gate. I was on my way to that most talked about city in the world. The journey was a nightmare – not because anything went wrong but it seemed to go on for ages - well six hours. Flying for so long but still being in the same country was weird. I couldn't sleep; the films were boring and the food inedible. I was so relieved to finally land at JFK, and bounded off the plane to collect my rucksack. All the other passengers collected their luggage whilst I waited, and waited and waited. At first you just think that your luggage will be one of the last to appear, then that somehow it's been left on the plane, and finally that it has gone off on its own to a different destination. I feared the latter, and was cross because I knew how little time I had in New York, and didn't want to spend what time I did have, shouting at airline officials. However, it then came trundling through the flap. Reunited, I struggled across the arrivals lounge which was the closest thing I have ever seen to a scrum outside a rugby field, and finally found the bus that would take me into the centre of Manhattan.

I had already booked a hotel for a couple of nights in the centre of the theatre district, just off Broadway, and trusting the driver knew where he was going, settled back to enjoy the journey. It took about an hour, and as we crossed over the bridge I got my first view of Manhattan with the skyscrapers sparkling in the summer sunshine. We slowly made our way into the centre, dropping off people at various hotels on the way. By then I was completely fed up with travelling and just wanted to get to my hotel. It seemed as though I was going be the last one. As I checked with the driver he said he didn't recognise the name of the hotel – oh good, here we go again I thought! He took me to 48th Street and to the number where the hotel was supposed to be, and lo and behold there was a hotel, but not with the same name as that one that I had found in my Berlitz guide, and booked. Fortunately it was the right one, despite its name, and they had my reservation. It had a stunning lobby with a sky-lit atrium and a waterfall, but I was more interested in dumping my stuff in my room, having a shower, changing and finding some dinner. After dinner in the hotel, which was the easiest option as I was now dead on my feet, I had an amble around the block to get my first taste of the atmosphere of New York. I then decided that I was going to have to go to bed and get up early to make the most of my day. It was my first proper bed in over a week; I'd been on a camp bed in Mexico and on a seat in San Francisco airport the night before, so it was feeling very spoilt that I stretched out on the enormous bed, and fell asleep immediately. Well, that's not exactly true. That's how I wanted it to happen. I had to contend with the air conditioning. What a bloody racket. I admit it was probably needed as it was in the 30s that weekend, but I would rather have been sticky than listening to the drone of the system all night. I tried every switch but nothing would turn the stupid thing off! Since then I have discovered the joy of earplugs, and for someone who wakes up if an alarm clock goes off in Australia, they are priceless. Whoever designed them should be knighted!

The next morning, rather blearily, I made myself get up early and set off to explore. Before that, of course, I needed fuelling. Where better than one of the famous coffee shops. I had a huge mug of coffee and a delicious muffin, and although continually distracted by everything happening around me, tried to plan the next couple of days to squeeze in as much as possible. I decided the first thing I had to do was to get an overall view of Manhattan and to see the Statue of Liberty; so headed towards the subway to catch a train. I have never been as confused on an underground system as I was that morning. It was easy to buy a ticket, the maps were clear as to the different lines; but what I couldn't figure out was which way I was supposed to be going. There didn't appear to be any signs at all. I pride myself on my sense of direction, and being able to find my way round new cities, regardless of the language spoken, but here I was in New York, completely baffled. I really don't know if it was just me or there was a complete lack of signs so I decided to get on, knowing I could always get off and go in the opposite direction! Purely, by luck, I choose the correct platform, and before long was deposited at Battery Park which had the most amazing view of New York Bay. There was a huge variety of boat and helicopter tours on offer, but I had inside information and being short of time and money, opted to take the advice I'd been given by my lovely companion on the flight from the UK and take the fifty cent ferry to Staten Island and back, for the best and cheapest view. It was a good choice. There was loads of room, ample opportunity to take photographs, and no throngs of tourists pushing and shoving. It was a stunningly clear day, and the Statue of Liberty shone out in the sun, with the skyscrapers of Manhattan in the background. Like so many people who saw them, it now feels all the more poignant when I look back at my photographs, and see the skyline dominated by the twin towers. However, on that day, it wasn't even a possibility anyone would consider, and everyone was blissfully unaware of the tragedy to follow seven years afterwards.

Sailing past the Statue of Liberty was incredible. She was enormous, but graceful at the same time and many years previously had symbolised reaching the New World for so many immigrants. I knew she had been a gift from France in recognition of the friendship between the two countries, but didn't know much more. Apparently, according to my book, Bartholdi had a dream to create the 151-foot-high structure, but realised that he needed some engineering expertise, so called in Eiffel to help translate his artistic vision into metal. Although I had come across Eiffel's work in Porto, in the form of a bridge, I had no idea that his handiwork was on display in America as well. The statue was erected in Paris in 1884 to the amazement of the Parisiennes, and then later disassembled and packed into two hundred and fourteen crates, and shipped over to Liberty Island to be reassembled. How mad is that? The Statue of "Liberty Enlightening the World", to give it its full name, was officially unveiled in October 1886 by President Cleveland, and has been an iconic symbol ever since.

I wasn't going to spend time on Staten Island, so having bought a disposable camera, as mine had decided to stop working – great timing – I took the return trip. In some ways, the view the second time round of Manhattan was more overpowering, as rather than the buildings getting smaller and smaller, they seemed to be gradually rising from the sea and looming over us. Disembarking from the ferry, I decided to avoid the subway to be able to see as much as possible of the city and caught a bus. It went through the heart of the World Trade Centre, then Soho and I hopped off in the middle of Greenwich Village. Although, not what it used to be like in its heyday in the 1920's and 30's, when it was the artists' quarter, there was still a fair amount of atmosphere, and I wandered about, soaking it up and poking around in interesting craft shops. I ended up in Washington Square, admiring Washington Arch, erected in 1889 to mark the centenary of George Washington's inauguration as President. As splendid as the arch was, it somehow seemed out of place, as the square had now become notorious for its drug dealers, of which there were some in evidence the day I was there.

Next on the itinerary was a trip up the Empire State Building. Although I hadn't been up the Statue of Liberty, this was something which I had to do. Fortunately, there was only a small queue and before I knew it was being whisked up to the eightieth floor in less than a minute, and from there took the second elevator to the eighty-sixth floor, some 1050 feet above street level. Once my internal organs had caught up with the rest of me I was able to enjoy the view. The panorama was truly amazing. You could see all the famous buildings of Manhattan itself, Central Park, which looked like a postage stamp of grass; then, on the other side of the Hudson and East Rivers, New Jersey, Brooklyn and Queens. And if you looked down lots of little ants, and yellow ant cars, all scurrying along. I spent a long time enjoying the view, and only tore myself away when the huge Macy's sign reminded me that New York was a shopper's dream.

The area around the Empire State Building contained some of the city's most famous stores, and I spent a couple of hours wandering around, amazed at the huge variety. I stopped only for refuelling – I couldn't believe how cheap it was to buy a quarter of pizza from a little take-away, and which was also delicious – and got back to the hotel a satisfied shopper. Being horizontal for a while helped my aching feet, and feeling re-energized I set off for the tour I'd booked. I knew that it was the only option if I really wanted to see as much of the city as possible. It was billed as a night excursion by bus of New York and lasted for about four hours. We covered a huge area of the city with a pleasant, informative guide, stopping off at many points to sample the local culinary delights and visit the sights. We went to Central Park, and had a wander as the sun was going down; we then headed towards the tip of Manhattan, stopping off in Chinatown to explore food markets, and Little Italy where we went to a traditional Italian café and ate homemade ice cream. After that we drove passed the Tribeca area, passing CBGB's, which, for anyone who doesn't know was one of the most formative venues for live music in the 1970's. I thought about The Ramones, Patti Smith, Blondie, Talking Heads and Tom Petty, all who had been 'discovered' there. Shame I hadn't been able to see them!

The last two places on the tour were the Twin Towers, and then over Brooklyn Bridge. In front of the towers, on the grass, we lay full-length on our backs with our feet pointing away, and looking back. I'm not sure this was on a normal tourist itinerary but it gave a spectacular angle to view the ill-fated towers. From there we drove over the bridge and into Brooklyn, where we experienced one of the archetypal views of New York – Manhattan by night. Although completely manmade you couldn't help but be struck by its beauty. So that was the end of my first day. I'd had a brilliant time and my personal impression was so different from many of those I'd heard. I know it's difficult to form a proper opinion in such a short time, but the noise, crime and grime just didn't seem that evident. Even the people were friendly – apart from the bus driver who got cross with me, as I didn't know I needed the exact change. That was counteracted by a passenger who paid my fare! New York had worked its magic on me!

The following day was equally packed, although much more indulgent. That indulgence was art. Following a gorgeous breakfast in the parasoled garden in front of the Rockefeller Center, overlooked by a gold-leaf covered statue of Prometheus (I never did discover why he was there) I made my way to St Patrick's Cathedral on Fifth Avenue. Although dwarfed by modern skyscrapers, the cathedral was magnificent. It had been modelled after the Gothic cathedrals of Cologne and Reims, but was only built in 1858. I made my way inside, to find a wedding had just taken place. What's more, the bride and groom were exiting to the music I'd heard the week before in Jalapa Cathedral – namely part of Beethoven's ninth symphony. The music may well have been ancient and serene; the same cannot be said of the wedding party. As they congregated on the steps of the cathedral for the photographs, a large crowd had gathered. Not only were there seven bridesmaids, and the same number of ushers, but all the women, including the bride were wearing the shortest dresses I have ever seen, let alone at a wedding. What a spectacle it was. Maybe I'd witnessed one of those fabled 'Only in New York' moments.

I decided I'd been getting distracted for too long, and went to find the Museum of Modern Art. I knew it held it the world's largest and most inclusive collection of modern painting and sculpture but wasn't really ready for the impact that it had. The MOMA, however, had had a very inauspicious start. The first exhibition was opened in 1929, only ten days after the stock market crash; it was held in a makeshift gallery and included four impressionist painters, who were scarcely known in the United States at that time. Said painters just happened to be *Cézanne, Gauguin, Seurat and van Gogh*! None of these factors deterred the museum founders, and over the following ten years they held further painting exhibitions, as well as ones for photography, architecture and design. A film library (the first of its kind) was further established in 1935. By this point the public's response was enthusiastic and the new building was opened on 53rd Street in 1939. By the time I visited the collection was known throughout the world.

I'd been to galleries before, where in one room there may be works on display from a number of artists, but the MOMA had rooms devoted to only a couple of artists, or in some cases, just one. The collection encompassed those post-impressionist painters who had been part of the first exhibition and covered Cubism, Fauvism, through surrealism, early abstract expressionism, and up to the abstract works of the 1960's. For you and me that means Picasso, Chagall, Kandinsky, Mondrian, Klee, Dali, Magritte, Pollack, Warhol and Lichtenstein. I spent ages enjoying all these artists but knew that it was one room in particular that I was really saving myself for. The Matisse room. A whole room just for him. It was stunning. I was completely overcome by being there and sat for ages surrounded by the most beautiful paintings. I particularly loved the paintings of the interiors of rooms with light flooding in through the windows, and from that day the painting entitled '*Interior with a violin case*' has been my favourite.

When I finally managed to tear myself away, I headed off to the sculpture garden. What a haven of peace and tranquillity it was, right in the heart of Manhattan. It was beautifully set with trees, fountains, reflecting pools, and of course magnificent sculptures by modern masters such as Moore, Picasso, Rodin, and luckily for me, Matisse. Having wandered around I sat in the Garden Café, where I had another divine New York sandwich, soaked up the atmosphere and rested my throbbing feet. Feeling suitable refreshed I had one more quick look in the Matisse room, and then remerged into the heat and confusion of Manhattan. It was another boiling hot, stuffy day, but I remember feeling so happy to be there. I only had a few hours left in the city, and rather than rush off to see other sights or museums, decided just to wander round the area, and poke about a bit, stopping where I fancied. I found a Doubleday Bookshop, which was enormous, and also a huge CD store, Sam Goody's, where I parted with more money. It would have been rude not to really. The prices were amazing, even compared to Portugal.

I wandered up Fifth Avenue, lined with the most outrageously priced shops selling designers jewels and clothes, and even went up the escalators in Trump Tower. It was so completely over the top, everything seemed to be gold, but you couldn't help but be awed by it; not least that it was air-conditioned.

Time was fast disappearing, and with some regret I plodded back to my hotel, knowing that my fantastic holiday was nearly at an end. I had accomplished so many of the things I wanted to do, eaten so much different food, seen so many sights, and experienced a lot of things I hadn't expected. The biggest shock I think must have been New York. Yes, it was noisy and dirty, but expensive it wasn't and friendly it was. The only regret of the entire trip was that I didn't get to see a professional baseball match (I don't think watching my cousin and his mates in a park in Vancouver really counts, although at least I started to understand the rules). The players were all on strike over money. How much did they need for God sake, and how thoughtless to strike when I was in the States?

So, that was it. I had a non-eventful journey back to the UK and was met at the airport by Dad, and we chatted happily about my trip and swapped notes about San Francisco and New York, both which he'd previously visited.

Those special places visited

Frankland Islands, Queensland, Australia

~

Ribeira, Porto, Portugal

~

Thira, Santorini, Greece

~

River Restaurant, Carrizal, Vera Cruz, Mexico

Part Seven

All change

Chapter 21

Final year in Guimarães

Term started and the familiar routine was quickly established; lots of dinners with friends, cinema trips and the occasional weekend in Porto. It was just what I needed to help bring some order and sense to my life, but I still had periods when I realised what people go through when they are suffering from depression. The analogy I can equate it to is a big black pit, with me standing on the edge looking in, feeling as though I was about to fall in. Things must have been bad because for the first time I had absolutely no interest in the opposite sex. The idea of being touched or kissed made me feel incredibly anxious. The reason for this has to do with the man I met on the plane. We met up in the UK a few days after I returned from the States, but shortly after that tragedy happened, and whilst I can't write about the details, suffice to say it was a very bleak time.

By Christmas, thankfully, I'd started to feel more positive, and was looking forward to being in the UK for the holiday. I saw many friends, and even met somebody at a New Year's Eve party who I felt comfortable enough with to start a relationship. On Christmas Eve I spent a mad evening in the local pub with my brother and his mate Richard (the same guy who I'd had a fun time with a couple of summers before). Waking up, and feeling as bad ever after Christmas Eve, there was more to deal with. We discovered that Dad hadn't been well the night before, and none of us knew how serious it was then.

I headed back to Portugal to start term and await news of Dad's test results. Unfortunately, when Mum phoned me it wasn't with good news. Dad had got colon cancer, and it wasn't in the early stages. Almost immediately he had an operation, then chemotherapy, and spent many weeks recuperating. I felt very far away, but at Dad's request he didn't want me to come rushing back then. He believed completely that he could beat it, and that life would return to normal. I went through all the usual emotions you feel when faced with such news – I tried to be as positive as Dad was, for his sake – but one of my main feelings was of how unfair it all was.

Around the same time I heard that I'd been accepted on a Masters course to study English Language Teaching Management, starting in October of that year. I'd reached the point in my teaching where I felt I needed more, and having previously done management it seemed the logical progression. Although I knew it would be hard to scrape together the money, and to leave Portugal, I felt that I had to return to the U.K.; as well as studying I could spend time with Dad. Although the course was accredited by Southampton University, it was actually being run at a local college, so it made sense that I would live with Mum and Dad for the year. Having made this major decision, I concentrated on my life in Portugal and living it to the full.

The first thing I did was to start having aerobics lessons with Clare once a week. The pair of us were incredibly unfit, and decided that something had to be done. The first lesson nearly killed us, and on the way home we realised how hungry we were. Some people would have been virtuous and gone home and made a salad, but being incredibly weak-willed, we stopped off at the takeaway on the way home, and got pizza and chips. That's the way to do it! When Russell arrived home later on, he was amazed that we had actually gone, and was full of admiration (being another resolute non-exerciser). However, despite our best efforts he discovered the empty pizza box, and we endured endless piss taking. We might have wobbled on that first day, but every week until August, Clare and I religiously went and leapt around! To my shame I have never been to an aerobics class since.

One positive thing during this hard period was that my love life was on the up again, and the guy (another naval officer) that I'd met at Christmas came out to Portugal for a holiday in February. Still being on a four-day week, and bribing someone to cover my Tuesday lessons we had four clear days. I don't need to go into details, but we had a great time and even managed to get to Porto, do some sightseeing, and sample some port.

Chapter 22

Lisbon at last

To make things even better, the Carnaval holiday was just round the corner, and after two years of living in Portugal I was finally going to visit Lisbon. I went with Cath and her daughter Caitlin, and not having a car used the coach which took forever. We did, however, finally arrive, and the wait was worth it. Having been deposited in a small square lined with palm trees, we huffed and puffed our way up a steep hill towards our shabby (but spotlessly clean) *pensão*. We were staying in one of the old areas of Lisbon, called Chiado, perched high above the central area and a delightful warren of narrow streets.

Although I knew a little history of the capital, mainly about the earthquake, I had no idea how drastically the city had been changed. As we walked down the windey roads, trying to avoid being run over by trams as the pavements were only about an inch wide, the whole area suddenly opened up. It was almost like being back in New York. The roads were wide, and organised in a grid system, and it was though we'd stumbled upon a different city. This area, called the Baixa (low area), which started by the river with the enormous Praça do Comércio, was surrounded by government buildings, and lots of little cafés nestling amongst the arches. Walking away from this, and up a few blocks, the road then opened up to another square, surrounded by restaurants and more cafés, and although named after a king is collectively known as Rossio. This square then led to a beautiful tree-lined avenue, graced with Art Noveau buildings. The city didn't obviously show its chequered past; not just because of the devastating effect of the earthquake but the fact that it had been invaded countless times. Legend has it that Ulysses founded the city, but it was probably the Phoenicians who settled here 3,000 years ago. However, others soon recognised the city's qualities, and the Greeks quickly arrived, who in turn were booted out by the Carthaginians. In 205 BC it was the turn of the Romans, and after a succession of northern tribes, the moors arrived from North Africa in 714. It was they who fortified the city, which they called Lissabona, and fended off the Christians for four hundred years. In 1147, though, after a four-month siege, Christian fighters under Dom Afonso Henriques recaptured the city. It was in 1260 that Afonso III made Lisbon his capital, having moved it from Coimbra.

Since then, Lisbon has definitely had its fair share of glory and tragedy. In the 15th and 16th centuries it was the opulent seat of a vast empire, after Vasco de Gama discovered a sea route to India. The city's importance was further increased when, in the 17th Century, gold was discovered in Brazil. Merchants flocked from all over the world, dealing in gold and spices. During the reign of Dom Manuel 1, the extravagant style of architecture that became known as Manueline, complemented Lisbon's role as the world's most prosperous trading centre. This all came crashing down (literally) in 1755, with the massive earthquake. Thirteen thousand people are thought to have died, although some say it may have been up to twenty thousand, and the lower area of the city was destroyed. Fortunately, the first Pombal de Marquis (equivalent of our Prime Minister) dealt with the crisis and rebuilt the city, but the damage was done, and Lisbon has never quite regained the glory of its early days.

I wasn't complaining though and was thoroughly enjoying being in the capital. Having wandered around the 'newer' part of the city we walked up the steep hill on the other side of the Baixa. This was Alfama, a chaotic warren of narrow streets where the Moors had settled, and its shape and atmosphere was defined by them. It was in complete contrast to the order of the Baixa. Some of the streets were so narrow you could almost touch the houses on either side. Despite this a tram still, somehow, made its way up the main street, and it was indeed a terrifying experience trying to jump out of its way, or travel on it feeling convinced that the tram couldn't possibly get round a corner without smashing into someone's living room. Having made it to the top, we were afforded a stunning view over the nearby roofs, the clearly organised streets below, and up to the Bairo Alto on the other side. We could also see way out across the River Tajo. Although obviously larger than Porto, it was the same mixture of a city being partly situated on a hill, overlooking a river and close to the sea, which I found so exhilarating. After soaking up the atmosphere we wandered round the Castelo de São Jorge. Although fairly touristy, climbing up and down the massive battlements, watching Caitlin stalking the peacocks, and looking at Lisbon from so many different angles was extremely pleasant.

I was intrigued by one area I could pick out on the other side of the Baixa. It was what appeared to be an iron tower, which rose up from the lower area, and whose top was parallel to what looked like a fairytale type ruined church. Cath filled me in with the details and we set off back down the hill to have a look. Suddenly we were back in the real world of shops, and before we reached the tower, Cath told me about a bookshop which sold books in English.

Still being starved of such shops in Guimarães, we made a detour, and Cath and I both left clutching bags. The tower I had seen was in fact the Elevador de Santa Justa which was an immense wrought-iron outdoor lift designed by Raul Mésnier du Posnard and completed in 1902. The style seemed very familiar, and I wasn't surprised to discover that Mésnier was a follower of Eiffel – the man was everywhere! We took the lift, which hoisted us thirty-two metres above ground level, and deposited us in the Chiado district, with the ruined church in front of us. It was the most spectacular of ruins, and to this day I still have a postcard of it pinned up in my kitchen. The Convento do Carmo stands as stunning testimony to the 1755 earthquake and only the gothic arches, walls and flying buttresses remain of what was once one of Lisbon's largest churches. I stood and looked at it for ages – it was memorising, and eerie, especially if you thought about how long it had been standing in such a sorry state.

Another way to avoid walking up the steep streets was to take the Elevador da Bica – except this wasn't an elevator but a funicular. What was it about the Portuguese language that they used one word for a variety of things? Talk about confusing! Take the word *massa*. It means pasta, and bread dough, but also any kind of paste, blu tac, and (as in English) is the slang for money. Someone might ask you for some blue tac, and you hand over a bag of tagliatelli. Mad!

Next day we took the tram (called an eléctrico!) six kilometres west of the centre to the district of Belém, one of the main launch places for the Portuguese discoverers. It was from here that Vasco de Gama left in 1497, and when he returned two years later, Dom Manuel I ordered the construction of a monastery on the site of a riverside chapel where da Gama and his officers had held an all-night vigil before leaving. The Mosteiro dos Jerónimos was stunning. In 1984 it was designated a UNESCO World Heritage Site, and rightly so.

It is one of the few structures in Lisbon to have survived the earthquake undamaged, and one of the finest examples of the Manueline style of architecture. Another structure that survived the earthquake was the Torre de Belém. Manuel I intended it to be a fortress to guard the entrance to Lisbon's harbour, but today it sits on the riverbank after the shoreline drifted south; symbolising the Age of Discoveries.

Having done the history thing, a pit stop was in order and we made our way to the *Antiga Confeitaria de Belém*, in English the Old Belem Cake House. It is a traditional café covered in the most beautifully painted blue tiles; famous since 1837 for serving *Pasteis de Belém*, the renowned custard tarts. We wolfed them down, topping up the calorie intake with thick, rich hot chocolate. So that was Lisbon – well until the next visit. We had only had a couple of days, and on following visits I discovered much more of this beautiful and captivating city.

Chapter 23

Last hot months

A couple of weeks later we all went to Braga for Russell's birthday. He'd heard about a new Russian restaurant that had opened, and being that there was a distinct lack of international restaurants, and because he'd studied in Russia for a while, decided it was the ideal venue for his birthday meal. About ten of us went, and settled ourselves around a large circular table, where we commenced to down shots of vodka whilst deciding what to eat. The novelty was all too much, and we became increasingly silly and rowdy. Towards the end of the meal Clare took Rosie into the toilets to change her nappy, and enlisted my help. I'm sure if social services had been there, they'd have had something to say. Rosie had decided she was in one of her 'no nappy changing' moods, and since there was no changing table, we had her pinned down on the marble floor while she screamed and squirmed. This wasn't helped by the fact that the pair of us were completely pissed and howling with laughter. To make matters worse we then managed to bang Rosie's head on the china basin – at least this distracted her for a moment and we were able to finally change her nappy. Things weren't much better back in the restaurant, and the vodka was still flowing. When we finally asked for the bill, we couldn't even get that right, and managed to loose it! What a spectacle it was – what's more Russ's Mum was there and not being a drinker and driving some of us home – had seen all the drunken antics. How embarrassing, and what hangovers the following day.

For the Easter holidays that year I decided to go back to England to see Dad. It was so good to be able to see with my own eyes the recovery he had made from the operation, but at the same time it made me realise that he had a terrible disease, and despite a successful initial operation had a long fight ahead. Although I spent a lot of the time at Mum and Dad's, I also managed to see friends, and even went to Bournemouth. Not a usual port of call, but after a gap of three years David and I had decided to meet up. Even after such a long time, and with all the unhappy feelings gone, I still felt somewhat nervous about seeing him again. It started off well enough; we had a good meal, and chatted away as we had always done. But then, completely unexpectedly, as I got into bed, well David's (he was on the sofa), and after everything that had happened between us, he made a pass at me! Men. Honestly! However, I resisted the temptation!

Back to Portugal and summer term followed the pattern of the previous two years. Lots of weekend evenings eating good meals, drinking beer by the pool, and listening to live music in the square. I made the most of it, as I knew that before too long I'd be back in chilly England, trying to remember how to study. As ever, the term whizzed passed us and before we knew it, it was the last day of term. Having just been paid Guy, Ros and myself decided we'd earned a lunch out, and drove to Braga to a favourite chicken and chips restaurant. By the time we got back to Guimarães, I had done considerable damage to the country's store of Vinho Verde; unfortunately we couldn't stay in our local but had to go to the traditional end of year meeting from hell, in a boiling hot classroom, listening to old 'cat's bum' (otherwise known as our director) warbling on. It was all completely hopeless – I hid behind my shades and tried to stifle the giggles as the same old ridiculous discussions reared their ugly heads (why was the spread on the break time bread rolls so rank; why weren't the toilets cleaned, why was the cleaner always pissed etc – all good academic topics) until all the things I'd ever wanted to say to the old bat suddenly appeared to be coming out in speech rather than in my mind. Oops! There went my two weeks intensive course which would earn me some holiday pennies. Our boss must have been even more stupid than we gave her credit for – she seemed to not mind me voicing my opinions – strange since she'd only ever had a yearly favourite 'blue-eyed boy', certainly never a brown-eyed girl!

And that was it. The end of an era. The school might have driven us all crazy most of the time, with a boss who was so far up her own arse I can't think of a suitable ending, but it was a cracking first job and I knew I wouldn't see the likes of it again. Apart from the two-week intensive course in the evening that somehow I'd managed to keep, I was as free as a bird for the next two months. The holiday started off in an extremely memorable way. I was going to be thirty that September but by then would have left Portugal. I therefore decided to be The Queen and have an official birthday, and since some of my friends were going to be away for the summer, choose the first weekend in July.

Invitations were designed by Clare, guests invited, food prepared (my friend Guy spent hours stuffing vine leaves using ones from our own vine), beer and wine bought, and music organised (Russell even made me a special birthday tape). We were going to have the party around the pool, and people were encouraged to arrive late afternoon to have a swim and stay for as long as the party continued. Problem. I woke up that Sunday morning to hear the extremely unwelcome sound of rain. It was the beginning of July for God sake, and the weather had been amazing for ages. PANIC. There was no way I could have a full-blown party in my shoe box of a flat. Fortunately Guy and Ros told me I could hold it in upstairs in their flat where there was plenty of room. And what a party it was - excellent fun! There were my teacher friends from work, other friends and some favourite students. What's more some of the sons from our local bar came too – including the gorgeous one, Reinaldo. And what a present he brought. A huge bunch of flowers and a crate of beer. What more could a girl want? Preferably not the enormous hangover I had the next morning. Apparently the weather hadn't dampened anybody's spirits and it was an excellent party – for me in many ways, including an overnight visitor in the form of said gorgeous barman.

My party set the tone for July, and apart from the two classes I taught in the evenings I was on holiday. The weather was hot and sunny and there was more of the usual lazing around by the pool, and sitting in the square in town listening to music, and sometimes attempting to dance to it (not easy on cobbles I can assure you). I was also seeing Reinaldo from time to time – nothing as official as boyfriend, girlfriend but on afternoons between his shifts he'd appear on his motorbike and we'd spend the afternoons having a 'siesta' (well, what else could you do in a hot afternoon) and messing around in the pool. One hot afternoon he took me for a long bike ride, and clinging on to him for dear life we swooped round the corners of the narrow back roads, and up into the hills near Braga. I think I was the envy of all the girls in Guimarães that summer, as he was obviously a real catch!

Halfway through July an old friend from my BT days came over for a week's holiday. That time I didn't have to worry about how to get to the airport in Porto as Gabrielle, Russ' Mum, had gone away for the summer and told me I could use her car. So, for my remaining two months I had a white Renault 5 that I nipped around in. My week was Phil was great, and filled with café, bar and restaurants visits, and naturally a couple of days in Porto. One afternoon we headed over the river to the port cellars, and being near the cathedral I decided we'd walk over the top bridge. I'd either completely forgotten, or never knew, because as we started to walk over, and the first bus came passed, causing the bridge to visibly shake, Phil stopped, turned green, and announced that there was no way in this world he was continuing. What a woss!

A couple of weeks later and we were into August. Clare, Russ, Rosie and I drove up into the mountains in Gêres, and had a picnic on the side of one of the reservoirs. The reservoir was surrounded by trees so we first had to battle our way through them, and then scramble down a slope with picnic stuff, swimming stuff and a two-year old! It was worth it though, and we had a narrow stretch of sand to sit on, surrounded by the most beautiful scenery. However, you couldn't see anything in the deep water, and there was no way I was getting in with what were undoubtedly sea monsters! I happily sat on the edge amusing Rosie whilst Clare and Russell paddled around. Now, never can it be said that Russell is a wimp. He is a big bloke. But I have never heard such a girly scream.

"F......ing hell! Snake! Get out!"

"Where, where?" Clare screamed as she scrambled out.

"Just there!"

Just there it was; a snake and a very big one. I know water snakes aren't supposed to be dangerous, but we weren't taking any chances. Which reminds me of another Portuguese snake story. Living where we did, we regularly saw a variety of insects and creepy crawlies, and there were often grass snakes around. One day, however, Adrian appeared home to say he had seen an enormous black and yellow snake on the road. Yeah, right. Adey was known for his exaggerating! However, on this occasion he wasn't. Although he'd forgotten to mention that the snake was squashed on the road, it was indeed very big, and yellow and black! After much discussion and visions of man-eating snakes making their way into the pool or our beds, we decided that it must have been a pet that had escaped. Bizarre!

A couple of days later, and Clare, Russ, Rosie and I headed off for a short camping holiday. A word of advice for anyone thinking of going on holiday in Portugal in August. Don't try and get three adults and a two-year old, plus two tents, cooking equipment, duvets and pillows into a Renault 5. Also, make sure the car has air-. conditioning. And stop the passenger (in our case who hadn't yet passed his driving test yet, and is called Russell) from necking red wine out of the carton and getting you lost. Tempers were frayed to say the least by the time we reached our first campsite in Figueira da Foz, and had struggled with the tents. To make matters worse, we had a little fight with somebody else's bumper. Clare and I went off to park the car with me in the passenger seat. Unfortunately the door had never closed very well, and as we were driving through the rows of tents, it flew open, smashing into a parked cars' bumper and the Renault was left with a large dent in its side. Woops! And, of course, it wasn't mine, but on loan from Gabrielle, Russ's mum. After everyone had calmed down we did manage to have a relaxing evening, and went into the old-fashioned seaside resort for a meal.

The following day we packed everything up and continued south. We stopped off at Batalha in order to visit the famous Mosteiro de Santa Maria da Vitória. The abbey was erected after the King called on God for help against the Spanish, and the Portuguese won the war. It was built in the Gothic style in 1434, with Manueline additions in the 15th and 16th centuries. Although now set in a huge, ugly concrete plaza, the abbey itself was amazing. Hued from ochre limestone, with pinnacles, parapets, buttresses and balustrades, it looked spectacular bathed in the bright summer light, and offset by the almost violet sky. Compared to the outside, the inside seemed plain. It was vast and vaulted, and in fact is my idea of how the interior of a church should be. So many of the catholic churches I have visited are so over the top, with gold leaf covering everything. It was also a bit of a history lesson as the abbey held the Capela do Fundador (the Founder's Chapel), a stark vaulted room where the tomb of João 1 and his wife Phillipa of Lancaster was, and also that of their famous son, Henry the Navigator. It was the alliance of João and Phillipa in 1387, which cemented the closeness of Great Britain and Portugal, and even today (as pub quizzers will know) we are the longest standing allies in Europe.

Having done the cultural bit, we squeezed back into the Renault, and in the sweltering heat headed off to Lisbon. We stayed in a campsite on the outskirts of the city, close to the estuary. Despite the fact that half of Portugal appeared to be trying to get into the campsite, it was so huge that we managed to find a spot where we could erect our tents in the usual loud, haphazard way, and not annoy any neighbours. First stop was the lovely swimming pool, and after that a gourmet meal by camping gas stove, and then availing ourselves of the campsite bar. Might not sound very glamorous but after the drive it was pure bliss!

We didn't do an awful lot whilst in Lisbon as it was so hot but did go to Belém as it was on the water. Since there was a breath of fresh air we wandered around the area, and then escaped into the cool interior of the monastery.

Another stop was Cascais, which is on the mouth of the River Tejo. It was originally a small fishing port, but in 1870 Luís I decided to make it his summer residence, and after that it became very fashionable. During World War II several kings and heads of state sought refuge both here, and in nearby Estoril. They were followed by aristocrats, politicians, actors and writers, and between 1939 and 1946 the population increased by 20,000. By the time we got there it was a fairly upmarket seaside resort with lots of expensive hotels. Fortunately though, there was a small area of the original town with narrow, interesting streets full of restaurants and bars, with a stunning view over the estuary.

And that was my last little jaunt in Portugal for a while. The next couple of weeks were full of boring arrangements to make for my return to the UK – battling with sending money back to the UK, and nervous moments when £2,000 didn't appear in Dad's account for over two weeks, sorting out bills, and booking a flight. And then there was all my stuff. After nearly three years I'd accumulated a flat load of it. Not one to travel with one suitcase I have carted the most ridiculous items around Europe with me. By this point it wasn't too bad as I just had belongings brought from the UK, or acquired in Portugal. My task was to figure out how to get the important things back; they were such priceless things as a cast iron fondue set (nice and light), a stereo (not compact and bijou), loads of books (also nice and light), and a variety of other impossible to leave behind items. Somehow I couldn't imagine BA being particularly sympathetic if I turned up at the airport with the luggage of a touring rock band. So, how to get it all back. It had started back at Easter when my friend Cath had gone to the UK for a holiday. Strictly against airport security she took a suitcase through for me. I imagine the conversation could have been like this.

"Did you pack your own suitcase?"

"No."

Are you carrying anything for somebody else?"

"Yes."

"Could anybody else have tampered with your suitcase?"

"ER, yes."

However, she got to Heathrow with no traumas where my friend Phil was waiting to collect the suitcase, as he lived nearby.

So, first load back in the UK. Second lot went back with a friend of Guy's, Simon who had come to stay in May. We'd hit it off the previous year when he'd been on a visit, and was more then happy to stuff his suitcase full of more of my junk. More lying at the airport. Second load in Cardiff. My stereo and speakers went back with Guy and family in the back of their car, as they were driving back through Spain and France and getting a ferry. More stuff in Cardiff! The last load went back with Phil after his holiday with me – yet more fibs at the airport. And there was still more left. Nothing for it but to pack up some boxes, take them to the airport and cargo them back to London so they arrived at Heathrow just before me. After I'd sold and given the last bits of stuff away there was a very empty flat, and the reality was sinking in. I had a last afternoon with Reinaldo, a final meal with Clare, Russ and Rosie, and then on the last but one day of August I left Portugal. I was slightly damp eyed that day when we had lunch in town, but was fairly together for the journey to the airport. That was probably helped by the fact that in the height of summer I was wearing my lace up winter boots rather than having to carry them. I looked ridiculous – not helped by the fact that I was also wearing a coat. I still got whacked for excess luggage, and on this occasion no amount of persuading would work and I had to cough up. By this point Clare was in tears and Rosie (being two) was refusing to say goodbye. I was still fine, but having started to go through into the departure lounge, I could hear Rosie shouting my name - well her version, which was like Riddle, Riddle. That was it. The tears came and I sobbed my way onto the plane, wondering when on earth I'd be back.

Chapter 24

Britain

Britain. Talk about culture shock. The beginning of September and it was already turning chilly, and what was even worse was that at eleven o'clock you got chucked out of the pub. What was going on? I threw myself into getting organised for my course and at the same time made trips to London and Cardiff to see friends and pick up my belongings. Well, some of my belongings. I couldn't carry everything back from Cardiff in one go on the train so it meant a return trip and, on one trip I forgot about my stereo! It wasn't that much of a problem returning though, as Simon was there. Towards the end of September I'd hooked up with Ewan (my naval officer friend) again – nothing heavy but it was great to have someone around to go out for meals, go to the cinema and have a bit of R & R.

October came around very quickly and that meant the first day of my new life. This was me, going back to education, voluntarily. What was going on? After day one, and for the first time ever I was thoroughly enjoying being in an academic environment. It was hard work, not least that I had to get up far too early for my liking, get a lift to the bus stop, get a bus to Chichester and then another bus to the college. When I got home I couldn't just slob on the sofa though. The deal for staying with Mum and Dad was that I would cook every night for them. At the time Mum was working full-time and Dad had recovered well enough from his operation to go to work part-time.

Although this period has nothing to do with travelling, it does however still have a very important bearing on my life now, and what happened immediately afterwards. The first term up to Christmas passed in a blur. I worked extremely hard as I found the course so stimulating – it took up an enormous amount of time with all the reading that had to be done, but it felt completely the right thing to be doing. I was also able to spend valuable time with Dad. One weekend I saw friends and even managed a trip to Cardiff again in November to see Simon, which was a great distraction – having said that I studied all the way there and back on the train.

That year, Christmas was especially important because of Dad, and also because I went down to Bournemouth as Clare and Russell were over for the holiday. It was great to see them and catch up on all the Portugal gossip, although it made me long for the sun and warmth, and sensible bar opening times. By the beginning of November I'd decided that all I really wanted to do was hibernate as the cold, dark mornings were disgusting!

The New Year started and things continued along the same vein for a while – I even managed a little trip away. To Oxford. I know, it's not abroad, but one incident has to be relayed for the pure embarrassment it caused. Simon and I agreed to have a weekend away somewhere, and had plumped on Oxford. As I vaguely knew it from when I was younger, I said I'd book us a B & B, which I duly did. The arrangement was that whoever arrived first would check in, leave a message and wait in the nearest pub. When I arrived I was told that Simon had arrived and was in a pub just down the road. I decided to go to the room to leave my bags – what I expected was a bog-standard double. Oh no! Far from it. As I opened the door I was faced with what I can only describe as a 'Barbie Honeymoon suite'. There was a white plastic four-poster bed, frilly bedclothes, pink towels, plastic flowers and other horrors. After I'd got over the giggles, I then wondered what on earth Simon would be thinking about the whole thing – whether it was some very unsubtle ploy on my behalf to suggest marriage. He had already been married twice by then! I cringed all the way to the pub, and gingerly made my way to where Simon was sitting at the bar. By this time I was in fits of giggles again. He was cool and we had a great weekend, despite that fact the bed creaked like you had never heard a bed creak, just by looking at it! What on earth were the owners thinking of. We ended up pulling the mattress and bedding off and 'sleeping' on the floor!

The weekend was a great interlude to what was rapidly becoming a very difficult time. By the end of February, Dad was becoming increasingly unwell, and I was very wary about being away at all. I did, however, go back to Oxford for a wedding at Christchurch College. It was an extremely posh do – Ewan's commanding officer marrying a Russian academic – but that didn't stop me sobbing my way through the introduction to Zadok the Priest, which is moving at the best of times, but a piece of music I had sung with Dad.

Soon, Dad's health had worsened still; he had stopped work and couldn't drive anymore. He had gone into the local hospice for a few days - although he was still fighting, and everybody was hoping for a miracle, he didn't come home. At least it was easy for me to see him everyday. I was able to use Mum's car as she was driving Dad's, so could drive to college the day I had lectures, and then visit Dad on the way home. He'd often be asleep so I'd just sit with him. I found it so hard to be strong and positive in front of him, and I cracked when I took in a birthday card for him to sign for Mum, as he couldn't do it properly. In the early weeks in the hospice the drugs were really affecting his personality. He became twitchy and argumentative, and this made it even harder. Fortunately this stage soon ended, and although he was so ill and weak, he was Dad again and we could talk about anything.

The pressure was on at college, but despite this I'd managed to do some extremely good assignments, and made Dad proud by being able to tell him that I'd got a couple of A grades. By the beginning of May I started my dissertation, and spent hours reading whilst Dad was asleep. He was becoming weaker and weaker and the end came very quickly when, during the middle of the night on the 16th May my lovely Dad died. It was him who mainly made me the way I am - my love of food and wine, of new adventures, of travelling, of living abroad, of music. I just hope that he is proud of me, and that I can be half the person he was. He was always so positive, so friendly, so gentle and got me out of so many scrapes when I was a teenager I can't remember most of them. The following month went by in a bit of a blur – the only way I could cope was to study as hard as I could, and this meant that I wasn't thinking of Dad all the time.

The next thing that helped immeasurably was ten days holiday to Portugal. I'd decided to go with Simon and his mate Hugh, and the first stop was Porto. We stayed in the same B & B that I'd stayed in many times, and having an early flight meant we were able to get to the port houses in the afternoon. I think the port drinking must have affected Hugh because the next morning he embarrassingly told us that he was a sleep-walker   and had had a little wander the night before. Needing a pee, but still asleep, he'd got out of bed, and gone in search of the loo. He went out into the corridor, trying all the door handles until he found an unlocked one. He went in, walked round the double bed were two people were asleep, and made his way over to the basin which was in the room itself and had a pee. By then the couple were awake, and extremely surprised to find someone naked in their room, relieving themselves. At this point Hugh woke up, said hello and went back to his room. Priceless. That night we locked him in and kept the key to stop a repeat performance. The ridiculous thing was that, unlike many of the rooms, he had his own toilet all the time!

The next day, we had my favourite chicken and chips meal in the Angolan restaurant, and then settled ourselves down at an outside café in my favourite square near the river, and watched some of the Euro 1996 football. Afterwards we walked, well staggered all the way along the river and up the steep hill towards the Solar do Vinho do Porto – otherwise known as the Port Wine Institute. It was hidden away in a park overlooking the river, and had a gorgeous rose garden from where you could see right down the river to the sea. As opposed to the port houses, the Institute sold a range of ports from each of the houses, and the great thing was that you could buy a glass of whatever you fancied, even if it was a vintage. It was a very formal place, with bizarre 70's orange and brown furnishings, and sommeliers serving you, but a great place for a civilised drink. Some years later when I moved to Porto itself, I lived just round the corner, and spent many happy hours there.

Happy is what the boys were. They couldn't believe such a place existed, and proceeded to try and drink their way through the wine list. Despite this, when we finally decided to leave, in good Portuguese fashion, and especially if you earned pounds, it wasn't really expensive at all. The rest of the evening continued in much the same vein, and there were a variety of hangovers to contend with the next morning as we drove up to Guimarães. It was great to see all my close friends again, but at the same time quite emotional, and during the week I had a few tearful moments. These thankfully were out numbered by happy days spent eating, drinking and chatting in the sun. It was a real antidote, not only to the sadness I felt about Dad but also how hard I'd been studying. The ten days came to an end all too quickly, and before I knew it I was back in the UK.

By this point I was concentrating solely on my dissertation which meant no more lectures to attend, just visits to college for research, and to see my tutor. I therefore had more free time, and was able to enjoy the summer in the UK. There were some local music festivals, and I went to blues, jazz and classical concerts, and spent weekends away seeing friends. By mid-August Mum had decided that she was ready for a holiday but didn't want to go on her own, or have to arrange any details.

She asked me if I'd like to go with her on a five-day trip to Normandy, visiting various gardens. Gardens! She then mentioned that one of the gardens was Monet's at Giverny, that we would be staying in Chantilly, and that there was a day trip to Paris included. Suddenly I became a gardener! For the first time ever I went on an organised coach trip where most of the other people were twice my age. Saying that, it was a stress free way to have a holiday for Mum, and exactly what she needed. We stayed in a beautiful hotel on the outskirts of Chantilly, grandly named the Château Montvillagenne. The château had been converted into a hotel and was set in the most beautiful grounds, surrounded by fir trees at the front, and at the back overlooking a series of terraced gardens which descended as far as the eye could see. The hotel served lovely meals, had a swimming pool and was a great base. Being so close to the château at Chantilly, we had a wander around the gardens one afternoon. It is most famous through its association with horses and of having two of the season's classiest flat races. The château was built in the late 19th Century and was instantly familiar to me. Having wracked my brain for ages, trying to work out which film I'd seen it in, I finally remembered it was in one of my least favourite Bond's – *A View to a Kill*. Beautiful locations, bad film. The building was incredibly graceful, surrounded by water and overlooking formal pools and pathways, and we had a slow walk round in the baking sun.

A couple of the gardens we visited, whilst obviously interesting for the gardeners didn't really do it for me, but Monet's was a different matter. We left the hotel early, in order to avoid the hordes, and were the first group admitted to the gardens. It was only about eight o'clock in the morning, there was dew everywhere, and whilst it was damp and fresh at that time, you could tell it was going to be scorching. The first thing we did was walk around the water garden, which focuses on the famous water-lily pond. With the sun coming through the trees and reflecting off the water, and just a hint of early morning mist left, it was magical – not surprising that Monet painted it so many times. Another famous image was the Japanese footbridge, again immortalised in paintings. From the water garden we made our way to the main flower garden in front of the house, not so instantly recognisable, but stunning in its design. There were trellised walkways running parallel to each other and each planted in a different colour.

The house itself was covered in a riot of colours, and it was here that Monet lived from 1883 until his death in 1926. Although few of the originals furnishings were there, many of the rooms were crammed with his collection of Japanese prints, and you could get a sense of how it used to be as the dining room was still painted bright yellow, and the upstairs rooms pale blue. We also visited the huge studio, built in 1915, where Monet painted his largest canvases depicting the water lilies. Although there were no original paintings, it was full of art books and gifts shouting 'buy me, buy me'!

Not seeing any originals in Monet's house wasn't really a disappointment as we did manage to see some elsewhere. As part of the holiday there was a day trip Paris. We headed for the Tuileries gardens, which housed the Orangerie, a private art collection inherited by the state. Although not a huge museum, it had two oval rooms arranged by Monet as panoramas for his largest waterlily paintings. Although I had previously seen an example in New York, it made a huge difference to have seen the actual subject, so closely followed by the artist's interpretation. As well as the Monet's there were other artists such as Sisley, Cézanne and Renoir, and luckily for me Matisse. For the rest of the day Mum and I snuck off from the rest of the group - we enjoyed the relative calm of the city in August, wandered around Galeries Lafayette, and stopped off in various cafés. It was a good break, and I'm sure helped both Mum and myself, especially since Paris had always been a favourite of Dad's.

Back to the UK and I had to start making some decisions about what to do for the new academic year. I'd already had an interview in Reading for a position as a lecturer of English at the university in Ankara, Turkey. Although I'd been offered the job, it was on the condition that I started in the second week of August. Since I had to submit my dissertation then the decision was made for me and I had to turn it down. I went up to London to International House, in Piccadilly (big cheese in the world of TEFL) to see if they could offer me something. There were lots of jobs as teachers, especially in Eastern Europe, but I hadn't slaved away for a year on a management course to teach. I wanted to manage, and was prepared to try somewhere different to Portugal. I've long realised it's worth sticking to your guns, and this was no exception – having left the interview saying that I wasn't interested in a pure teaching position, wherever it may be, I had a phone call asking me if I was interested in a senior teaching position, with responsibility for all the business teaching. The position was in a place called Bielsko Biała, in the south of Poland, and since the first two letters were the same as those of Portugal, I decided to give it a go.

That sorted out, I concentrated on getting my dissertation finished, and preparing to move again. I managed one last little break – friend Guy from Portugal was in Wales for the summer, so along with Simon we spent the August Bank Holiday weekend on the Pembroke coast, in Broadhaven, in Guy's Dad's mobile home. It pissed down for three days so we went to the pub and got pissed for three days! One morning we even sat outside waiting for the pub to open – sad!

Before I knew it my dissertation was done, I heard that I'd passed (yippee), and I spent a week celebrating my birthday and saying good-bye to family and friends. I knew that I had to move abroad again, to put into practice what I'd learnt on my Master's course, and Mum fully understood this need. She knew I was my Dad's daughter. However, there was one moment of doubt. For one of my assignments I'd done some research into the cultural problems of foreign students studying with British undergraduates at the college. Apparently, not only had it earned me an 'A' but the 'powers that be' decided that area had to be looked at in much more depth. They had therefore decided to offer a fee-paid and bursaried PhD to do the research, and wanted to know if I was interested. I couldn't believe it – this was me who had walked out on her maths 'O' level, spent ages avoiding lessons, and was being given the opportunity to apply for a PhD. Although I was very flattered, I knew that I had to go and earn money abroad, but was delighted to have been asked.

Favourite cities

Paris

~

Sydney

~

San Francisco

~

Porto

View from the Botanical Gardens, Sydney

Part Eight

Polish pursuits

Chapter 25

Bielsko-Biała

After a final week of rushing round, I was on my way to Poland. I think it was the first time I actually felt tearful about going somewhere – hardly surprisingly after the year we'd all had. Mum had kindly driven me to the airport, and I knew that since we had given each other so much support over Dad, that she was going to find it tough. Fortunately, I wasn't flying on my own as there was a group of teachers going to work for the same group of schools as I was, and some to the town I was going to be teaching in. I sat next to one teacher, Andrew, who although lived in a different town, became a friend, and also someone who was called Sarah, who quickly became a soul mate. We drank our free drinks and swapped stories, and the flight passed happily enough. At Krakow airport we were herded into mini-buses and dispatched to our different locations.

By the time we arrived in Bielsko-Biała, although it was only September, it was dark and cold. It took ages to drop everyone off, and naturally, at about midnight I was the last one. It seemed I was going to be living in the middle of nowhere. I did little apart from take myself to my room, have a quick look around and crash out. Well, not immediately. First I had to figure out about the Polish bed system. In a small room off my main room there was an incredibly hard sofa, which, since there didn't seem to be a bed obviously doubled up. After lots of heaving and shoving, and quite a bit of swearing, I finally managed to get the back down, and 'hey presto', there was a bed. It was nothing like any sofa bed I was used to which is probably why it took so long to work it out, as there was nothing to pull out! Down the centre of it was the joint of the sofa, which, however you slept on it kept sticking into you. I decided that they couldn't have had time to deliver a bed – of course, this wasn't the case, and I quickly realised that all beds were like this! I climbed in 'bed', tired and emotional, feeling very different from when I'd first arrived in Portugal, wondering if I'd made a huge mistake. This wasn't helped when I read a card Mum had given me to open when I arrived. It thanked me for all my support and wished me good luck in my latest adventure – I promptly burst into tears.

Things seemed a little better the following morning, and I was able to have a proper look at my surroundings. The house I was staying in was someone's summerhouse and on the edge of a field, and as I had suspected in the middle of nowhere. The downstairs was enormous, and didn't seem to be used much, apart from a tiny kitchen, with lots of hideous red plastic pots and utensils. The room I had was almost like a loft conversion. It was very large and wide, and had the most beautiful sprung beech floor. It also had another sofa and a large table so I didn't have to worry about space. The bathroom was modern and clean, but full of someone's stuff. I discovered later that day, that although being a senior teacher, entitled me, if I wanted, to have my own place that it only meant not sharing with another teacher. My flat mate, who I rarely saw (thank God) was completely humourless, and a control freak. On being introduced to her for the first time she announced that all the red items in the kitchen were hers, so I knew not to use them!!

After a few hours of unpacking my suitcases (more excess baggage money shelled out), I'd had enough of my own company, and decided to go into town earlier than necessary to have a look round. First of all I had to figure out how to get there. It had been so dark the previous night I had no idea where I was in relation to the town and nothing had been provided by the school. I set off up the hill, and when I came to a small road, stood there for a bit. Not a clue. I eventually turned right, and followed the road for about ten minutes, until it came to a small opening where there was a bus stop. I waited, and waited, and eventually a bus came. For the next three months I was completely at the mercy of the bus timetable. There was often only one every hour and a half, so everything had to planned with military precision. After about ten minutes the bus seemed to be in the centre of the town, so I jumped off. Just as I was crossing over the road I bumped into a couple of the teachers so we spent a few hours wandering around, and familiarising ourselves with the town. Not much of a problem since it wasn't exactly large. It seemed to be split in two by a four-lane, fearsomely busy road, with fumes swirling in all directions. There were very few places to cross it, and even then you had to wait for ages, as jay walking was a complete no-no. I didn't fancy having a run in with a traffic policeman, especially if they were women. They looked terrifying.

It turned out that the town had indeed been two separate places and was divided by the river, well stream would be more appropriate. It had only been in 1951 that the towns were united, having spent most of their history in different countries. It is all very long and complicated, suffice to say that Bielsko was part of the Duchy of Cieskyn and annexed to Bohemia in the 14th Century and Biała came under the Polish crown until Austria had its turn in the 18th Century. Complicated stuff – history had never been my strong point, but it was obvious in the architecture that there had been a variety of influences at work. Both towns had flourished and were very prosperous; mainly due to wool and textiles, and rich merchants had built themselves appropriate houses. Many were built in the Viennese Secessionist style, and added an air of grace to the town, despite the fact that lots of them lined the dirty, noisy main road.

We discovered a main square, where there was a Renaissance Town Hall, and in a nearby square a house which had two stone frogs who looked as if they were straight out of *The Wind in the Willows*, sitting above a window mantle. Adding to the mixture of styles was the castle, which was built in the Gothic style, but rebuilt in the 19th Century. What a bizarre place I'd picked to live in for the year.

My first week in Poland consisted of an induction week, so nothing too taxing. We had various sessions, including a trip to nearby Katowice for the day. What a depressing place, especially in the grey. It is in the heart of Poland's industrial zone, and the pollution was legendary because of the old fashioned factories. In fact it had been named as an environmental disaster area by the Polish Academy of Science -when we got there we realised why. All the buildings were dark and dirty, not helped by the general greyness of the place. I pitied some of the teachers who we had flown out with who were based there. It might have been fairly grey a lot of the time we were in Bielsko, but at least on sunny days we could escape into the nearby mountains.

The weekend before we started teaching was spent checking out local bars and cafés. When we first arrived in Poland, bar culture was still relatively new and people tended to drink at home or in hotels. We found and adopted one near to the school. It was a health and safety nightmare – you descended into a low-ceilinged cellar, where there were no windows and no air-conditioning so you had to fight your way through the smoke and there was definitely no fire exit.

Every evening the one loo overflowed, seeping under the door which led straight into the main bar, and smelling delightful. However, the owner was great fun, the drink was cheap, and after a while the locals were more than happy to indulge our attempts at conversing in Polish. As we became regulars, it became a second home. During the time we were there, other bars opened which were far more salubrious, and although we regularly went to a variety of them, it was to Dziupla that we returned the most often. Possibly something to do with it being the closest to school after a day of battling with students - especially when it was minus twenty-one outside!

The day before we started teaching was bright and sunny so we decided to take a trip to the nearby mountains. All we had to do was take a local bus and suddenly we were transported from the grey tower blocks of the town, and into greenery and fresh air. For some mad reason we decided not to take the fifteen minute ride by cable car up to the top of Mount Szyndzielnia, some 1,026 metres high, but to walk up the trail, which took about three hours! Despite moaning most of the way up, the trek was worth it, and the panoramic view was stunning. The walk had made us hungry and we ventured into the hostel at the top. We had a disgusting lunch of lard and grease, washed down by some beer (much better), and then walked up a bit further.

Having had a complete day of escape, the reality hit the next day with the start of term. As I was in charge of the company classes it meant that also I taught most of them, so I spent the first week being completely bemused by the local buses; getting off too soon; going in the wrong direction and generally getting lost. What's more, there was absolutely no system – in fact the bus system made that of Portugal look organised (no mean feat I can tell you) – and you could get on through any of the three sets of doors, making getting a seat a complete lottery. Saying it was a smelly experience would be putting it politely. At least all the company classes I had were great, and I thoroughly enjoyed teaching them. After Portugal, where there was a high proportion of spoilt kids, it was so refreshing to have classes of people who were grateful that they had the opportunity to learn, and were continually thanking you.

Although the setting and weather was completely different to Portugal, we quickly settled down into a routine, and there were some great teachers to spend time with. Our social life tended to centre on bars, and having meals at each other's houses. There wasn't a lot to do culturally, although we were lucky enough to have two cinemas, which showed films dubbed into Polish, but with English sub-titles! I could understand that in Portugal the English films were subtitled in Portuguese, but this way. How mad is that?

One slight interlude in the trying out of bars was going to a concert. I'd discovered that at one of the local churches there was going to be a performance of Górecki's Symphony No. 3, or, as it was better known, 'Symphony of Sorrowful Songs'. I'd been introduced to this piece of music by Dad, and hadn't been able to listen to it since he'd died, as I knew it would set me off. However, the possibility of seeing the symphony performed live was too good an opportunity to miss. Górecki himself had been born in Katowice, so somehow he had been inspired by the greyness! What's more, he was going to be conducting the orchestra. The atmosphere was amazing, and I enjoyed myself despite the fact that throughout most of the performance the tears were rolling down my face.

After a month of living in Bielsko, we were starting to get used to polish living. One thing I found particularly hard was the availability of particular foods – there was a lack of fresh peppers, tomatoes or anything slightly Mediterranean

– not surprising I know, but difficult if you really dislike cabbage and all the associated vegetables which the Poles lived on. When we first arrived there wasn't a supermarket, so shopping was an experience in itself. In the basement of the local department store there was a small food area which sold tinned and dried food. It wasn't particularly inspiring, and positively unpleasant when the security guard followed you up and down the aisles, literally on your heels. I saw one of the mildest mannered, sweet teachers turning into a screaming banshee one day, when she'd had enough of being suspected of shoplifting. Once the dried food ordeal was over, it was on to the bread counter, where you had to ask for what you wanted, and ended up with something else (well, in my case as I was really struggling with Polish, and using a mixture of Portuguese and French - always useful when you're in Poland!). It was the same for eggs, vegetables, fruit, etc, with a different stall for each – I'm surprised there was any time left for going to the pub.

Eating out wasn't much more inspiring. Everything was really heavy, and appeared to consist of potatoes and lard. Another delight was *bigos*, a greasy stew with cabbage in it. Yum! However, they seemed to have the snacks completely sorted out. In most of the pedestrian streets there were portable snack outlets – they sold hotdogs with the biggest array of pickles you could imagine; something called *Zapiekanki* which was like cheese on toast but with tomatoes, and my favourite, a torpedo roll, with the insides taken out, and filled with hot mushrooms. Wandering round one Saturday lunchtime, suffering from evil hangovers due to more excess from the previous night, we discovered a Turkish fast food café. How weird but oh joy. We staggered in to find the most delightful dishes of Turkish food on show, with the highlight being chicken kebabs – lovely soft pitta breads stuffed with proper pieces of chicken, lots of salad and an amazing garlicky, yoghurt sauce. We got talking to the owner, who spoke perfect English, and before long were regulars on a Saturday. We also found a pizza restaurant, which was a regular haunt on a Friday after work. This probably doesn't look too bad, but that was it. There were no different places to eat, and so we always went to the same restaurants and cafés.

The range of pubs to frequent may have been limited in the early months of living in Poland but the nightclub array was even direr. There was one small club in the centre of town, imaginatively called *Number One*. It took lack of class to a new low. The total area was about the size of a couple of living rooms; the dance area was so small if you held hands and stretched out with one other person you could reach both sides; the pictures on the walls were cut out of Vogue and framed; the music came from a pre-recorded tape; the upstairs was a brothel and the whole outfit was manned by seriously nasty looking guys, and was apparently run by the Mafia. Nice! However, when there's nowhere else to go, that's where we went. To say that there were some incidents would be a huge understatement; however, among them were flashing, lesbian kisses, scuffles on the dance floor, and general misbehaving - but to protect the innocent, and not so innocent, no details here.

After a couple of weeks, we discovered that there was an even more inviting club. The *pièce de resistance* in this dark and dingy, but slightly larger club was a huge illuminous spider, which dangled from the ceiling. We had a few interesting evenings there, one that involved one of the teachers, Jen, a lovely girl but so completely dippy, who managed to walk into the toilet door and break her nose. Another happening centred on the trait of Polish clubs of having to leave your coats on the door, and pay a paltry amount to retrieve them. One evening the coat man obviously decided he was going to chance his luck, and wouldn't let us have them until we paid a small fortune. As well as being illegal, there was a real undercurrent of menace. Not being completely sober and not able to communicate in Polish wasn't helping matters, and everybody was getting irate and shouting. After ages, when we had demanded to see the manager, who refused to talk to us, we literally had to remove our coats by force before we could leave. Not a pleasant experience. What we had realised in our short time in Poland was, that while most of the people were incredibly friendly and generous, there were some really nasty characters around, who made no effort to hide their malevolence. We decided better the devil you know, and returned to *Number One* for our post-pub nights.

Being in Poland obviously meant vodka. I had never been able to drink it, and despite liking it, got a headache after one. I therefore stuck to the local beer, Żywiec. One of the teachers taught at the factory where it was brewed, and frequently came back to school clutching cans. Although it tasted lovely, it was obviously laden with chemicals, and the hangovers it caused were terrible. After a couple of months, most of us gave up drinking it, and I tried once again with the vodka. I don't know whether vodka in Poland is any different from that sold in the UK, but suddenly the headaches had gone. Maybe it was because of the brand which we were drinking – namely Żubrówka. This particular vodka is legendry and is infused with the taste of bison grass from the eastern Białowieza forest – in fact each bottle has a stem of it in it. Mixed traditionally with natural apple juice, it was exceedingly easy too drink, and far too quickly came our staple diet!

We did, of course, have to fit in work around all the partying – also, we frequently had to drag ourselves out of bed on a Saturday morning for special clubs or training days. One beautifully sunny morning towards the end of October it was the turn of our school to host a training day. What we really wanted to do was get the cable car up to the top of the local mountain, take in the view and drink beer. We struggled through the day, and then along with some teachers from other schools, who were staying overnight, went out to party.

We arranged that Andrew, who I'd met on the flight, would stay with me. Oh dear, what a night. The following morning, feeling very delicate, and having, for some reason, refused Andrew's advances of the night before, we decided that the only cure on offer (no Mickey D's anywhere) was to get some mountain air. There was no way we could do the three hour walk, so we got the fifteen minute cable car, and were soon sitting on a bench swigging coke, taking lots of deep breaths of the air, and swiftly deciding that hair of the dog was the only way forward. No vodka, but bottled beer, which helped to ease the pain.

Chapter 26

Weekends away

At the end of the following week we had a day off for All Souls Day. We decided that it was a fitting day to visit Auschwitz, (or as the Poles know it Oświęcim), and was only thirty minutes away from Bielsko. We took a local bus there and arrived in a fairly non-descript town which looked like other places we had visited. Of course, this all changed as we approached the camp gates. I'd seen so many pictures of the camp, and especially the main gate and felt moved by it, but in reality it was such a profoundly gut-wrenching experience that I don't think you can really feel it unless you have been there. Before we entered the camp itself, we watched a solemn film which was taken by the Soviet troops who liberated the camp in May 1945, and which showed harrowing footage of the survivors and the dead. I then read the brief history in the guidebook which described how Hess was made the commander of the camp after orders to begin work on it were made in late 1940. By June of the same year the Gestapo dispatched the first political prisoners there – 724 Poles from Tarnów. Before long it had been turned from a detention centre into a full-scale death camp.

However, neither the film nor reading from the guidebook really prepared me for what we were about to see. It was a grey, bitterly cold day, and suddenly we were standing looking at the cellblocks, shivering. The first thing that struck me was that it all looked too ordinary for such horrors to have happened there. The blocks looked similar to naval bases I'd visited; that was because the main buildings had been an old Polish army barracks – it had been chosen as the location as it was away from prying eyes. It was when we went inside what were the prison cell blocks that the evidence was all too clear - rooms full of suitcases, toothbrushes, glasses, shoes, dentures, and what made me break down, mounds of women's hair. Feeling very emotional we then made our way to the "Death Block", which was separated from the rest of the camp, so the executions couldn't be seen by other inmates. We finally came to the gas chambers, where prisoners thought they were being showered, but were in fact gassed with Cyclon B. What completely finished me off were the ovens where the bodies were incinerated - the opening looked like that of a large pizza oven. It's estimated that between one and a half to two million people were killed here in those few years - a number too large to comprehend. As we slowly left the camp, with no-one speaking, and the grey sky weighing down so heavily I realised that what I'd heard was true. The birds don't sing there.

We plodded towards the train station, and for a while the mood was lifted when we tried to figure out which platform we needed to be on get back to Bielsko. Obviously all the signs were in Polish, the numbers were written in full rather than characters, the ticket seller told us something, and the board appeared to say something else. Just when we thought we'd cracked it, and were waiting with other expectant passengers, a train with Bielsko on it pulled into another platform, and to the amusement – yet again – of the locals we careered up and over the bridge. In Poland, it's not a question of catching the next train in thirty minutes – it could be thirty days. Finally, seated on the creaking, groaning train, which I have to say makes even the old-fashioned 'slam-door' type trains look modern, we left Oświęcim and the horrors. However, it had made a huge mark, not least that evening when we fell into the pub and downed numerous vodkas to try to ease the pain, and I also fell into the comforting arms of an English guy who happened to be working in the area, and who I'd met a few weeks before. The last thing to say about Auschwitz is that I feel everyone should go there, or to another concentration camp, to try to understand what happened, and to stop it ever happening again.

Happier distractions were needed, so the following day we decided to visit Krakow for the first time. Sarah and I had pored over my rough guide, lapping up the description of Poland's second city, and it sounded like the tonic we needed. The city's position at the junction of several important east-west trade routes had helped commercial development, and by the end of the 10th Century it was a major market centre. By 1038 it had been made the capital of the country, and the founding of a university in 1364 by King Kazimierz enhanced it still. He also rebuilt much of the city and allowed the Jews to settle, and for centuries there was a thriving Jewish community, until World War II when most were sent to Auschwitz.

With the Renaissance, Krakow became an important centre of learning, with Nicolas Copernicus being its most famous student. However, in 1596 King Zygmunt III decided to move the capital to Warsaw, following the Union of Poland and Lithuania and the city started to decline, aided by the Swedish invasion of 1655 – 57. After the Partitions, the city was incorporated into the Austro-Hungarian province of Galicia, and being the least repressive of the occupying powers, Krakow became a relatively liberal place allowing underground movements to form.

It certainly sounded like an interesting city, and myself,

Sarah, Anna and Jen happily endured the torturously bumpy bus ride to get there. I would like to say that as soon as we reached the bus station we headed straight for the main square to look at some of the places we'd read about. However, you must remember that our choice of food had been limited, and as we walked though the city walls and up a pedestrianised street we noticed a MacDonald's. I know how bad it is, bla, bla, bla, but there was no stopping us, and apparently the rest of Poland. I have never seen a Mickey D's like it – complete bedlam everywhere. Naturally, we persisted and were rewarded with burgers and fries. Delicious.

Having done the important thing, we walked up the street towards the main square. Well – bloody hell! It was huge, and beautiful. The Rynek Główny was the largest square of medieval Europe, and today is still extremely impressive. Magnificent houses and towering spires ringed a huge expanse of flagstones, and in the middle was, what looked to me, an Eastern palace. It was in fact a medieval cloth market, the Sukiennice, rebuilt in the Renaissance and topped with gargoyles. We went to have a closer look and found that it still served as a market, but this time aimed for the tourists. Having said that it had some beautiful stalls, full of painted wooden toys, ceramic art, and best of all, silver jewellery. We decided that we needed a pit stop to soak up the atmosphere and found a café on the edge of the square where we could happily watch the world go by. Well, that was until someone started to play the most mournful tune you have ever heard on the trumpet. We looked around, to discover that the noise was coming from the top of a nearby church, and as quickly as it had started, stopped mid-melody. How bizarre! So, it was back to the guide book to try and discover what it was all about. The church was the Mariacki Church, and the current building was begun in 1355 and was a stunning example of Gothic architecture. The taller of the towers was topped by an amazing array of spires. It was from this tower that the trumpeter had been doing his stuff; the story was that during one of the early Tartar raids the watchman used his trumpet to raise the alarm when he saw the invaders approaching. Unfortunately for him, he got an arrow through his throat, and the warning was cut short. The legend continues, and a trumpeter plays the sombre melody on the hour, every hour, stopping abruptly at the precise point when the watchman was supposed to have been hit. Good story.

We didn't do anything specific with the rest of our day; just wandered around the passageways and courtyards and enjoyed the grand centre. However, there was a little mission I wanted to accomplish and that was to find the house where Joseph Conrad had spent his childhood. Having found it and looked at the outside for a while, we all became rather distracted when we noticed a few doors down that there was a Mexican restaurant. A MEXICAN! Oh joy of joys. All thoughts of Conrad vanished! We ventured into a warm room painted in lovely earthy colours, and decided without any discussion that this was where would have an early supper before getting the train back. I'm not sure Mexican food has ever tasted so good (perhaps with the exception of Mexican food in Mexico itself) and we settled down to huge bowls of nachos and cold bottled Mexican beer. I couldn't wipe the stupid smile off my face for days.

So, that was Krakow, well at least for that visit. The castle and cathedral would have to wait for a future one. The following weekend was another long one, so whilst the weather was still not too cold we decided to head to the mountains south of Krakow. We took a train early on a Saturday morning and headed through gentle valleys, and up into the hills. Everything was beautifully green, and the fields were liberally dotted with the traditional Polish pointed wooden houses. We were heading towards Zakopane which is the main base for the Tatras. These days a major mountain resort, it had first attracted the Poles in 1870, when the purity of the air began to interest doctors who sent their consumptive patients there. Within a few years it was transformed, as artists and intellectuals followed, creating a fashionable colony, and by the 1920s and 1930s the town grew to become one of the country's major tourist spots.

Apart from the lovely scenery, we were also hysterically entertained for part of the journey, and had that joy of laughing so hard you really can't stop and ache all over. We had obviously been overheard speaking English, as suddenly a tall, late middle-aged man started talking to us. He introduced himself as a Pole, called Walt and said he had been a translator. He spoke a wonderful antiquated form of English, as though taken from a 19th Century book, and was also extremely opinionated. On hearing an American accent further along the train he loudly announced that all American girls had 'broad buttocks and cow's bosoms', and repeated this on a number of occasions. I guess he'd been to San Francisco and seen old those 'purple and pink' shell-suited tourists I'd been so surprised by. He was also old fashioned and a gentleman, and explained that 'the age of rivalry' wasn't dead. We think he was talking about chivalry. His parting shot as we pulled into the station late was that the train was 'retarded'.

When we arrived in Zakopane it was a beautiful, sunny early November day, and as neither in the summer season or the winter season we easily found somewhere to stay. Not glamorous by any means but on the edge of the town, the hostel was quiet and clean. The main problem was that it was dormitory style rooms in the most enormous wooden building and so no privacy. None of this really mattered though, as all around us were the most amazing mountains. The Tatras are eighty miles long, with some peaks of over 8,200 feet; however the Polish part makes up only a small part of the range, with the majority across the border in Slovakia. Having arrived in the afternoon we had a gentle walk around the town, and made the most of the sunny, but not too freezing weather. In the evening we met up, as planned, with teachers from some of the other IH schools, and spent a silly night trying out the local bars. We also looked through various guides and decided to go for a major walk the following day.

We took a local bus to a well-known beauty spot the following morning, and got off in Kiry. From there we paid to get into the national park, and had a wonderful walk along the Dolina Kościeliska, a valley following the course of the stream deep into the park. It was a stunning valley, completely flat where we were, but with the sides rising dramatically away from us. After a couple of hours we came to the end of the valley floor, and then had to decide what to do. Some sensibly (including Sarah, who in hindsight I should have followed) decided to go for the eastern route, a gentle walk a short distance to a tiny mountain lake surrounded by the forest, others (me included who decided she wasn't going to follow her head but Andrew) decided to take the western route which followed a high ridge over to the next valley and back to the main road. I must have been mad, as I hate walking up hill.

And that's where our adventure began. Looking back I can honestly say that for five minutes I really believed that we might die, and all I could think of was how on earth Mum would cope so soon after Dad. It started off well enough; we walked up the beautiful mountains, through open patches of green and clumps of trees. At one point we even met a mountain ranger, who did nothing to dissuade us from carrying on. After another couple of hours we came to the edge of the tree line. From there the views spectacularly opened up. We were practically opposite the most amazing, imposing peaks rising in Slovakia. There was no greenery, just dark mountains topped with snow. We continued up the narrow path, at one point having to slither over a small glacier, and as we turned a bend, were hit with the most incredible wind. It seemed to be coming from all directions. Using low bushes to hold onto, we turned another corner to find that we still didn't appear to be anywhere near the top, and that the first traces of ice and snow were appearing on the path. Did we really know what we were doing? No. We all had strong boots on, but having left for a walk, rather than a hike didn't have all the things you're supposed to have; no whistle, waterproof clothing or anything useful like that. We continued up the narrow, slippery path, by which point the wind was buffeting us from all angles. Even if we did get to the top, then what on earth would it be like up there. By this point it was about two thirty, dusk was falling, and I remembered that that was another walker's 'no, no'. By the time we finally reached the summit there was a good half-foot of snow, the wind was gale force, and the signpost showing where the path went down had been blown over.

I was convinced that the wind was going to blow me right of the mountain, so crouched down low whilst we decided what to do. My friend Rob was playing the typical, macho role assuring us everything would be ok - together with Andrew he slithered a little further down the other side to see if he could see the path. At this point all we could see was snow, and in the distance the mountain peaks rapidly disappearing into the night. As the boys went over the crest I was convinced I was never going to see them again. After a couple of minutes they returned saying they couldn't really see a path, but that it must be that way. So, we sat there, huddled together, trying to agree on what to do. At least we had the sense to stay together. I told Andrew that I was sure I would get blown off the mountain if we went any further, and that in the dark we wouldn't be able to see a thing. Rob was still saying we should press on and that all would be ok.

"I'm scared now," I told Andrew.

"So am I," he replied.

Not exactly what you want to hear, but at least he realised the danger. By then it was three o'clock and the darkness was quickly descending. Those five minutes when we huddled together were probably the most terrifying of my life. All I wanted to do was turn back – all we had to do was avoid being blown off by the wind, navigate the glacier, then once we reached the tree line we'd be ok. It would be another five-hour walk, but rather knackered then dead. So, that's what we did. We held hands going down the path, grabbing the gorse bushes with the other, had a very anxious time trying to get back over the glacier. By the time we finally reached the tree line it was dark, really dark and there wasn't a light anywhere. Despite feeling knackered, at least we were safe and all we had to do was keep walking. After another three hours, where we either walked in silence, or played silly games to keep our spirits up, we finally came to the end of the valley. Not a chance of a bus, so we waited for ages, and then thankfully managed to hitch back to the town. We headed straight for the bar where we had arranged to meet the others an hour previously. We looked the most sorry bunch ever; in fact I have a photo where we appear completely shell shocked. It was great to be in a warm, protective atmosphere, and with a hug from Sarah, who had starting to think about alerting the rescue people, we downed a couple of hot drinks each, and then hit the vodka.

I was completely knackered, so didn't stay out long. My brain though had other ideas – I felt completely alive and my head was crammed full of thoughts and mountains. As I wriggled around on my top bunk, Rob whispered from his.

"Can't you sleep?"

"Not a chance," I replied.

"Shall we get up and go out again, to see if that helps?"

"Yeah, why not? Lying here is driving me crazy!"

So, up we got, and finally went to bed and sleep some hours later.

I wrote a poem about the experience, and never again will underestimate the power of the mountains. Going back to work the following week seemed unimportant in comparison, although by the weekend I was shaking in my proverbial boots again. This time for a very different reason. Every Sunday evening a couple of the teachers were invited to do an hour-long slot on the local radio station. This consisted of giving the show a theme, and playing records. After dinner at Jen's house, Anna and I left for the radio station, and arrived in time to be briefed about what to do, in time for the ten o'clock start. I have always been impressed by presenters who can chat so naturally when on air, and flow from one idea to the next with no awkward gaps or cutting off records. I was incredibly nervous beforehand, and worried about not concentrating on the system of lights which told us when to start talking. Although I'm sure it wasn't the most scintillating hour it was enjoyable and we got to choose the music we wanted. David Bowie please step forward.

Maybe having a little drink beforehand would have made things easier. By the time it was my turn again, we had got a well-established routine of the 'Sunday Seven'. This meant that we would all meet at someone's house, and they would cook Sunday lunch, and we'd drink a lot. One Sunday it was my turn to cook, and to do the radio show. Sarah came round mid-morning to help me prepare, and I nagged her to make sure I didn't drink too much, at the same time pouring us both generous glasses of port. Wise move!! We had a lovely roast chicken, and drank the house, and most of the local shop dry. Anna was trying to get us both to stop, as she was my co-host for the evening for the second time. We all piled onto the bus, dropping off the others on route to go and listen in someone else's flat, and Anna and I fell off the bus at the radio station. The controller or whatever his name was, you know, the guy who plays the records, and turns the lights on, didn't seem too concerned. Being obviously unable to focus on lights going on and off and him telling us when to talk, he helped us by waving through the studio window whenever we needed to do anything. I, of course, have very little recollection of anything that was said, but was assured it was hysterical. Waking up the following morning with a frightful headache, I then started to worry that maybe the school owner had heard the programme, or been told about it, and I was in for a right bollocking. Finally managing to open my eyes, I made it into school for a lunchtime start, and apart from comments from other teachers no-one else seem bothered.

Our school was fairly active in organising events and a couple of weeks later we went to see a production of *The Importance of Being Earnest*, which Sarah had helped produce. It was somewhat bizarre seeing it done in a hall in a small town, especially as most of the actors were Polish, but was quirky and very enjoyable.

By now we were into December, and everyone was busy with all the end of term stuff that had to be done. I was also busy as had a weekend in grey, depressing Katowice being trained to be an oral examiner for the Cambridge English exams, and then a couple of weekends after that examining. It meant that I didn't have days off but at least I'd have the money to fly home for Christmas, rather than take the horrible bus which some people were having to contemplate.

That left one free weekend in December so we decided to

treat ourselves to an overnight stay in Krakow. Somehow European cities seem to do Christmas so well, incorporating traditional markets, and food, and Krakow was no exception. Together with Sarah, Anna and Jen we took the familiar, bumpy bus on the Saturday morning, spent quite a long time looking for somewhere to stay which was cheap (ending up in the Hotel Warsawa, which reminded me of the place I stayed in Porto, with huge rooms with lots of beds in them) and then headed for MacDonald's as a reward, and to escape from the cold. It was freezing, and made Christmas shopping a whole new experience. You could just about stand being outside for a bit, and then had to dive inside a café to revive yourself. There weren't department stores, just small, local, interesting shops, all of which had their doors open, and the lovely square was full of market stores. We spent ages soaking up the lovely Christmassy atmosphere, looking at the beautiful wooden decorations, and following our noses towards enticing smells. Aah, mulled wine. It helped take away the numbness of the fingers, and really warmed your insides. Especially if you had a lot. We did. What I didn't try was the hot beer, which they were also selling. I couldn't quite get my head round the thought of it. Beer was supposed to be cold, and drunk on a hot day, not the other way round.

For the first three months in Poland I felt as though I was a student, behaviour wise. There had been far too much drinking, staying out, clubbing on school nights and generally misbehaving. A final part of what seemed to be slightly rebellious was, that at the grand of old age of thirty-one I decided to have a tattoo. Sarah had two, which I admired, and here I was, on a freezing Saturday afternoon in Krakow, standing outside a tattoo plaour, knowing that going inside meant a tattoo, and a good hour of warmth. Surprisingly, I didn't have to try and explain what I wanted in Polish, as the tatooist was a graphic designer from the States who had been disillusioned by his homeland, and after a holiday had moved to Krakow. He showed me various pictures, but none of them were what I was after. I had set my mind on a dove, as a symbol of peace, but didn't want a traditional depiction of a dove. Being a designer, the tattooist told me he'd design one himself, and happy with the results, he got started. With encouragement from the girls, as I knew it might hurt, I lay down (tattoo was to be on my bum) and waited for the worst. Well, it tickled quite a bit and black was supposed to be the colour which hurt the most but it really wasn't a problem. The tattooist made me laugh by saying that it made a change to be doing one on soft skin with someone who was happy to chat, rather than on a hairy bottom with a male who winged all the time about how much it hurt. So, there I was, with tattoo.

Back to the hotel (if you could call it that) we changed in readiness for an evening out, and made our way back to the same Mexican restaurant we'd discovered on the visit before. Full of lovely food, we then sampled some of the famous Krakow bars, which put the ones in Bielsko to shame, and from time to time, no doubt fuelled by vodka, I apparently squeaked to anyone in earshot, "Hey, I've got a tattoo!"

For a couple of hours the next morning, to clear our heads, we wandered around the quiet centre, understanding completely why UNESCO had named it one its significant historic sites that year, due to the various monuments. Unfortunately, the government has also named the locality as an official 'ecological disaster area' because of the damage done by the steelworks in the suburbs. Not only is it damaging the health of the locals, but the high toxic levels are causing incalculable damage to the ancient centre we were so admiring.

There were only a couple of weeks to go to the end of term, and I was well and truly counting the days. Although it sounds as though we were having a fun time, I was still finding the transition hard from Portugal to Poland. I was fed up with the cold, and having to rely on a terrible bus service and then a dark walk back to the huge uninviting house I was living in. Before the end of term I brought this up again with the school owner, who, as she was in my proficiency level class, I knew quite well. She agreed that as a teacher was leaving at Christmas I could move into her flat, much closer to the centre, in January.

On the last Wednesday before the end of term I moved the majority of my stuff into my new flat. It was on a more regular bus service, with a bus stop round the corner, and was completely self contained. It was the ground floor of a house, had its own kitchen, bathroom, a spare room and a little balcony, and the very friendly landlady and her husband lived on the floor. The following morning, I woke for one of the last times in my house in the middle of nowhere to discover a couple of feet of snow had fallen overnight. I skidded my way to the bus stop, to discover lots of people wandering around looking bemused and no sign of a bus. I eventually plodded back home to phone school to say it looked unlikely I'd make it in. However, they were having none of it and said they would try and organise a taxi. So, I finally managed to get to work, without a clue how I was going to get back. Things were no better the next day as it had snowed more, and there was talk that the airport would have to be closed. Nooooooo!!!

However, on the Saturday morning the mini-bus we'd arranged turned up, and we left for the airport. It was a terrible journey, with abandoned cars everywhere, the snow was still coming down, and there were lots of heavy hearts when we realised that we might be stuck in Poland for Christmas. By the time we reached the airport it had stopped snowing, and it looked like flights were leaving.

Having checked in successfully we settled ourselves down in the bar for a holiday beer – for many just topping up from the night before. As our flight was called we made our way to the minute departure lounge and discovered that being in Poland meant that they had squeezed a vodka bar in. We quickly realised we weren't boarding as the runway kept freezing, so decided to avail ourselves of said bar. When we finally boarded, to say we were happy would be a huge understatement. Being fuelled by vodka meant that we didn't panic too much on take-off when there were still de-icers on the runaway.

Poland's national airline, LOT, did themselves proud. No only did they provide a little menu of the very palatable meals they served, but the stewardesses wandered up and down the aisle pouring as much vodka as people wanted. They didn't even mind as Sarah, Rob and I squeezed into two seats in order to chat. When we finally landed, we literally fell off the plane, and staggered to the baggage reclaim area. Oh my God, it all took ages. Trying to find which carousel had our luggage took a while, and when we finally got it, co-ordinating brains and arms to grab suitcases was a marathon task. I know I fell over my trolley a couple of times and rammed it into lots of people. We eventually we made it through customs weaving and stinking of booze. And there waiting for me, was friend Amanda who I was going to stay with for the night.

"Do you want to come to a party at a neighbour's house tonight?" she enquired

sweetly.

"I think I'd better pass," I slurred happily.

Chapter 27

Another new home

After a lovely Christmas break when I saw lots of all friends, ate lovely food and enjoyed being outside without freezing half to death, it was soon back to Poland. It was good catching up with new friends on the flight, and we discussed what the options were for our winter break coming up at the end of January. It was a very civilised two-week holiday, traditionally given to workers to save on fuel costs in companies during the coldest part of the year. Rather than staying at home and having huge heating bills ourselves we decided that since we were in a perfect location to visit other Eastern European countries, a little trip was in order.

However, I am rushing ahead of myself. On retuning to Bielsko we discovered that it was a good thing we hadn't been stuck in Poland, as on Christmas Day the temperature dipped to minus twenty-seven. Nice! I arrived in my new flat, to find it was like being in the tropics and was about thirty-seven degrees. I really hate overheated houses, especially having lived in Portugal where there was no central heating, but this was ridiculous. My new pad was great; if slightly mad as all the Polish flats seemed to be. Although I had another hard, Polish sofa bed, at least it was a double so I could sleep on one side and avoid the ridge in the middle.

In the living room, where the bed was, I had the ubiquitous glass fronted cupboard stuffed full with hideous glassware (why on earth every flat needed five sets of vodka glasses I don't know) and in the bathroom I discovered the washing machine. I suppose I should have been grateful I had one, but I have never known such an torturous process – at least this one didn't boil all my clothes, burn them and turn them grey like my previous machine had! Anyway, the machine wasn't plumbed in so the first thing you had to do was fill it with hot water. Using the shower attachment stretched as far as possible and aimed towards the top of the machine you could nearly reach the top; but not quite. It meant filling the washing up bowl with hot water and emptying it in endless times. You then had to mix in the powder, and finally put the clothes in. There weren't any particular programmes, you just turned the clockwork knob, and then every three minutes had to do it again until you thought the clothes were clean. Then it was time to remove the dripping clothes, and get rid of the water. This time the process was in reverse, emptying water into the bowl, repeated a thousand times. I might have just as well got in myself as I was always completely soaked through. The final process was spinning. The spinner was tiny, so I could only do a sock at a time, and it would rock all over the kitchen with me trying to catch the water in the bowl. I tell you, who needs TV when you have a machine like the one I had! Kevin Costner and *Waterworld* eat your heart out!

On a Sunday my sweet landlady would always bring me down a bowl of soup. It was typical of so many Poles, always giving. Unfortunately, it was always horrible, but I'd try and make the right appreciative noises. After three months I hadn't made a lot of progress with the language, but could at least exchange pleasantries. My landlady took this to mean I was fluent and when I bumped into her, she'd settle down for a good chat. She'd tell me all sort of things, and no doubt when she told me her sister was at death's door, I'd say how nice, when her dog got run over I'd say how pleased I was, and when she said her husband had been murdered I'd say what nice weather we were having. Bonkers, all of our conversations, but we enjoyed them.

Another mad Polish trait was to have a thermometer outside the house, just so you knew that once you left your tropical paradise any body part not covered would freeze. Morning after morning I'd peep through the curtains, to discover, oh joy, it was minus twenty-one again. Jesus H Christ; this was ridiculous. Have you ever tried to look nice, dress up a little, but need to wear at least twenty layers, so you resemble the Michelin man on a fat day, then wait at the bus stop, by which time your eye lashes and snot has frozen solid. Gorgeous, everyone thinks as you enter the bar!

The cold weather did have a positive side though, and for our first weekend back we went skiing. One of my students was a (very handsome) skiing instructor who had promised to give some of the teachers a lesson. At eight in the morning, a time previously unknown to exist in Poland on a Saturday, we waited at the bus station along with the rest of Bielsko, and then fought our way onto the bus. We headed for the little ski resort, and were soon having more mad conversations to try and get boots to fit. I hadn't been on skis for ages and it felt great. Whilst the others had a beginner's lesson on the plateau, I skied down the beautiful run through the trees, feeling alive as only you can when skiing.

One of the main benefits of being in my new flat was that there were more regular buses, so I could go out at the weekends and in the evenings without always having to wait for ages for a bus or get a taxi. The following weekend we again went into the mountains, but this time used the cable car up to the top of our local mountain, where we went for a long walk, and generally messed around. We also started to

243

go to the local cinema a lot. Somewhat surprisingly, the Poles were more advanced than Portugal in the cinema stakes and although there was only one screen, at least the film changed every week. What's more, the films weren't dubbed, but subtitled so we had no problems; apart from the time when during a particularly tense point in *The English Patient* the sound went. We were all frantically whispering to a Polish friend who was with us, to translate, but he couldn't really keep up, so although the sound came back after a while, I was never really the wiser as to what had happened.

Chapter 28

Three cities on the Danube

After the grand total of three weeks back at work, it was holiday time again. Sarah, Anna, Jen and I set off in freezing temperatures for Hungary. We decided that Budapest was a must, and then on the way back we'd stop in Bratislava. First, we had to take the local train north (which seemed ridiculous) to Katowice and from there take the international train south, back through Bielsko and on to Budapest. We knew we were in for a long journey, and would go though four countries in the same day before arriving late in the evening. The trip was both enjoyable, excruciatingly boring when we sat at borders for ages, and at times rather frightening. We thought that by travelling together we wouldn't have any major problems, and could look out for each other. After crossing over easily into the Czech Republic and getting a variety of stamps with pictures of trains on them in our passports, we continued over the flat plain which was covered with snow. At the time I was listening to *Four seasons in one day* by Crowded House, and looking at the blue sky contrasted with the white snow, sparkling in the sunlight, I had one of those 'happy moments' when you feel completely at peace and joyful with the world. If I hear the track again, I just have to shut my eyes and I'm back on that train.

And then, as were enjoying the journey some different guards came into our compartment and asked to see our passports, despite the fact that they had already been shown at the border and stamped. Although fine with the British ones, they started making a fuss about Jen's American one. With Anna being able to speak some Russian, it seemed that they thought Jen couldn't travel out of Poland on it, although she had clearly got a stamp in it. When they tried to take the passport away, I decided that enough was enough, and told Jen that no way was she to give it to anyone or let it out of her sight. We'd all heard stories about money being extorted from foreigners travelling in the Eastern block, and didn't want to get into that situation on the first day of our holiday. When they realised we weren't going to back down they went away to consult, and returned to say it was ok. Whether they were genuinely confused by the American passport, or were trying it on I don't know, although I tend to err toward the later after a similar incident which happened on another international train a couple of months later.

After another two, tortuous border crossings, when we were stamped out of a country, and then stamped into the next one, namely, Slovakia, then Hungary, we finally arrived at Budapest station at about ten o'clock at night. We'd had trouble booking anywhere to stay from Poland so had taken the first vacant rooms, which happened to be in one of the youth hostels, but unfortunately was on the outskirts, another bus ride away. This was exactly what we didn't need after a day's travelling, and that was after we had to try and find the machine to buy our tickets. The machine, of course, only took change which we didn't have, so had to go in search of a kiosk where we could change one of the Hungarian notes we had got in Poland. Working the ticket machine was another mystery. Why is nothing ever easy where ticket machines are concerned? Clutching our tickets and bags we finally walked outside into the freezing cold to try and find the bus stop. I have always had a good sense of direction so when the others plonked their bags down at the number 7 bus stop, I was confused to say the least.

"Why have we stopped here? We need to be on the other side of the road, going in the other direction."

"No we don't," they chorused.

"Look", I said, pointing at the map," we need to get across the river, and then go left; if we go this way we are going in completely the wrong direction. You're all mad!"

After a fair amount of persuading, and of course doubting myself by this time, the others agreed that perhaps we should be on the other side of the road. We crossed over, the bus came along, we jumped on and looking at the street names I could see it was a good thing we'd followed my sense of direction otherwise we could have ended up bloody knows where. The bus seemed to take ages when, finally, we recognised a road name and got off into slushy, cold puddles in the middle of nowhere, and found the hostel. What followed was one of the most terrible night's sleep I have ever had. Apart from being in a dormitory with at least ten other people who all came in at different times during the night, waking me up every time, there were noises from the creaky old house, and worst of all, the room was freezing. The bedclothes were suitable if you happened to be in the south of Spain in August, and there was nothing inviting about the entire place – not even a huge mural of Bob Marley on the wall helped.

In the morning I announced that I was too old to be staying in a dump like this and was going into the centre, bags and all to find something half decent. Sarah was with me all the way, and with a little encouragement the others agreed. Despite being cold, tired and fed up, seeing Budapest for the first time in the daylight and bright sun was a real treat. The bus went back over the Danube from where we could see a variety of beautiful buildings, and dropped us on the main road. From there we walked up to one of the squares and found an office which dealt with accommodation, and thankfully, since the girl spoke English, we were able to have a sensible conversation. She told us about other youth hostels which were in the centre, but they seemed really expensive for what they were. Feeling very pissed off, we wondered what on earth we were going to do, when the lady then said that we could, of course, rent an apartment. Yeah right, so we couldn't afford a youth hostel, but we could afford an apartment! However, there was a brilliant scheme in Budapest, which involved local flat owners renting out their homes when they were away, and not charging the earth. We were shown pictures of a modern flat, in a lovely old building, and for three nights it was cheaper than a youth hostel. A done deal. So we set off, bags and all to find the flat. Did we get lost? Completely! We found the correct street but there was no right number. We went up and down blocks of flats, trying to explain to locals what we were looking for, and finally gave up and despatched Anna and Jen to go back to the office. The poor lady eventually appeared, showed us where the flat was, which she admitted was virtually impossible to find with the given address, and we had a home. What a glorious difference from the yucky youth hostel. It was modern and clean, and best of all, warm.

Having wasted a fair few hours we set off immediately to have a look round the city. We were in the Pest side, and across the Danube was Buda, set on the hills. It was only in 1873 that the city was born, when the two towns merged. The architecture was stunning, and a mixture of baroque, neoclassical and art noveau amongst others. First stop was the State Opera House, designed in 1884 and a beautiful building. We discovered there was a performance of Eugenie Onedin on the Thursday evening and since the tickets were a ridiculously low price, decided to buy some and have a look at the interior at the same time. From there it was a short walk to the stunning Parliament building. From close up it was amazing, but its full beauty wouldn't be apparent until we viewed it from the other side of the Danube the following day. It was built as recently as 1902 in a mixture of styles, which worked well, but it was its colossal size which was memorising.

By this time the cold was starting to seep in, so we headed for a café and some warmth. Budapest is almost as famous for its cafés and cakes as Vienna is. We stopped off at the most famous one, the Gerbeaud, on the west side of a large square, which had been a fashionable place for the elite to meet since 1870. Being in an historic café meant it was time to find out a bit of history. Hungary's past seemed complicated, not helped in the least by the fact that the word 'Hun' as in Attila, has nothing to do with 'Hungary'. What was certain was that the Magyars, part of the Finno-Ugric group of peoples, lived in the forests somewhere between the Volga River and the Ural mountains in western Siberia as early as 4000 BC and that by the mid-eighth century, nomadic groups of Magyars reached the Carpathian Basin. The country had a long and bloody history, which has continued up to the very recent past.

It was in 1956 that there was an anti-Soviet uprising by the students of Budapest, who demanded that Nagy be made prime minister. Two days later, on the 25th October he formed a government, and just when it seemed possible that he might transform Hungary into a neutral state, the Soviets arrived. On the 1st November the tanks rolled over the border and before long had begun attacking Budapest and other major centres. Fierce street fighting continued for several days and when it was over 25,000 people were dead. This wasn't the end though, and the reprisals started. It was estimated that 20,000 were arrested, and 2,000 including Nagy and his associates were executed. I obviously couldn't remember it happening but reading about it and looking at the bullet holes and shrapnel in so many of the buildings in Pest, it wasn't hard to remember was a terrible tragedy it had been.

Dinner that evening wasn't, I'm afraid to say, eaten in a local restaurant but somewhere called 'Chicago' which was bright and warm, and sold a tempting array of American diner food, unavailable in Bielsko. The meal was washed down with lots of local beer, accompanied by laughing at our abysmal attempt to speak a work of Hungarian. The Hungarians themselves admit it is one of the world's most difficult languages to learn, a good example being that it took me four days just to remember how to say 'thank you'! Fuelled by food and booze we thankfully remembered where our flat was, and gratefully went to bed not surrounded by lots of strangers but in the quiet and warm. Bliss!

We woke up the next day to another gloriously bright, blue-skied day. It meant that the snow sparkled in the sunshine but the temperature had dropped and it was freezing walking around. Another day of sightseeing, and rushing into bars and cafés to keep warm was in order. We walked along the bank of the Danube, which was nearly blue, and then slowly ambled across Chain Bridge to visit the Buda part of the Budapest. Jen and Anna hadn't been able to drag themselves from their warm beds so Sarah and I chatted away happily, and were content to take things at the same pace, stopping often to admire the views. On reaching the other side of the river, we decided to take the funicular up to the kilometre-long plateau, one hundred and seventy metres above the river. The view from the top was stunning, but even better was to come. We walked through the old town, full of medieval buildings, and came to Matthias Church. Some parts dated back some five hundred years, but the main church was designed in the neo-Gothic style in the late 19th Century. I loved the amazingly ornate tower and the colourful tiled roof which looked as though it was covered in material. The interior was similarly stunning, and had remarkable stained-glass windows and frescos. Leaving the church and heading towards the river we came to the Fisherman's Bastion. This again was a Gothic pretence, but looked medieval. It was built as a viewing platform in 1905, and the views all round, but especially over the river and towards the Parliament, were stunning. Connected by walkways there were seven white turrets, which represent the Magyar tribes who entered the Carpathian basin. Close by was the Hilton hotel, apparently very controversial in its design. One side of it was covered in brown reflective glass, and although it wasn't in harmony with the surrounding buildings, it perfectly reflected the white towers, silhouetted against the blue sky, at quirky angles. I thought it was amazing and wasn't sure what all the fuss was about.

It was all so peaceful and quiet, looking over the snowy scenes, but just so cold; another café was needed. This one has to be given the 'all time smallest café' award, with all of two tables, but in the middle of a lovely bookshop. Afterwards we had a quick look at the Royal Palace, destroyed countless times over the last seven centuries, scrambled down the bank, went back over the river and found somewhere for lunch. Hungarian food was unhealthy in the same heavy, lard type way as the Polish food, but there was more of a range, and lots of dishes were flavoured with paprika. Delicious. We ate in a small, traditional place full of loud, happy Hungarians all talking noisily about God knows what, and being refuelled wandered around for most of the afternoon.

Our perfect day was spoilt by a bloody, washing machine disaster. Getting back to the flat we discovered that the machine had emptied its contents all over the floor. Having paddled around and mopped up, we cooked dinner at the flat rather than eating out as we'd been getting through money at an alarming rate, and then set off for a bar close to the Opera House. Sometimes those amazing things happen, completely out of the blue, and I guess that night was one of those occasions where you happen to be in the right place at the right time, and you happen to be with an American who will talk to anyone, even if it is in Japanese.

We were happily drinking and chatting away when Jen went over to the bar to get another round. Next time we looked over, there she was, talking away to the first person she came across; except this time she was talking to some Japanese men in suits. She finally returned, with a drink for each of us which they'd brought. Not being a shy retiring wallflower, when she heard them talking in Japanese she said hello and obviously dazzled them. They explained that they were thinking of opening a Japanese restaurant in Budapest and were doing some research. They also mentioned that they owned one in Vienna. Vienna! That just happened to be where we were heading for a day trip three days later, which Jen, of course, mentioned to them. On the spot they invited us to drop into the restaurant and have some Sushi. Well – it would be rude to refuse, so we said that we would hopefully see them on Saturday. A few beers later, and we decided that eating sushi in Vienna would be the height of extravagance and that we'd have to do everything to make it happen.

The following morning we did what all respectable Hungarians do, and that was to take the waters. The locals had been bathing in the thermal waters since Roman times, so if it was good enough for them! We crossed over the river to find the Gellért Baths. They were housed in a splendid

Art Noveau building, and the main entrance hall was worth the visit in its own right. However, we weren't distracted for long, and began the hysterical task of trying to figure out what to do. There was nothing in English, and no one spoke any, so it was complete chaos. I'm sure we can't have been the first foreign visitors, but from the looks we got it seemed that way. By the ornate ticket office there was a huge board with a long list of different prices. The problem was that we had no idea which treatments were which. All we wanted to do was to have a soak in the baths – no swimming, massages or anything. Having mimed what we thought was bathing, the lady broke into a smile, asked for some money and gave us some tickets. Good. We then wandered around trying to figure out which door to go through – it was like something out of a children's book. We watched where other people were going and then followed a group of women in.

We were suddenly plunged into a world of torture, or that's what it looked like. We were in an enormous room full of women lying on massage tables, being pummelled half to death by Hungarian shot putters. I prayed that we hadn't ended up with tickets for this. We wove our way through the tables; no individual treatment rooms here, and were pointed to a steep flight of stairs to go down. We had arrived in the changing rooms, and were met by a smiley lady who tried to explain what to do. She eventually led us to a cubicle each, drew a number in chalk on the door and handed us a tag with the same number. As we started getting changed into our swimming costumes, she threw an apron over the door to each of us.

"Why have we got an apron?" we chorused.

We peered out of our cubicles to see if we could work out what the other women were doing. There was no-one around, apart from the smiley lady who came rushing back, motioning that we needed to take everything off, leave all our possessions in the cubicle which she then locked, keeping the keys and putting the tags around our wrists. So there we were, butt naked wearing aprons. It was all too much, and we collapsed into fits of giggles – this was before we had to walk back up the steps. I was suddenly concerned that, for some irrational reason, tattoos were a 'no, no' in Hungary, and had my hand firmly clamped over my left bum cheek, which Sarah decided was particularly funny! We gingerly made our way back through the 'pummelled ones', convinced that everyone was looking at our bits. They weren't of course! We then reached the showers, where another attendant demanded our aprons and pushed us underneath. It was all so embarrassing – being naked in front of friends and loads of Hungarians. Having showered, it soon became apparent that that was the last we'd see of the aprons until after a dip. We rushed like mad things to get into the water and cover ourselves up. The embarrassment must have lasted all of a minute. What a place. The water was gorgeously warm, and the baths were in the most beautiful room with a stunning vaulted ceiling. It was like having a bath in a cathedral. We wallowed for ages, soaking up the benefits, only raising our eyebrows once when a nearby lady decided to lean against a pillar, and do leg raises. That we didn't need to see! We eventually dragged ourselves out of the soothing water, put our aprons back on and did the process in reverse.

After a quick lunch, and another wander around, we headed back to the apartment to put on our glad rags in readiness for the opera. We had seats in the front row of the circle, which afforded an amazing view of the interior of the building. It had been overhauled in 1980 and was spectacular. The opera itself was mesmerising, although we didn't have a clue what was going on for most of the time. At the interval we treated ourselves to a glass of *Tokay*, the sweet white local wine. Although not a huge fan of sweet wine, it seemed appropriate to drink it as most other people were. At the end of the second half we clapped enthusiastically and prepared to leave – except that other people didn't seem to be doing so! Apparently the opera wasn't in two parts, but three. When it was over I felt exhilarated as only opera can make you feel; not least by the fact that rather than costing £50 it had cost about £1!

So, that was Budapest. The following morning we jumped on another international train, which took us back through Hungary and into Slovakia, and we filled yet more pages of our passports with pictures of trains. Apart from travelling through Slovakia briefly on the way to Budapest, the last time I'd been anywhere near it was when I was faced with a range of mountaintops, and worried about seeing another day. It was therefore, with just the tiniest amount of trepidation I got off the train in Bratislava. Naturally, my fears were ridiculous, and the most difficult challenge was trying to organise somewhere to stay, and doing it in Slovakian. Anna had already left to go back to Poland, and being without someone who spoke even a little Russian was proving interesting. We managed it though, and found a large room at the youth hostel for the three of us, with central heating – memories of the hostel in Budapest were forgotten.

Slovakia. Apart from knowing that it had split from The Czech Republic in 1993, only four years previously, my history of the country was woefully inadequate. A quick look at my guidebook, and I was a little wiser. There had been another independent Slovakia before, and that was when the Slovaks split from the Czechs in 1938, forming an independent state allied to nazi Germany – still a contentious topic today. Before 1918 it was known as Upper Hungary and for roughly a millennium lay under Magyar rule. By the time we got there, Bratislava had been the capital of the new Slovakia for four years, and restoration was well under way.

We entered the old town across a footbridge and under a

double gateway with a tower perched on top, which was rather an impressive way to arrive. Inside there was a warren of narrow old streets, busting with shoppers and students. There didn't seem to be any other tourists which suited us just fine. After a short walk our stomachs and the cold got the better of us and we went in search of lunch. Slovakian food seemed to be a mixture of Hungarian and Polish fare, heavy and filling, but we struck lucky with our first sampling. We found a restaurant which had been converted from what appeared to be the crypt of an old church. It was a beautiful setting, and apart from the grumpy waiter who refused to let us keep our coats, demanding instead that we hung them up, and then had to pay to get them back, we had a lovely lunch. I went for the national dish; *bryndzové halušky* – gnocchi with a thick sheep's cheese sauce and crumbled grilled bacon. It tasted a bit like *carbonara* but was tangier and fuelled me until a late dinner.

Feeing very soporific we finally dragged ourselves away from the cosy restaurant and set off to explore the rest of the city. It was tiny and took little time to get from one end to the other. We walked through old residential streets which the money obviously hadn't yet reached as there were numerous old houses desperately in need of repair. We came to the two main squares, namely Hlavné námestie and Františkánske námestie, on the east side of which was the Old Town Hall, an amazing mixture of Gothic, Renaissance and nineteenth-century styles. It was a ridiculous building, with sections from completely different eras, but mesmerising, and I stood and stared at it for ages. This was in stark comparison to the next area we came to. On the west side of the old town had been the Jewish quarter, but after the Nazi's had annihilated the people, the Communists did the same to the buildings, and erected a horrible showpiece bridge spanning the Danube. We spent little time there, before wandering off again through the old streets, enjoying mingling with the locals and peering in shop windows. Taking a wide loop back in the direction of the hostel we suddenly all squeaked in unison.

"Oh my God, that's a Tesco's!"

This no doubt sounds completely inappropriate – firstly that there should be a modern shop in this beautiful centre, or that we were excited by it. But, if you have lived abroad, even if it is for a long time, you still pine for things from home. I was already dreaming about pork pies, Branston's and Marmite by the time we went in. Unfortunately it wasn't a 'proper' Tesco's. It was more similar to a small department store, with a dried food section. But even that was enough to excite us; and we pored over the shelves for an indecent amount of time. No pork pies, but I did come away with Marmite and pickle!

After a poke around the Kostel Trinitárov, one of the city's finest churches, we walked   back through the modern, residential streets and to the hostel where were crashed out for a while. The next issue was where to go for dinner. We'd had a traditional, Slovakian meal, and although other people might be horrified we were sorely temped by the Chinese restaurant we'd just walked passed. We didn't know the next opportunity we'd get, so it was a foregone conclusion, and before long we were sitting in a bright restaurant, full of plastic flowers and illuminated pictures of waterfalls, trying to figure out what sweet and sour chicken was in Slovakian. It was proving far too complicated – the waitress couldn't speak Slovakian, let alone English, and had decided that she was going to communicate in Mandarin. Madness. We eventually choose what looked like a meal for three, and waited to find you what we'd be eating. Delicious! A huge amount of food and no MSG in sight. I was so full that moving was impossible for ages and I really feared that I'd end up doing an impression of Mr Creosote (for those not in the know he was the exploding 'wafer thin mint' man in *The Meaning of Life*).

The following morning we got up early to catch a train to Vienna. It was only half an hour away and since none of us had ever been, and I especially had always wanted to, we had decided that a day trip was in order. Having arrived at the main station we took a local tram towards the centre of the city. As we got closer in, the majesty of the place quickly became apparent. I'd seen many pictures before – of Hapsburg palaces, white horses, women in fur coats, and endless cafés – the reality was the same. The city was stunning. Set against blue sky, and with the roofs covered in snow, the buildings were clean and gleamed in the sunlight. The first building we came across was the Opera House. Having just been to see an opera we were keen to have a look inside; that however, wasn't possible. The outside was stunning, and the museum shop was open so we could look at pictures of the inside. The golden staircase was magnificent, and apparently the only part of the building which wasn't destroyed by a bomb in 1945. The Opera House was originally opened in 1869 with a performance of Don Giovanni, and then reopened nearly a hundred years later after a ten-year build. Apart from some beautiful postcards, the best find in the shop was a little book summarising opera plots. How we could have done with it a couple of evenings previously. Reading the story of Eugenie Onegin, everything finally slotted into place.

From the Opera House we walked up one of the main pedestrian streets, Karnternstrasse. The difference from Poland, Slovakia, and to a lesser extent Budapest, was beyond belief. The shops were crammed with expensive goods and there were upmarket deli type places everywhere – even the air smelt affluent. It didn't take long for me to stop with my nose pressed up against a window selling sandwiches. These weren't any old sandwiches but open, colourful ones with a huge array of toppings. I hadn't seen a prawn since Christmas in the UK, and so treated myself to a prawn and salad one. It might have been ridiculously expensive but was worth every penny. Walking up to the end of the street we found ourselves face to face with the stunning St Stephen's Cathedral – yet another example of my favourite architectural style, Gothic. It was beautiful, with a 450 feet high steeple and had a roof covered in glazed tiles in an intricate design. We went inside and wandered slowly around. Suddenly memories of Dad came flooding back – he had always loved Vienna and I knew had been inside the cathedral. Deciding that it wasn't the time for tears, I lit a candle for him, promising that I would go and fulfil one of his wishes; that I'd have coffee and cakes in one of the traditional Viennese cafés.

I didn't quite have enough room for any food then so we went round the corner from the cathedral in order to find the Figorohaus. This was where Mozart had lived from 1784 – 1787, and composed some of his finest works, including *The Marriage of Figaro*. It was a small house, but despite that had a wealth of information and items on display related to the great composer. By the time we'd finished looking round I had a space in my tummy so we decided a stop in a warm café. We wandered down Grabben, an even more elegant pedestrianised street and peered through the windows of a couple of contesters, finally settling on one which was the epitome of a Viennese *Kaffehaus*. Inside, it was traditionally furnished with lots of dark furniture and deep coloured fabrics; the waiters were formally dressed, did everything to perfection, and there was generally an atmosphere of elegance and sophistication. Knowing that it would cost us far more than we could really afford, we felt complete frauds, but nevertheless played the part, and immensely enjoyed the thick slab of *Sachertorte* and strong coffee whilst behaving with unusual decorum. More sightseeing was in order afterwards, and knowing that we didn't have time to go into any more buildings we made do with a long, slow amble through the other parts of the city.

First we walked along to The Hofburg, originally the Imperial Palace complex that now housed the famous Spanish Riding School, a variety of state apartments and museums. The whole area was enormous, and so incredibly stately and grand. Waiting in one of the large forecourts were the obligatory horses and traps – trying to take a photogenic shot of Jen next to one with the palace in the background I managed to include a huge pile of greying, slushy snow! From The Hofburg we walked onto the Ringstrasse, otherwise known as the ring road, but it wasn't what you imagined a ring road was like. On either side it was graced by the most beautiful buildings which included the National Gallery of Art, the Parliament building which was built in the style of a Greek temple as a tribute to Athenian democracy, and the City Hall which was neo-Gothic. Somewhat buildinged out we headed for the exquisite café next to the Opera House, where we drank tea from incredibly delicate china, and Sarah had a barny with the old lady in the toilet who wanting paying for the experience. We were used to paying in Poland for a pee, and didn't mind as it was probably the only source of income for some, but in Vienna it seemed a tourist rip-off, and Sarah had told the old lady this; well, waved her arms around a lot.

The next decision was whether it was worth trying to find the Japanese restaurant which belonged to the owner we'd met a couple of evenings before in Budapest. We looked up the street on our map, and found that it was only about ten minutes walk away. Deciding that we had nothing to loose, and that it was only very early in the evening, we set off. Having found it and peered in through the window at the beautiful decor and at the exorbitant prices, we wavered, wondering whether the offer of a free meal was really the case. We walked in, were greeted enthusiastically by the hosts, and told that they would indeed like to give us a set dinner for free. Who were we to complain? We ate our way through a selection of beautifully presented sushi and sashimi, amongst other things, washing it all down with green tea. Jen continued to impress our hosts with her Japanese, but otherwise they left us to it, and we ventured in the cold, crisp night, extremely happy bunnies. With some time left before our train back to Bratislava, we found another warm, plush café where there was an amazing array of fur-coated women with lots of shopping bags, and because I suddenly felt decadent, we all had a glass of champagne. A whole week's Polish budget gone in a gulp of bubbles, some prawns and chocolate cake, but we didn't care, and felt like royalty.

We had a last morning in Bratislava, and then were on a train back to Poland. Of course, it wasn't as easy as that. We should have known after the journey from Poland that it would be eventful. Having boarded the train, and settled ourselves down in a compartment, a man suddenly opened the door and handed me my little purse. We'd already been sitting down for a couple of minutes, so he can't have watched me drop it, picked it up and rushed after me. The only thing we could think of was that he'd actually pickpocketed my purse, discovered that it only had some Polish and Hungarian currency in, and no plastic (which was in my wallet), had maybe had a pang of conscience and brought it back. Very strange. The whole episode disquieted me somewhat, and when a group of soldiers came into our compartment a while later I sat quietly in the corner, not feeling like chatting at all. Jen, on the other hand, positively encouraged conversation, so much that they went to collect other colleagues, and before too long I felt the atmosphere had changed for the worse. The subject matter wasn't exactly what you'd expect from people you didn't know, and when we tried to extricate ourselves from talking to them, the situation got more threatening. I don't really know what might have happened, but there were lots of them, only three of us, and we were in an unknown country. Eventually I decided I wasn't in the mood to put up with it – we had hours more of the journey, and I didn't want to have these guys in our compartment all the way. Whilst they had gone to do something I found the guard, explained the situation, well tried to, and he found us another compartment and told us he'd keep an eye on us. Everything was fine, and we finally got back to Bielsko in the early hours.

The next day was Monday, but joy of joys we still had another week off. It all got a bit tearful though, on the Wednesday, as we gathered at the station to put Jen on a train. Except that we were all there, including the train, and no Jen. The taxi she'd booked hadn't arrived! After Christmas in the UK she'd done some soul searching, and decided that as her British boyfriend had proposed, she should be there, and not leading a mad life with us, partying a lot of the time, and invariably getting into scrapes. I did understand how she felt, and although we pleaded with her to stay, her mind was made up. The taxi finally pulled up, with literally a couple of minutes to spare. Being Jen she hadn't booked a ticket, so rushed off to get one whilst we very slowly loaded her luggage aboard the train, hoping that this would stop the train leaving without her. I stayed on the train, so that if it did leave I could throw her luggage off and then jump off myself. Chaos. She made it; we all burst into tears, and then the train left for Krakow and the airport.

I guess that one of the really hard things about living in different places, especially different countries where you tend to meet like-minded peopled, is that you are always saying goodbye. Working abroad in fairly tight knit groups the friends you make are more like family, and bonds are made very quickly. Jen leaving was no exception and we all knew that the staff room and our evenings out would suffer from the lack of her dizzy, naïve sweetness.

To counteract our despondency, Sarah and I had a day trip to Krakow the weekend before we went back to work. We did the usual café stopping and wandering but decided that it was time we did something cultural and visited the famous Wawel castle and cathedral. We approached them up an old cobbled path, where they majestically looked over the river and the city. On closer view it seemed strange that the capital had been moved to Warsaw. The buildings were beautiful, and had natural defences. Apparently, even after the capital was moved the monarchs were still buried in the cathedral – along with heroes and poets. Its origins date back to 1020, of which there were a few fragments, and the current cathedral was built in the Gothic style in the 14th Century. The inside was incredibly ornate, and the side chapels held the tombs of all but four of the forty-five monarchs.

Leaving the cathedral we walked towards the castle, passing through a beautiful courtyard, built in the Italian palazzo style by a Florentine architect in the 15th Century. It was stunning, and if it hadn't been so cold, you could almost have imagined that you were in Italy. Everything was so stately and grand; well, until we went into the castle. We were promptly handed two plastic bags each, and told that to view the interior we had to put them on our feet. How elegant. But it wasn't just that we looked ridiculous, inducing the giggles, but that walking down the highly polished marble staircases was a bloody death trap! I have always been reduced to hysterics when watching slapdash humour on telly, and seeing it in front of me was hopeless. We did try and do justice to the castle; marvelled at the lavish state rooms and the treasury, but I think the entrance fee was worth it just for the skidding it caused.

Chapter 29

More trips away

After the distraction of a winter holiday, the reality of cold, grey Poland set in. Although it didn't snow that much more, it was so cold that the snow that had fallen never melted, and apart from the main roads wasn't cleared. The result was pavements covered with a foot of grey snow, tinged with a suspicious yellow colour. With a lack of sun, everything appeared grey and February and March were a bit of a slog. At least, being in my new flat meant that it was much more convenient for meeting up in town and, furthermore, Sarah and Anna had moved into a flat right in the centre so there was always company. What's more, just round the corner from them a new supermarket had opened. It was apparently owned by Tesco's and the day it opened we rushed to see what delights there were. Unfortunately, not exactly the British idea of Tesco's – but unlike its counterpart in Bratislava it was organised and did sell products we associated with supermarkets such as yoghurt and cheese, and frozen vegetables. But it had something else that British supermarkets definitely don't have – SAS style store detectives. We had got used to being followed around the department store food area by a non-scary guy, but this was ridiculous. Outside the supermarket, completely clad in black, and carrying guns were two men. Another one paraded up and down the aisles. The only thing that they lacked were balaclavas. It certainly gave an edge to the weekly shop!

One morning when I got into work my boss asked me if I was interested in going with her and the Assistant Director of Studies to that year's IH management conference in Budapest for three days. She obviously didn't know me that well – as if I needed to be asked if I wanted to spend some more time in a beautiful city and not have to pay for it. We took the same route as I'd used in January, except that this time we took the overnight train. It was all very jolly, drinking, chatting and playing cards in the buffet car, but the reality was that we did have to try and get some sleep. I was already expecting that it wouldn't happen for me, and was proved right. Crammed in to a six-person couchette the others were snoring away happily, whilst I tossed and turned all night – not helped by two sets of guards who came in to stamp our passports as we passed over the borders. Arriving at Budapest station the next morning I blearily followed the others, and we eventually managed to figure out how to get to our hotel. No cold, noisy youth hostel this time, but a modern hotel right in the centre.

As with all conferences, everybody pays a decent amount of attention to what is being said during the sessions, but it was at the meals and during the evenings where the fun was to be had. We partied hard, went to bed late, drank too much, snogged other managers and generally misbehaved. One evening we went to the local Irish bar, where there was a D.J. I finally wore him down and he played some Bowie to which I leapt around the tiny dance floor like a complete loon. I also managed to seriously bend the ear of one of the big cheeses in IH, about a bugbear that I had about the lack of any management training for academic directors in our EFL profession. I knew I'd been ranting drunkenly, and had suspected that he'd give me a wide berth for the rest of the conference, but what I'd said had obviously touched a nerve, and he even suggested that I could lecture on some of the modules which they had been thinking about introducing for managers. Hurrah! Drunken rants do work sometimes!

After all the partying, some might say we got our comeuppance. I travelled back to Poland with one of my colleagues, and the guy I'd been condoling with, on another overnight train. After a few drinks we wobbled back to our couchette, and just as we were settling down for the night, there was a loud hammering on the door, and two officious guards barged in. We showed them our tickets, (although we had, of course, already showed them to other guards), but they weren't happy, and one of them explained in very broken English that they weren't the correct tickets for this train. I knew that the school owner had booked the tickets and being Polish and very efficient I was sure she couldn't have made a mistake - added to the fact that we'd managed to use them on the way down. The guards weren't interested and told us that we had to get off the train – in the middle of the night, in the middle of nowhere. Being the girl I tried the tearful approach but that didn't have any effect. We began to get increasingly worried, and knew that guards sometimes tried to extort money from passengers, especially if they thought they had money.

Suddenly the guards changed tack when they realised there was no way we were going to get off the train, and told us that we could pay some extra money to make up the difference in the price of the tickets. They then announced that we had to pay in Deutsch Marks, making us even more suspicious. As we tried to explain that there was no way we'd have this currency as we lived in Poland and had come from Hungary, they said we could go to the bar and change the money. We couldn't believe that they were really trying this on – the whole episode was a complete scam. We steadfastly refused to go to the bar, or to give them money of any currency, and after a couple of hours they finally gave up. I was incredibly relieved that all this had happened when I was with two lads; I would have felt so much more vulnerable if the same thing had happened when I'd been travelling with my group of girlfriends, two months previously.

We finally got home early on Sunday morning, and by then I was feeling shocking. I was supposed to be going to Sarah's for one of our Sunday Seven lunches, but the combination of too much booze, and not enough sleep meant that I as soon as I got home to my boiling flat I knew I wasn't going anywhere. I'd like to say that I had a complete break from drinking and partying, but we only had a three-day week and were then on holiday for Easter.

Hoping that we'd get some bright, sunny weather in the mountains, Anna and I decided to go back to Zakopane for the break, do some gentle walking (absolutely no mountain hikes for me) and enjoy the fresh air and views. As we approached the mountain resort the clouds rolled in, and we could barely see each other, let alone the views. Groping our way to the youth hostel, we managed to find a twin-bedded room, rather than sharing with scores of other people, and feeling positive that luck would be with us regarding the weather, wandered around the town, looking at all the little shops. We re-visited one from our previous stay, namely a silver jewellery shop, and both came away with rings. I think it must be an addiction – I am physically unable to walk passed a shop or stall, which has silver rings. I'd even been seduced in Vienna. Vienna! How ridiculous was that? But I had my credit card, so bought myself a beautiful ring with three different bands and a gorgeous moonstone, and on Sarah's behalf bought a lapis one. Needless to say, as with the majority of my jewellery it didn't survive. I lost one of the silver bands some weeks after I'd bought it, taking my gloves off, and the moonstone part, the following year when drunk in Porto. Serves me right, I suppose. I guess I should either give up buying silver jewellery, or booze but I can't see either of those happening anytime soon.

The shopping came to an abrupt stop when it started snowing – horizontally. The force of the wind was amazing, and looking like cartoon characters we fought our way through the weather and into the nearest bar – where we stayed. Walking back to the hostel through the newly laid snow, we were looking forward to what we thought would be a beautiful, clear day with everything covered in new sparkly snow. Wrong! The next day was cold and damp, and everything was shrouded in cloud. We spent   another day going from one bar to the next, but by the next day, Easter Saturday, we realised that the weather wasn't going to change so decided we might as well go to Krakow for the rest of the break. We thought there might be something interesting to see in Krakow at the weekend so caught an early train on the Saturday morning. Things weren't much better there – although there wasn't a blizzard, it was sleeting, and freezing cold. To add to our misery, very few of the shops were open, so we opted for the cinema, and ended up seeing *Fierce Creatures* – unfortunately nowhere near as funny as *A Fish called Wanda*. By Easter Day we'd had enough – even fewer places were open, so we decided to go home and caught a bus back to Bielsko.

Anna came and stayed for a couple of days, as Sarah had a male friend staying and they needed space to sort various issues out. The weather was better, so we met up in town with some other friends for our lovely kebabs, discovered a newly opened Greek style café, which made the most delicious milk shakes, and even had some ice-cream. We're not talking a *Feast* or anything like that, but a bowl. One of the traditions that we had noticed in Bielsko, and other

Polish towns was the amount of ice-cream parlours there were. On a freezing Sunday afternoon there would literally be a queue of people waiting to get in. Completely mad. We decided to see what all the fuss was about and went in. Not only did they serve a huge variety of different flavours but also sold delicious hot chocolate. We had both, and while the ice cream was indeed delicious, I feel it was better suited to warmer weather – if that ever happened!

Chapter 30

Joints and lumps

Up until Easter I'd felt remarkably fit and healthy, but for the previous couple of weeks had felt the familiar pain returning in my hips, and now spreading to my feet. In my early twenties I'd been diagnosed with Juvenile Rheumatoid Arthritis, and after a really bad period when I could hardly walk, had had two sessions at UCH in London where I'd had a series of injections into the base of my spine. Ow, did that hurt! Afterwards, I'd sometimes taken anti-inflammatory drugs when the aches were bad, but on the whole it had been bearable, and the warmth of living in Portugal had really eased the pain. But this was back with a vengeance. I tried to persuade myself it would go away, but after a couple of weeks realised I needed help. However, I wasn't the only one with problems. Sarah had been feeling increasingly unwell, and had a lot of pain in her tummy. She was eventually taken to hospital where they diagnosed a cyst on one of her ovaries. She needed to have an immediate course of pills to try and shrink the cyst, and then have it removed. Sarah and I battled on for a week, feeling increasingly unwell and sorry for ourselves, and after a special dinner Sarah flew back to the UK for treatment. I was feeling doubly miserable – my best friend was really poorly, I was without her and feeling fairly ill myself.

My boss decided to have a Spanish tapas party to try and lift the mood a little. It was the day after Sarah had left, so although not feeling much like partying, I knew it would be good therapy to go. I woke up on the Sunday morning feeling very cold, and opening the curtains saw it was snowing. Bloody hell, it was nearly the end of April, and I was really getting fed up with it – not least that it seemed it was the cold, rather than the damp which was really affecting my joints. I struggled to the party, but knew that there was only one outcome and that was that I'd be following Sarah to hospital.

Although I'd experienced visiting someone in hospital in Portugal, I hadn't been near a Polish one. Sarah had described what it had been like for her, and so it wasn't an experience I was looking forward to at all. One of the secretaries took me, and translated (thank God) and the first thing I needed was a blood test. Well, I am a huge baby about this and always work myself up into a complete state – I've even fainted before! Apparently I have very faint veins, so whenever I have had a blood test done, I end up with an arm that looks like that of a heroin user. I always bruise as well and resemble someone's punch bag. Nice! Being in Poland wasn't helping, and I worryingly looked round to make sure that the needle was a new one.

After the blood test it was a case of waiting for the results, although I knew exactly what the problem was. By this point I was beside myself. Because the toes of my left foot were so racked with pain every time I walked anywhere, I'd been walking badly which had put extra pressure on one hip - the pain then spread to my back, and going out for a pizza that evening, I could barely reach out to eat or drink. I was thoroughly miserable, went home, burst into tears and spent the beginning of the following week off work. On the Wednesday I went to a local clinic, which the school had, amazingly, managed to get an appointment at for me, and with the blood tests back and the arthritis confirmed, I was given a much needed shot of steroids.

The following day was May 1st and a public holiday, and we also had the 2nd off which meant we had a four day weekend. Although I still felt terrible there was no way I was staying at home on my own for four days, and so when a couple of friends said they were going to Krakow I went too. It happened to coincide with Labour gaining power in the UK for the first time in years, and amongst the English teachers there was a bit of a party atmosphere. We hooked up with some local teachers, were offered sofas for the night, so decided to stay and party. Well, they partied and I watched. Absolutely no dancing for me. Getting to sleep on someone's sofa wasn't any good for my poor joints, but despite that it had been fun.

During the following week the weather suddenly changed, and from the snow of a couple of weeks previously we were able to sit outside in the sun. It was also the day Sarah was due back, and Rob and I had arranged to meet her at the station. There was no way I wasn't going to be there so I slowly hobbled after Rob. The treatment Sarah had received was a success, and although she needed to be on medication for some time, and there was a doubt about her long-term fertility, she was well, and had wanted to return to Poland for the remainder of term. It was great to have her back, and we duly celebrated that weekend, not least that it was Sarah's birthday on the Monday.

With another shot of steroids, this time into my foot itself, I also began to feel better, and with the warmer weather we were all much happier. What's more, the long waited bar at school finally opened. It had supposedly been almost ready for months, and then, towards the end of our contract was opened. It was located in the basement (as all Polish bars seemed to be) of the school and very originally called 'The Shakespeare Bar'. The *pièce de resistance* was a garish picture of the Bard, with various lights on it. The students, however, loved it, and probably thought that all British bars were similar. What we liked about it, was that it was even nearer than our local, and that it sold Guinness and Czech Budwar.

The end of our contracts were rapidly coming to and end, and before we knew it, it was the beginning of June and we only had a month left. Although the school had offered me the position of Assistant Director of Studies, which was a step in the right direction career wise, it just wasn't in the right direction location wise. I'd decided that I really needed to be somewhere warm for my poor joints, and although had spent the year drinking and partying as though I was a student, was missing the lifestyle of Portugal.

Being an examiner for the Cambridge oral exams meant that I spent two of the final weekends working in Katowice which wasn't the ideal place to be. One of the evenings I went to the hen party of a Polish girl who was marrying one of the English teachers. It was held in someone's flat, with hardly any booze and was the most sedate hen night I have ever been to – very strange!

Krakow was calling for a final visit, so Sarah and I decided to go early one Saturday morning, with me then getting an afternoon train to Katowice for yet more examining. Those mornings was my first, and thankfully, last scrape with the local transport police. Jumping on the local bus to get to the bus station at the horrible time of eight o'clock on a Saturday morning, I didn't bother stamping my ticket in the machine. Very naughty I know – but hey, we've all done it, and it's very tempting. Big mistake. Out of nowhere, two, incredibly butch and scary female shot putters, masquerading as transport cops, got on the bus to check peoples' tickets. What could I do? In my purse I had half a dozen unstamped tickets and thinking it would show that at least I had bought some tickets, and that I could pretend I couldn't find the stamped one, that there wouldn't be a problem. Oh no! Obviously the language caused the first problem – I showed them the tickets, looked for the 'stamped' one, acted like a stupid tourist, which didn't work when they asked for identification and my passport clearly showed I had a work permit. They told me I had to go to the police station with them – no way, I'd miss the bus to Krakow and that would be it. By then some of the other passengers had joined in, and apparently decided that even if I hadn't bothered to stamp a ticket that they were on my side, and that it wasn't worth carting me off for. After much discussion, the policewomen agreed and said I'd have to pay a fine. OK – I deserved it. As I reached for my wallet, one of the women grabbed the rest of my tickets, and very angrily stamped all of them as a punishment. A lucky escape. There is definitely a moral there!

The final day in Krakow with Sarah was lovely. We revisited favourite places, enjoying the city in the sun and warmth but the day went passed far too quickly and then I was catching yet another snail train. And that was it virtually. The last week of term was a write-off teaching wise. We went out with our respective groups of students, drank way too much, and partied very hard. On the last day we saw Rob and Sarah (who had been an item for a couple of months but where now just friends) off at the train station, as they were taking the train to Italy for a holiday, and then in the afternoon the rest of us flew home. We were nearly all over weight (luggage wise, although most had piled on the pounds with all the lard and vodka) but the LOT check-in attendants were sympathetic and no one had to pay any excess. Can't imagine that happening with BA. We landed in Gatwick, somewhat soberer than at Christmas, there were lots of goodbyes, and that was another foreign stage in my life finished.

There were times when I had wondered what on earth I was doing in Poland, especially when I'd been in such pain, when it was so cold and grey and when I had to eat the scary, greasy, sausage soup which my sweet landlady gave me each Sunday. On the whole, though, it had been a wonderful experience - I had had some great classes, made some good friends, enjoyed getting to know the lovely Polish people and visited some amazing places.

Dodgy quotes collected from Poland

(mostly alcohol induced)

I wasn't born for straight curves and flat! (I was born to be curvaceous)

Thumbs up to the space models (Whilst discussing diets, actually meant fingers to the super models)

I don't smoke Russian vodka!

I've spilt my biscuit

He's my shite in knighting armour

I'm not remotely Sarah (apparently she meant 'sober')

The queue for the toilet was busy

I used to have a big minge (apparently she used to whinge a lot)

I thought it was going to be solid (after stepping in a puddle)

The world is nigh!

I'm pacing my nibbles

Part Nine

Port in Portugal

Chapter 31

Getting there

The sun was beating down, and I was enjoying yet another cold, Portuguese beer in the old square in Guimarães. It was heaven – the only problem was that I was only there on holiday. I'd spent a lot of time during the previous three weeks seeing if there were any jobs in Portugal – although there were teaching positions there were very few management ones, and this was what I wanted. I'd already decided to have a holiday though, and it looked as though I'd be job searching in situ - in fact I'd booked the holiday the day after returning from Poland. Having heard so much about Portugal, Sarah had decided to join me.

As well as being back, amongst friends, and showing Sarah my favourite places, it was a break from the three weeks of running around in the UK. As well as job searching, one of my friends, Amanda, was getting married and as chief bridesmaid I was very involved. The three previous weekends had consisted of the hen party, the registry office formality, and then the lovely blessing ceremony at the beautiful abbey in Milton Abbas in Dorset. As bridesmaid, it was the next best thing to being the bride, and as well as being fussed over, my glass was continually being filled up.

I had just over two weeks in Portugal, and was so relaxed

and content I'd almost forgotten about the fact that I still didn't have a job. And then, out of the blue, one of the new teachers in Guimarães said that her mother had noticed an advert in the Guardian for a Director of Studies at a language school in Porto. I phoned them up, said I was in Portugal, and was asked to go for an interview. So, on the way back to the airport I stopped off in the centre of Porto for a job interview. What's more, I got it! It was to start at the beginning of September, which meant that I had a month in the UK to catch up with family and friends. I also managed a trip down to Cardiff. I had finally managed to collect all my stuff (just to ship it all back!) so this was just a social visit. I stayed with Simon, and on the second evening we had a big Portuguese reunion. Guy and Ros, and their children were already in Cardiff for the summer, and it was the first time I'd seem them for over a year. Clare and Russ had come to the UK for a holiday the day before I left their house in Portugal so I'd only just seen them, but we had arranged for them to come to Wales for all of us to meet up. Needless to say, there was lots of catching up, eating of good food, beer drinking, and we finished off by doing some serious damage to a few bottles of port. Saying goodbye was no trauma at all, for a change, as I knew that I'd only be an hour away from them within a couple of weeks.

Chapter 32

Porto

I flew to Portugal on the 29th August, full of optimism for the future. It was slightly strange, though, not continuing on to Guimarães, but instead remaining in Porto. I stayed with my new boss and his family for the first couple of days whilst I looked for a flat – it was there that I woke up on the Sunday morning to find that the Portuguese news was broadcasting something about Diana, Princess of Wales. Despite not being a royalist I reacted in a way I imagine was very similar to many other people – a mixture of complete disbelief and sadness. It was a strange beginning to my second sojourn in Portugal, and the following week it was all everyone talked about.

On a happier note I soon found a flat in an area of Porto called Boavista, very close to the centre. Being a rented property in Portugal there was nothing in it at all; no bed, washing machine or even a teaspoon. I had expected this though, and close by found a local shop, which sold a mug, spoon and saucepan so I could have a cup of tea. My landlady appeared soon after with a new double bed, and a table and chairs. The lack of anything was counteracted by the fact that it was a lovely flat, with a wooden floor throughout, marble surfaces in the kitchen and bathroom, and the crowning glory, a large balcony. It instantly felt right, and, must have been as I lived there for five years.

Talking to my boss the first week he mentioned the new teachers who would be arriving the following week.

"…. and the final teacher is Adrian," he said.

"Where's he from? I asked.

"Stoke on Trent," Steve asked.

"What?" I spluttered. "Is his surname Smith?"

"Err, yes. Why?"

Why? It was Adrian from Guimarães – who I shared a flat with, who got hopelessly pissed, brought in cups of tea in the middle of the night because he wanted to chat, and left trails of blood in the kitchen. I couldn't believe it. From not knowing anyone in Porto, I was going to be working with an old sparring partner – but hang on, that meant that I was going to be his boss. How on earth was Adey going to cope with that? That evening I phoned up Clare and Russ to make them guess who was going to be working with me. They had no idea, and when I finally told them Russ thought it was the most hysterical thing he had heard for ages. So, when Adey arrived the following week, and was told he'd soon meet the Director if Studies for induction, it was me he was introduced to! His face was a complete picture.

I quickly settled into life and being back in Portugal. I had Adrian around for cinema visits, and bar crawling. I had made a new friend called Jen who was Australian, and spent various weekends in Guimarães. It seemed that friends back in the UK also wanted to make the most of my returning. Now single, Lisa came back to Portugal for a visit at the end of October. Having suffered from the most terrible weather when she'd visited four and a half years earlier, the sun came out and it was warm and bright. Everything was going swimmingly. We had a lovely weekend, wandering around in the sun, meeting up with Jen for dinner at the new Mexican restaurant, then on the Sunday walking along the seafront in lovely Foz. And then, when I got back from work on the Tuesday I discovered Lisa in bed. She had eaten something which didn't agree with her and spent the rest of the week in bed. What a disaster!

More successful were other visits. Friend Rob, who I'd met in Poland, was now living in Viseu, a town east of Porto. He came to stay one weekend with some other teachers. We had a great time, and partied one Saturday from lunchtime to the following morning – the downside was one of the biggest hangovers I have ever had! Normally I could have curled up on the sofa and not ventured out – it wasn't the current houseguest who was the problem as Rob was feeling as bad as I was – but I had another one on the way. On the Sunday evening, Stuart, an old school friend's husband arrived. He had been working in Lisbon, and since I hadn't seen either him or Isabel for years he decided to come up to Porto for a couple of days. I'm sure I wasn't the best company the first evening, but did at least manage to take Stuart to the popular haunts the following one.

Porto was still proving popular and the following weekend I had yet more visitors – this time in the form of Amanda and Clive. After all the running round they'd done that summer with the wedding preparations, it was good to be able to relax together. Although Amanda had been to Porto with me before, it was Clive's first time, and we both enjoyed being tourist guides. And then, finally, it was my turn to get away. It was only to Guimarães to stay with Clare and Russ, but it was very jolly as I took Rob with me as well. As well as wanting to see another town, it also gave him the opportunity to see the mad Pinheiro night – that of the bulls pulling an immense fir tree through the town. The somewhat bedraggled tree was then erected in the centre, as a phallic symbol of new life, and then we all staggered home, having stopped off in way too many cafés as we followed the tree round!

Throughout December and over Christmas back in the UK, life was all I could hope for. I'd seen old friends, and had a drunken New Year's Eve with Sarah and Anna, my friends from Poland. I'd made some new friends in Porto and was enjoying the social life. Unfortunately, all was not well at work – although the actual job was what I thought it would be, it was what was going on underneath the apparently friendly surface that was causing the problem. Not really wanting to waste time writing about it, it's enough to say that I believe there was malice around. I realised that I couldn't stay, but felt that I had to see the academic year out, so hung on to July. It wasn't just me, as Adrian and the other new teachers all felt the same.

It wasn't all doom and gloom though. I spent a few weekends visiting Rob in Viseu, a small town fairly close to the only mountain range in Portugal. The town wasn't that inspiring in itself but what it did have was the biggest nightclub in Portugal, housing various rooms for different styles of music. It was about seven thirty one Saturday morning as we emerged into the dazzling light after an all nighter, and fell into a local café for breakfast. It was warm, and as well as being packed full of bleary eyed clubbers, also had lots of hunters with guns slung over their shoulders, drinking strong coffee and the local hooch to fortify themselves against the cold. A very bizarre breakfast experience it was. We decided that being such a beautiful day we shouldn't waste it, so grabbed a few hours sleep, and then, despite the hangovers piled into one of the teacher's cars to drive up to the *Serra de Estrela*.

It was a lovely drive up the mountain roads and passed the small rural town of Guarda, after which we suddenly came to a plateau where the moisture in the air was crystallising and making everything sparkle. It was the most beautiful sight, especially set against the blue of the sky. Having felt serene for a while we decided to brave the cold, and along with many other people tobogganed down a slope on bin bags. The hangovers were all gone, which set us up for some more all night dancing!

As well as weekends away, I was sort of seeing a teacher from the British Council, and we had a new teacher start at school, Adam, who turned out to be a really good friend. The only thing I really had to sort out was work. I knew I had to leave, but desperately wanted to stay in Porto. The problem was that management jobs were hard to come by, and I knew it was going to be a slog. Obviously the gods were smiling on me – I met my future boss whilst doing some examining. He owned a school in the centre of Porto but told me there were no vacancies as he did the academic management. However, the school was due to move to new, shortly to be modernised premises, and Alex said it was always worth me popping in to see him. Although I didn't want to work as a teacher, there didn't seem to be any harm. Showing me round the premises which were to be done up, and with me being enthused by the whole project, I think the enormity of it sunk in for him. Alex asked me back for a second more formal interview, and starting talking about me having a management role. When I saw him for the third meeting he'd offered me the job of School Manager, to start in the September. Yippee.

The thought that I had a job sorted out made the time left at my current school bearable, and I made the most of summer in Porto. There was so much more on offer than there had been in Guimarães – lots of festivals, concerts, a much better selection of bars and restaurants, and almost best of all, the sea. I did have to drag myself away from it all for a while, and once I finished work at the 'E' place as it became known afterwards (E for the name of the school, and more fittingly 'evil') returned to the UK for a couple of weeks. Apart from seeing friends, the most important thing I had to do was sort out the remaining belongings that I had at Mum's. After two years she'd decided to sell the house – it was too big for her on her own, and I think the memories of Dad were still too painful. Although I supported her fully in this decision it was a really sad day when I left the house for the last time to fly back to Portugal, as it had been my childhood house since I was six.

Being back in Portugal, and starting a new job was the best way to banish any blues. The day I started was also the day that we moved school to the now finished premises around the corner. Bedlam is the only word that can really describe that first day. The positive side of being seriously thrown in at the deep end was that the position I held (loftily called School Manager) had been created for me, and being in a completely new building meant that the job was there for me to mould.

A routine was quickly established, and although working hard I easily grew into the job, had a great boss and some good teachers. There was lots of time to go out and party, I had lots of partners in crime and although I didn't manage to do much travelling, or visit new places it didn't really matter. Life was good. It continued this way into 1999, when I had various visitors, which meant that there were many excuses to frequent all my favourite haunts, and drink lots of port. I even managed a few concerts, ranging from a production of Don Giovanni to Deep Purple! The biggest change to this easy routine came in October when I had two new additions to my household, in the form of two five-week-old kittens.

I'd spent ages deliberating about getting a cat – especially because Portugal didn't really have catteries as we know them, and it meant finding someone to look after them when I went away. Going to see some kittens that a friend's landlady had, and the decision was completely taken out of my hands. I fell in love, instantly, with a little ginger kitten and her tabby sister, and a few weeks later took them home. The first test came at Christmas, when my cleaning lady said she would go in and feed them for some of the time I was away, and my boss, also a cat person, volunteered to cover the other days. When I returned on the 30th they were alive and well, although they'd managed to get into every cupboard in the flat, and cause chaos!

I'd decided to come back to Portugal for the celebrations of the new millennium. The thought of being in the UK in some ticketed pub, and struggling to get a drink and then get home, or having a quiet drink at someone's house didn't really appeal. Then the perfect solution appeared. My Australian friend, Jen, whose partner ran the very civilised and modern youth hostel overlooking the sea in Foz, decided to have a dinner party. We started early, and celebrated midnight in Australia in the middle of the afternoon and continued from there. There was no battle for the bar as the booze was in the kitchen, which was great. Later in the evening we wandered up onto the roof to watch a variety of fireworks being let off over the water and at some unearthly hour in the morning only had to walk up the corridor to stay in one of the hostel bedrooms. The worst thing, obviously, was the following day. It was a beautifully bright, sunny day, and I decided to take the old, rickety tram home. It ran alongside the sea, (with the fresh air seeming to do the trick), before it turned into the majestic Avenida da Boavista and headed towards home. Away from the sea air, with the stop start motion of the tram and that was enough for the full extent of the previous day to kick in. I am embarrassed to say that

I didn't make it home, got off the tram and threw up in the gutter. I spent the rest of the first day of the new millennium, with my shutters closed, blocking out the beautiful sunlight, lying in bed!

Chapter 33

The New Millennium

Christenings are normally fairly routine occasions – a baby shouting because it's had water thrown all over it, and a rather dodgy buffet. Not the one I went to a couple of days into the New Year. It was for Hugo, Jen and Pedro's new baby. Fortunately the surroundings were somewhat more auspicious then the hospital where Hugo had been born, which was privately run by nuns, and didn't seem to have any medical equipment in evidence when I visited.

The ceremony was conducted in a beautiful little chapel near the sea in Foz. The best part was the lunch. It was held in a private dining room in the gardens of Taylor's Port Lodge, and overlooking the river Douro. There were peacocks strutting around outside, and a few waiters doing the same inside. Course after course arrived; each accompanied with a different wine, with the meal rounded off by a huge platter of cheese and the ubiquitous port. Some four hours after we'd started, we trooped out into the dark, starry evening, having celebrated Hugo's Christening in a way that he would never remember!

The start of the new Millennium continued well with lots of going out and partying. We'd also had some interesting students at school in the form of two employees of FC Porto.

When they'd first started Alex (my boss) and I decided that we would take turns teaching them, despite their class being at 8.30 on a Friday morning. Over the months I learnt more about football and really enjoyed teaching the pair of them – one was the PR guy and the other the scout. That March, FC Porto were in the Champion's League and we were offered free tickets. We went to a fair few matches, a memorable one being the draw against Liverpool. As usual I had gone to the special ticket office before the match and Anteiro (the PR guy) handed me the half dozen tickets he'd promised. They weren't exactly what I was expecting though!

"These tickets are for Liverpool supporters," I wailed to Anteiro.

"Yes" he agreed, "I thought it was best as Alex's friends from England are Liverpool

supporters."

"Oh", I answered," and what about us, I've got my Porto Mac on!"

"Maybe that will have to come off" he helpfully suggested.

It was therefore with much trepidation that we queued up, not going in the familiar entrance but being herded into the away fan stand. It all seemed fairly good humoured and there was no apparent lout element. However, how would the Liverpool supporters feel when they had the opposition in their midst. I have never been able to sit down quietly when watching any kind of sporting event, and watching a crucial tie live was going to be virtually impossible. One of Alex's friends had the seat directly behind me and whenever Porto got anywhere near the goal he grabbed me sharply by the scruff of my jacket to keep me down. The pretence vanished at halftime though, when we heard friends shouting hello from the Porto family area which was next door, and went over to talk to them. The second half passed uneventfully, both on and off the field, and having waited for the Porto fans to leave we then filed out. We were directed up a narrow lane towards the main road where the Liverpool supporter coaches were ready to take them back to the airport or their hotels. We really didn't want to go to the airport with a coach load of Liverpool supporters so spoke to the security guards to let us sneak underneath the railing so we could go a get a local bus back into the centre. The guy we spoke to was completely thrown as to why we were speaking Portuguese, and in the middle of the Liverpool supporters. After explaining what had happened, and with some suspicious Liverpool supporters wondering what on earth we were doing, we were finally allowed under the barrier!

At the beginning of March, Mum came out for the Carnaval holiday, and as a surprise for her 60th birthday, I took her to Santiago de Compostella. Although I'd been there many times, it was somewhere she'd long wanted to go to, so having been up to see Clare in Guimarães for a late breakfast, instead of turning south at the motorway junction, we turned north towards Spain. Mum figured it out fairly quickly, but it didn't spoil the surprise and we had a great couple of days.

Spring was well on the way and full of all things new. I was lucky enough to see Travis in concert. Unluckily for them, no-one in Porto seemed to have heard of them apart from a handful of ex-pats, and despite all the noise we made and jumping up and down in front of the stage, there was no hiding the fact that there were only about a hundred people in the audience! Also, at a St Patrick's Day Party at Sam and Mark's, friends I'd made at New Year, I hooked up with rather a yummy half Dutchman who entertained me into the summer.

Along with the summer came Euro 2000. Yippee! Another

opportunity to hang out with friends in bars, all screaming for a different country. And we did a lot of that. We found a great bar with a huge screen, tucked away down a back street, which also did a free bottle of beer after the second one. For a few of the matches we went to Sam and Mark's as they were trying to get rid of their stock of booze before moving back to the UK. No mean feat I can tell you. One night when England played Romania we were doing a good job. Alex, my boss, had also come along, bringing with him a very pregnant Filipa. Many melon liqueurs later and everyone staggered home. The next morning I crawled into work, and discovered no Alex. A couple of house later I had a phone call from him - very sore headed, but ecstatic as he'd just become a father! In the early hours Filipa had woken him up, and was driven very slowly to the hospital.

We watched the final between France and Italy in the above mentioned bar, with just about every European nationality sitting side by side. Steph, my French friend, had her face painted in the colours of the French flag, and I of course was more than happy to support France. On the next table to ours were three Italian guys, who amazed us when France won, by buying us all a beer! Why can't it always be like that?

More fun was had at cocktail parties held on the naval ships which were docked in nearby Matosinhos, before returning to the UK. Because the school also taught Portuguese as a foreign language for diplomats, naval personnel etc, we got to know a fair few, and in return we'd get invited to parties. They were great – endless posh canapés which were served along with buckets of booze. And then when the formal part of the evening was over we'd sometimes be invited down to the officers mess, and carry on there, or go a find a bar or club in Porto. I won't go into the details, needless to say there were lots of antics, and kissing sailor jokes in the week after a party.

By now, summer was into its stride, and there were lots of parties, barbecues and other gatherings. None of this could match the madness of St João at the end of June. The festival was held every year to celebrate the patron saint of Porto, and basically, every inhabitant of the city turned out and crammed into the narrow streets. People congregated in the main square, where there was a stage with live music, and then towards midnight shoved their way toward the river to see the fireworks. After a few years of this, I realised there was no point as you could see the fireworks from further back, and get into the bars for a drink. What made fighting your way through the crowds in search of a beer even more difficult was the mad head banging that went on. Not the rock variety, but literally, using a plastic hammer or a long stem of garlic with a purple flower at the end, and smashing every person who walked passed you over the head. Completely bonkers, and something I can't imagine that could ever happen in the UK.

Unfortunately, some things come to an end, and in the line of work I was in, it meant that people did tend to move on. The first departure was that of Jen and Pedro, and baby Hugo. After lots of soul searching, and form filling in, they decided to move to Australia. That was home for Jen, but emigration for Pedro, and for me loosing two really special friends. I told them I'd come out to see them at some point in the future, but saying goodbye had to wonder whether I'd ever see them all again. Shortly after that Thomas left for London and whilst it had been fun going out him, it wasn't the end of the world for either of us. After a few further weeks of summer partying, friends Sam and Mark left. They left on a high after we spent their last day visiting port houses in the morning and downing as much port as we possibly could in the afternoon - and found time to squeeze in a lovely *Cataplana* (a dish of pork and clams in a spicy tomato sauce) for lunch in a local restaurant near the river. The next morning was somewhat chaotic, and in a huge rush we squeezed them and their enormous suitcases into my little Corsa and I took them to the airport. Despite all the football parties they still had some booze left, so I luckily inherited a nice little bar.

Two weeks later, and at the start of August, it was me leaving Porto. It was only for a few weeks, and the main reason was that Lisa, my oldest friend was getting married. Obviously I had to be there. But before that, was the thunderbolt that had made me realise I had to live in France, when I was in that small café in St Malo with Steph. The day after I arrived in the UK was when I took the fateful overnight ferry to France. It was great being back in France, and spending time with Steph and her family. We wandered round markets, lazed around in the boiling sunshine and ate gorgeous food. I had yet another treat in store, in the form of an overnight stay in St Malo. I had an eight am ferry to catch, and as Steph couldn't take me as she was leaving for Brittany the day before, I got a train up the previous afternoon. I spent the evening walking round the town, had *moules frites* for supper and spent the night in a hotel perched on the top end of the town overlooking the sea. I knew then that the thunderbolt had been real, and that at some time I would indeed move to France.

But before that there were many other things to enjoy, and two years to fill! Firstly, were Lisa and Ed's two wedding celebrations (one at the registry office, the other a traditional church blessing) and after an emotional service an extremely drunken evening followed. Soon after that it was back to Portugal, and another academic year to sort out. Work distracted me for a while, but then the reality of being back there and not having two close sets of friends, and Thomas being in Lisbon, really dragged me down - at least I still had Steph and Adam in Porto for regular nights out. On the recommendation of a friend I did something I'd never done before and went to visit a fortune teller in the November - not someone at a fair but a respected lady who rented a room at a local health shop. Although rather sceptical I really needed some help from elsewhere. I was struggling with feelings I had for two men. One was a friend in the UK, Will, who I spent time with every visit and always wondered 'what if?' The other was Adam, who had always been more than a friend as far as I was concerned; there had been some 'moments' and I had been in love with him for ages. The session lasted an hour and centred on Tarot cards, and also my birth date. What made it even more interesting was that the fortune teller was Brazilian, and although by then my Portuguese was good, I had always struggled with the Brazilian accent and use of different words. Anyway, she made complete sense, predicted various things that happened to me, and reassured me about my feelings and concerns about these two men in my life. Whatever anybody else might think she was amazing and I felt much more positive afterwards.

Chapter 34

A Swiss jaunt

In fact, one of the things that she'd predicted was that I'd go abroad, but that it was to do with work, and not just a trip back to the UK. Literally, the next day my boss asked me if I'd like to go to Switzerland the following February for a training session on our school's methodology. Would I like to go – what a silly question! The training course itself was interesting, but the journey there, and general travelling around much more note worthy. The Saturday before I'd over indulged slightly, and instead of walking down some steps into a favourite club down by the river, I managed to fall down, and land on my ankle. It hurt so much I howled like a baby, got a taxi home, gulped down some paracetemols and passed out. Unfortunately I hadn't remembered about the bag of frozen peas. The following day I had an enormous ankle, but didn't really think I needed to do anything about it. The day after, I hobbled on board a plane for Switzerland, and by the time I had changed planes twice, once in Lisbon and then again in Basle to board a scary propeller plane, I could hardly walk. What made it worse was that on the second day it snowed, and then became icy, and I was skidding around little a baby giraffe. To top it all, the girl who did the training with whom I'd become friendly was spending the Saturday skiing. Because I couldn't get a flight back until the Sunday, I could have gone with her. Instead I hobbled around Berne for the day on my own, bemoaning my lack of skiing, but fortunately meeting up in the evening for some good old après ski. Returning to Porto, and now with a bruise from my toes right up to my knee (and that's no exaggeration) I realised that I needed to have it looked at. Unfortunately, that meant a visit to a Portuguese hospital. It had been bad enough visiting people, but actually having to go to casualty was a completely different ball game.

People think that they have it bad in the UK. Trust me; with regards to Europe you haven't seen anything until you've visited a Portuguese casualty department. It was supposedly a new part of the hospital, but despite the fact that the building was new, nothing else was. Before I could get anywhere near a doctor I had to fill in two different forms, in different places, and was only then ushered to the waiting area. This all took ages, not helped by the fact I had obviously banged my head as well, and kept forgetting how to say 'I'd sprained my ankle' in Portuguese. Hours later, surrounded by people who were obviously very unwell, lying around on trolleys in the corridor, I was still waiting, and convinced that people who had arrived later than me were being seen to first, I started to make a fuss. Hey presto, it worked. Before long I saw the specialist, who was horrified by the extent of my bruising, and even more when I told him I'd been hobbling around for a week. I was wheeled off to x-ray, which was the easy part, and then had another endless wait. The outcome was that nothing was broken, but I had pulled all the ligaments really badly. Apparently this was worse, and I would probably always have a weakened ankle. You're not kidding. Two years later, I fell off my heels at my brother's wedding, and did it all again! It still aches regularly, is always slightly swollen and I'll never be able to sit in the lotus position at yoga. That's the demon drink for you!

Memories of the snow in Switzerland faded more quickly than the pain of my ankle, and before long it was spring again in Porto. There were various action packed weekends, including a joint party I had with friend Charlie on a beautiful May Sunday, a lovely trip up the river Douro where the port grapes come from, with Adam, and what turned out to be my last consulate party. Over the years I'd been to various parties there to celebrate Queenie's birthday. They always started off in a very civilised manner, with canapés being passed round and toasts made. And, they always finished in the same way with most people getting trashed on the free booze, falling over, embarrassing themselves, throwing up, etc, etc. This was one was no exception.

Some places not yet visited & on the list

India (for the food)

~

Barcelona

~

St. Petersburg (for the art)

~

Thailand

~

Rome

~

Nice (for the Matisse museum)

~

Cape Town

~

Jordan (for Petra)

Part Ten

The digging finally paid off!

Chapter 35

A long way

Everyone's got their own stories about Australia, be it the spectacular scenery or the beautiful cities, but how many people can say that on their first day there, jet lagged and a little pissed after a lunchtime drink, that they have met a future Prime Minister? I can!

I'd been counting down the days for my month away, and it had finally arrived. I'd decided ages before that I was going to take the opportunity to visit Australia, as Jen and Pedro were now there. The day before I left I had a farewell dinner with Steph, and her family who were on holiday. It was Steph's last summer before leaving Portugal, and I had no idea when I would see her again. At least the thought of Australia made yet another friend's departure more bearable.

With the type of flight I'd booked I had a stop over each way. On the way back I'd opted to have a couple of days in Singapore, but on the way there went for one in the slightly less glamorous UK. Not your usual stopover, but it meant that I had three nights to catch up with Mum and friends.

My flight to Australia was a night one and I turned up at Heathrow, at what I thought was particularly early to check in. I'd always left this part of travelling to the last minute, and felt I was making a special effort this time so I could get a good seat. Obviously my two hours beforehand wasn't anywhere near enough, and most people had already checked in. I pulled out the stops, and truthfully told the check-in guy that I had problems with my joints and back and that I needed somewhere to sit where I could stretch out, and not have to keep moving for people to get out. After a few calls he told me he'd got me a seat he thought I'd be happy with. Indeed he was right; I was at the back of the plane, with only one seat next to me and space between me and the window to spread out. What a star!

Having secured a good seat, the next battle was trying to sleep. Other people seem able just to shut their eyes and that's it. Not me! I did have a plan of attack though. I'd avoided caffeine for most of the day, took two herbal sleeping tablets, downed a double whisky and choose the most boring looking film available. Obviously '*The Wedding Planner*' did the trick and I slept for six hours. I woke up to find most people were still fast asleep but the cabin crew were obviously used to the insomniacs and early risers, and provided orange juice and coffee. Some hours later and we arrived in Singapore where I had a four-hour stop over. I'd already done my homework on the Internet and found out about Changi airport. It was like a little town. My luggage had been checked all the way through at Heathrow so I didn't have to cart it around. I found the on-site hotel, and bought myself a ticket to use the roof top pool. Bloody hell! Talk about heat – I thought I'd walked into a sauna. The temperature was incredible but the pool was bliss. I paddled around surrounded by the landscaped garden watching the planes soaring overhead – all very surreal. There was even somewhere to have a shower, dry your hair and get changed. I felt like a new girl. This was helped by a beer in the poolside bar. Afterwards, I munched some samosas, checked my emails, did some window-shopping and even watched the BBC news in one of the many TV areas.

The next part of the flight was incredibly boring. I couldn't sleep at all, and we then had to disembark at Darwin, hang round in a small lounge for forty-five minutes and then get back on the same plane. I still don't know why! Taking off for the third time in twenty-four hours I felt that I was finally getting near Queensland. I really wasn't prepared for my first proper view of Australia though. We flew in over the Coral Sea as the sun was coming up, and the water was of the most intense turquoise colour I had ever seen. There soon appeared a thin line of white sand, and then dense forest. It was stunningly beautiful and I was completely lost in it. Not only was I flying over one UNESCO World Heritage Site, namely the Great Barrier Reef, but it was also the only place in world where two met; the other being Queensland's wet tropics, apparently containing the oldest surviving tracts of rainforest in the world – to be visited in a couple of days.

For the moment, though, I was finally coming in to land at Cairns airport. As usual, it took ages for my suitcase to come round, and then I had the wait to go through immigration. Not surprisingly, the Australians are very strict about who and what come into their country. I was obviously no exception. Having a new style computerised visa helped, but my passport being full of Eastern European pictures of trains was proving very interesting. When I finally persuaded them that I wasn't anyone apart from Rachael, it was only customs I had to persuade that my suitcase wasn't full of apples, sausages, or any other fresh food.

Chapter 36

Cairns

I finally escaped the customs men, and there, in the arrival's lounge were Jen, Pedro and a now walking Hugo. It was great to see them; if slightly bizarre as the last time it had been a year before and on the other side of the world in Portugal. There was also a really buzz at the airport, as the mayor (who Jen worked for) was on my flight – or should I say I was on his! Obviously he came through customs first, accompanied by the yet, unnamed famous person I was going to meet. The mayor was delighted that Jen had turned up to meet him; until she told him that in fact she was there to meet a friend.

Before long we were on the highway heading towards Jen and Pedro's house. They lived on the outskirts of Cairns in an area called Whitfield, in a largish bungalow surrounded by loads of space, and with the most fantastic backdrop to a garden I had ever seen - tropical plants and palms instead of a fence or wall. I was practically in the rain forest! A sun lounger in the garden was pleading with me so I made a beeline for it. Jen, however, had other ideas. Quite rightly she told me that the best way to beat jet lag was to stay awake and try to adjust immediately to the new time zone. This was made easier by Hugo, who despite only being two and obviously not really remembering me, recognised an adult who was willing to play games and mess around. I'd have been quite happy just chilling out there for the day, but Jen and Pedro were having none of it. After all, what should you do on your first day in Australia, if not go out for a lovely lunch, washed down with some chilled white wine, overlooking the water? So now I was jet lagged and somewhat merry. Yippee!

After lunch we went over to the council headquarters where Jen worked. There was an important reception and the mayor really wanted her there to check that all the arrangements went smoothly. Nobody seemed bothered that Pedro and I were there, and as a reward for rearranging some chairs, we then joined the reception and had yet more wine. Pedro was ridiculously excited about the guest of honour and I soon realised why. It was Xanana Gusmão. Perhaps his name isn't that well known, but for anyone who knows and cares about East Timor he is a god. As a former Portuguese colony, and then province of Indonesia, the Timorese people had tried for years to overthrow the illegal occupation of their country. It was Gusmão, a poet and rebel leader, who for fourteen years had led the resistance, until he was captured and imprisoned in 1992, who changed all this. He remained in prison for seven years, when, a year after the then Indonesian president had been forced to resign because of social unrest and chaos in the economy, he was granted early release. He was taken into UN custody and to the British Embassy. Eight months later and he was finally able to return to East Timor as a hero. The following year, in 2000, he devoted himself to guiding the country to unity, and two years later in April 2002 was elected president.

And here he was, in front of me, being introduced to Pedro and myself. I don't suppose that we'd have been able to get that close if it had been nine months later and he was

President, but then he stopped and wanted to chat. He was interested as to why Pedro was so far from home, asked me about why I was living in Portugal, and even congratulated me on my Portuguese. As we stood there chatting away in his and Pedro's mother tongue, you could see all the VIP guests wondering what was so special about us that he had picked us out!

After all this excitement we dropped Pedro off at work, picked Hugo up from nursery, and went home. The three of us sat outside on the terrace enjoying the last of the sun, and sipped a glass of wine – well Hugo had juice! I'd always imagined doing this in Australia, but somehow imagined long, light evenings. What I couldn't believe was that it suddenly started to get dark at six o'clock, the mosquitoes appeared on mass, and Jen rushed us all inside. Despite a myriad of anti-midge candles, and other devices, the mosquitoes were very persistent, and not easily deterred. Now that it was dark, my jet lag was really taking its toll, although it was only half six. Jen tempted me to stay awake by announcing she was going to get a takeaway Thai curry. I couldn't argue against that. There were no Thai restaurants in Portugal, let alone a takeaway just around the corner. The food was excellent, not expensive, and fully contented, at eight thirty, I crawled into the spare bed in Hugo's room.

I was rudely awakened by what sounded like the inhabitants of a zoo having a party on the roof of the bedroom. They were the oddest sounds. Since everybody else was fast asleep I could only presume that all this was normal. I did have to check in the morning though.

"Jen" I asked the following morning, "I think I heard tigers last night!" Obviously I knew full well it couldn't have been. "Oh, that's just the possums scampering around, and the birds you could hear were kookaburras." That was all right then.

That morning we went to the annual Cairns show. There was all the usual crap you expect at fairs, but it was Australian crap and Hugo and I loved it. There were also lots of interesting stalls, indigenous animals and delicious food outlets. It was incredibly hot though, so we escaped early afternoon and I then had my first experience of the sea. We went to a local beach, Holloway's, which was deserted apart from us. There was just a narrow strip of white sand which was shaded by palm trees; we wandered slowly up, kicking the football to Hugo from time to time. The view was amazing – simply miles of coastline and immense sea and then, just as it had the night before, the light disappeared.

The next day was Saturday, and although Jen had taken some holiday whilst I was there, she still needed to do her weekly 'boring' shop. Not at all boring for me. The supermarket was great and full of amazing food – lots of Asian stuff, little of which I could get in Portugal. Apart from that, the other interesting fact was that I kept seeing people doing their shopping barefoot. I'd have been worried about getting my toes run over!

Having chilled out at home for the afternoon, Jen and I then went to a cocktail party connected with her work. We drank loads of champagne and I tried to keep up with the names of all the people Jen introduced me to. Afterwards we were persuaded to go to a café in town where we drank red wine and I flirted with the waiter. Well, that's what you're supposed to do on holiday, isn't it?

Despite that fact that we were a little sore headed the following morning, Jen and I took Hugo (poor Pedro had to work) for a drive. We went north of Cairns along the Captain Cook Highway towards Yorkey's Knob (I don't know who came up with that name but it had me sniggering for ages) and it was on the side of the road that I saw my first bright yellow sign warning of kangaroos. Unfortunately

I didn't see any in the wild in Queensland; I would have to wait for that until I got to Victoria.

Jen and Pedro had lived for a short while in Yorkey's Knob when they'd first moved from Portugal and were still members of the yacht club. That meant that we were able to have Sunday lunch sitting outside, overlooking the beautiful water and deciding which boat to buy. Afterwards, we drove a bit further to Ellis beach where we sunbathed and swam. Jen told me about the box jellyfish season, from October to May when you couldn't go in the water at all, as a sting could be fatal! Good thing I had come on holiday in August then!

When we were all beached out we headed home, stopping on the way for some huge fresh prawns from a specialist shellfish shop, and some wine. Well, I have brought wine from a huge variety of places but never like this. I couldn't really see where we were going to park, and then it became clear. It was a drive thru! To buy booze! What a mad idea. Having had our booze passed through the car window we went home, had a glass of wine, some crisps and a dip (the food variety) on the terrace, and then retreated from the mosquitoes, to cook the prawns.

It was Monday, and I was going to get my first real taste of the rainforest. Both Pedro and Jen weren't working, Hugo wasn't in nursery, and we all set off for a day trip. We were going to take a trip to Kuranda which was up in the tablelands. We decided to get the train the whole way from Cairns and got on one to take us to the terminal – a normal journey for most, but made so different by the addition of a two-year who was so excited he could hardly talk. And this was just a normal train – little did he know what other delights there were in store. The next train we boarded was a rickety old thing which joined the plains to the tableland high above. These days it is purely a tourist attraction, but had been built for very different reasons. Back in 1882, the tin miners couldn't get supplies because of the bad weather and terrible road conditions, and a crisis was imminent. They demanded a way through, a new route was found, and nine years later in 1891 the railway was opened. I can hardly imagine what it must have been like trying to lay the track, surrounded by sheer drops, let alone dig the fifteen tunnels where laying track was impossible.

The journey up was spectacular. The train twisted through gorges and rainforest, and the views were amazing. The most incredible sight was seeing a waterfall cascading down, and this was in the dry season. I'm not sure that all parts of the journey are for the faint hearted though. The old train rattled for most of the way, and in one place crossed over a ravine on an even older wooden bridge which was perched on extremely long supports. We could hardly contain Hugo, who made it a little more exciting, as two-year olds do, by trying to lean through the open window, and giving everyone around heart failure! After about forty minutes we reached the top, and walked the short way to the local village. Obviously, it had become very touristy over the years because of all the visitors, but I wasn't bothered by any of it. There were interesting shops selling gorgeous opal and silver jewellery, and more delicious food stalls. Being organised, Jen and I had packed a picnic which we duly ate, washed down with some more delicious Australian wine.

As well as shops there were also attractions in the resort, including Birdworld, which was a superb aviary with nothing between you and the most spectacular-coloured birds. What was even better was that Jen knew the owners really well so it was all free. The highlights were the Mandarin Ducks, not exotic since they live in the UK, but always my favourite, and then something that looked as though it had come out of *Jurassic Park*. It was a cassowary. It was securely sectioned off from the other birds and was enormous, black and had the most evil looking claw on each front foot I had ever seen. If you come face to face with one in the wild, and it's in a bad mood then basically your time is up! Jen did tell me that when she was younger, and walking near the sea in the mangrove areas with friends that they did come across one. Fortunately it was a fairly happy cassowary, and they very slowly walked away, and lived to tell the tale.

Having come face to face with one of Australia's killers, and heard about the box jellyfish, I then wanted to hear about the other ones. There were the freshwater crocodiles that would bite your head off if given half the chance, the sharks that would have you for lunch and the spiders that might come up the toilet and bite you on the bum. As many know, Australia has the highest percentage of killers in the world and in Queensland there were more killers than anywhere else in the country. There were stonefish whose spikes could paralyse you if you trod on one, the Green Tree Snake whose bite was fatal, the blue-ringed octopus and the numb ray (who did exactly that). Oh bugger! Of course, as every non-tourist knows, you rarely see a spider or snake in the built up areas, but have to choose where you swim very carefully.

Anyway, we were now on our way to The Skyrail, the world's longest gondola cable car. The trip takes you over the canopy of the rainforest and is almost five miles long. Before I'd even thought about the huge variety of wildlife and plants that lived there, I was trying to figure out how a cable car could be suspended above something in that way. Apparently the tallest tower was forty metres, and they all had to be lifted into place by helicopter. Quite a feat of engineering, and each time Hugo, who was obviously far more interested in the cable car than the rainforest, asked how it worked, I was also hoping someone would be able to answer the question. Not being a scientist I don't really understand anything like that, and still wonder how on earth a piece of metal can transport people from continent to continent in the air.

Finally, I managed to concentrate on the matter at hand. As well as enjoying the stunning scenery, especially the waterfall, you could peer at the trees below and try and figure out which type they were. After a while the cable car headed towards a platform and we leapt off. From here there were three lookouts with views over the Barron River, Gorge and Falls, and inside, an excellent display of the flora and fauna. Having jumped back on, and after another ride the second stop was even more interesting. With a ranger you could actually walk some way through the rainforest, experiencing the dark, hot, wet atmosphere that it so typified. From here it was back onto the cable car, which suddenly dipped incredibly steeply, and began its descent to the terminal. A different world appeared in front of me with the coastal plain and beyond that the open expanse of the blue sea.

One of the good things about staying with friends when on holiday is that you can do normal things – you don't always feel you have to be rushing around being a tourist. For the following two days I just hung out, and it was great. I spent time in Cairns, and enjoyed mooching round, either on my own or with Jen. Cairns itself doesn't seem to get a good press in the guides, but for me it had a variety of cafés, restaurants and shops which I couldn't get in Portugal. It was all very new, and although gold had been discovered in 1876, it was only when The Barrier Reef itself was discovered that the tourists appeared and the town grew to accommodate them. One evening Jen's mum looked after Hugo, and Jen, Pedro and I went to the cinema. It seemed fitting that we saw *Moulin Rouge*, which was an Australian made film, and had partly been filmed there. Despite the freezing air conditioning, the film was excellent and afterwards we strolled down to the Esplanade, which was lined with palm and fig trees, and ate the most delicious fish overlooking the bay.

The following day Jen took me to a travel agent where she

knew someone, and I booked my round ticket to Melbourne, Sydney and back to Cairns. I practically had a heart attack at the cost, but there was no way I wasn't doing it, and what are credit cards for if not for maxing out? Having sorted that out Jen and I spent the afternoon doing errands and bought some food for supper. I cooked a tasty fish dish for the three of us and a friend of theirs; we drank loads of wine and fell into bed in the small hours. This was followed by a late start the next morning, so Jen and I took Hugo to the nearby Botanical Gardens for brunch. The little café was nested in amongst a variety of tropical trees, and was a haven of cool and calm. Feeing revived by food and a couple of glasses of wine we then managed to take Hugo for a wander around the gardens.

The next day we were back on the tourist trail, and I got to cuddle a real koala. Before that I had a run in with another creature – a mosquito. My leg swelled up quite horribly, Jen packed me off to the chemist who had a look and prescribed me something strong for it. Ouch – the desire to scratch was incredible. Although malaria isn't endemic, you apparently have to be careful with a bad bite, just in case it's something nasty.

Before going to 'Wild World' Jen and I did some good old girlie shopping at a local shopping centre. A department store was having a closing down sale and there were massive reductions. Jen brought most of the shop, and despite knowing that I was rapidly filling up any space I had in my case, couldn't resist some cut-price Clinique goodies. Having had our fun we then took Hugo for a promised Mickey D's drive thru' to sustain us for the zoo.

'Wild World' was well known as a rehabilitation centre and a successful breeding programme, and was designed so that people could get close to the animals –well, most of them. The first thing we came across were the koalas. It was amazing how cute they were; wedged into the forks of eucalyptus trees, high on eating the leaves, and spending most of their days sleeping. What a life!

I rarely get swayed by touristy things but decided that I too was going to pay to have a picture of me holding a koala. I just couldn't resist it! I wasn't really sure what to expect, but once I was cuddling one was completely smitten. The koala was much heavier then I'd expected, and had really powerful claws. He seemed very happy to be cuddled and Jen was able to take lots of pictures. Hugo wasn't so sure, and eyed the koala very suspiciously. He was much happy with the kangaroos, and the pair of us stood in the enclosure surrounded by them, being hassled for the bags of seeds we had bought. The best sight was of a tiny joey peeking his head out from his mother's pouch. Australia might do dangerous, but it also did extremely cute. Not quite so cut were the crocs though. Hugo and I were mesmerised by one, and he whispered to me.

"Is it real?" I honestly wasn't sure as it was so long and still. "I don't know, but I guess it must be." I replied. Suddenly it moved, and Hugo and I both jumped about a foot in the air, screeching.

The other highlight was the snake house. It was fascinating, especially realising that the large, brightly coloured, scary looking ones were harmless, but that the brown, innocuous ones were the baddies. I was glad they were on the other side of the glass.

That evening Jen and I went out to celebrate the birthday of a friend of hers. Having dropped off Hugo at Jen's sister, after a mad rush to get ready, we arrived at the hotel where people were meeting. Normally you think of hotel bars as being quiet, staid places. Not this one. It was six o'clock on a Friday evening, and the fight to get to the bar was just like being in a pub. Some glasses of wine later, we staggered down to the esplanade and stuffed ourselves full of pizza to soak up the booze. We bumped into one of Jen's ex's who tried to persuade us to go for another drink. Although up for it, duty called, as we had to pick Hugo up. Probably a good thing!

The next day was one of those days that you just feel is going to be special. Even now I have only to shut my eyes to be transported back, and remember all the sensations I felt. It was my first experience of an Australian Island. Not being a diver, and hating having water over my head, there was no point going to the Outer Reef. Jen had therefore told me about various island trips you could go on. Having dragged ourselves out of bed at a horrible time in the morning, we drove for forty-five minutes south of Cairns towards the Mulgrave River. The sun was just coming up and it was a spectacular morning. Pedro, unfortunately, had to work, so it was Jen and I and a very excited Hugo who arrived at the boat at seven thirty. We had got there first and were greeted by rather cute crew member who rushed around making hot tea for us.

Our destination was the Frankland Islands, which were a group of sand cays off the coast. We left at eight o'clock, and initially cruised down the Mulgrave River which was edged by mangrove swamps. Having seen a croc the day before in the zoo, we were hoping to catch a glimpse of a wild one but they were obviously still snoozing. It was a beautiful place, so quiet and still, with that chill to the air which you know, before long, will turn into a baking day. After a while the creek opened out, and in front us was the most amazing view of the open sea and islands in the distance, with white beaches either side of us. Thirty minutes later and we approached the islands which were surrounded by the most incredibly coloured water I had ever seen. It seemed to keep changing colour depending on the depth, and close to the beach was turquoise.

We precariously boarded a small launch and were deposited on the beach, wading through the lovely water. There were no jetties or anything manmade as the islands were protected and nothing permanent was allowed to be left there. Consequently, it was the most perfect natural place I have ever been to. Furthermore, only a certain number of people were allowed each day - on the day we were there, there can only have been about forty or so we were certainly privileged. This obviously came at a cost. In the brochure the list price was a hundred and forty Australian dollars. Ouch! Fortunately, as well as being involved in the SkyRail project before living in Portugal, Jen had also worked for Quicksilver tours, and still knew one of the owners, so we got the trip for free!

We dumped our stuff on the beautiful white sand, and I spent ages looking all around me at the fantastic scenery. In the distance all you could see were other islands and the hills of the coastline, not a car or building in site. The only thing I could hear was the sound of the water breaking over the coral, making the most exquisite tinkling noise, like a glass xylophone. I decided that despite the fact that I wasn't a natural water baby I couldn't resist what was in front of me. As the water was so calm and clear I didn't have any of my usual fears of waves or killer seaweed and paddled around for ages out of my depth. I worked up an appetite and before long lunch was served. There was a lovely barbecue, mountains of fresh prawns, and salad and fruit, and buckets of white wine. Delicious!

Whilst Jen and Hugo remained on the beach I decided I needed some exercise and joined the walk which had been arranged through the rainforest and out onto the other side of the island where there were rock pools and reef flats. The guide also happened to be the cute crew member who had given Jen and I early cups of tea that morning. We spotted one spider which everyone gave a wide berth, and apart from that saw lots of interesting sea creatures. I was fascinated by all of them, and enjoyed poking around. Having done his guided tour bit, said crew member, whose name was Brett, walked back with me slowly to the others and we amiably chatted about travelling and teaching. As everyone knows, a perfect place is also that bit more special if there is a sexy and interesting companion at your side.

Before leaving the island there was the opportunity to go on a glass bottomed boat tour, which I naturally jumped at. Although I'd been to the aquarium in Cairns, which, I have to say was excellent, there was nothing like looking at the sea life for real. I saw the most beautiful fish swimming around the coral – including parrotfish and angelfish, but the best site was seeing Manta rays; there were so graceful as they glided thorough the water. Unfortunately, I didn't spot any Maori rasse, the huge blue fish which I'd seen in the aquarium, but I guess you can't have everything. At the end of the afternoon we piled back onto the boat and were served with hot tea and chocolate as we watched the islands disappearing behind us. In the promotional brochure it comes up with the trite lines '….five hours in our natural paradise. You'll leave with memories that will last you a lifetime.' Well, they were right. It was a truly amazing day.

Luckily for me, the next day had yet more fantastic views. We drove an hour north of Cairns up the Captain Cook Highway towards Port Douglas. The road hugged the coastline and at one point where it climbed high up the cliff, there was a curve in the road with a look out point. What a place to be able to stop. The view over the bay was incredible. Shortly after we found a secluded beach where we stopped for a quick sunbathe and Sunday morning paddle. Continuing north we arrived in Port Douglas, and drove down a wide avenue lined with huge palm trees. Once a fishing village, the town had been turned into a tourist attraction, but it had been done very well. Apparently, even Bill Clinton had visited in 1996. There was a very laid back atmosphere and we made the most if it. After a wander around the town, full of little boutiques and interesting restaurants, we headed to the marina. I was so busy looking at the boats, and different restaurants I hadn't even realised that I was walking on the pier with water underneath. Of course as soon as I did I scampered to the edge, completely confusing Hugo who couldn't work what was going on. I have always had a head for heights, am not scared of spiders etc, but hate piers or bridges that have gaps so you can see the water below. After my narrow escape we headed for the excellently named Hog's Breath Restaurant. Having stuffed our faces we then went to where Jen's sister and husband were staying for the weekend in one of the landscaped, poolside apartments, and went for a swim. Talk about pure hedonism!

The next morning I had my baby-sitting hat on, as having had a week off, Jen had to go back to work. No disasters, and with Hugo duly deposited at nursery for the afternoon, Pedro dropped me off at the council building so I could have Jen's car for the afternoon. Bloody hell I'd forgotten what it was like driving an automatic and combined with driving on the left my brain was doing all manner of strange things. Good thing the roads were wide and there was little traffic, otherwise I'm sure I'd have been taking bus stops out! Having done all my tasks I then picked Jen up from work, and the pair of us prepared dinner. Her Dad, his infamous girlfriend (much younger, originally from The Philippines and hoping to stay in Australia), with her two young, naughty children were coming. They were guaranteed to get Jen going so swigging a few big glasses of wine before they arrived was necessary!

Since Jen and Pedro both had to work for the rest of the week, I took up an offer of spending a few days on one of the islands. Jen's sister Jackie also had a friend staying, and although British, had been living in New Zealand for ages. We'd met a few times over the previous few days, and I could tell she'd be an easy person to be with. At the crack of dawn the following morning I crawled out of bed, and Jen very kindly dropped me off at the ferry terminal. We were heading to Fitzroy Island, which was a continental island, and had a low-key, inexpensive resort. It was a large island and there were few people, so the ideal opportunity to do absolutely nothing for a bit. Although I'd been having a completely brilliant time, it had been really busy, and knowing that I was heading off to Melbourne in a few days with everything a big city had, I was glad to be able to do nothing for a while.

Helena and I spent the morning sunbathing and swimming. Unlike on the Frankland Islands, where although I'd seen fish, hadn't had them swimming around me, there were brightly coloured fish everywhere. I was particularly struck by the black and white stripped, sergeant majors. All that swimming and an early start soon took us to the outdoor restaurant area, where we had a picnic with the food we packed, and demolished a bottle of cold wine. Jen had very thoughtfully liberated a Cairns City Council rucksack, which came complete with glasses, plates, cutlery and most importantly, a corkscrew.

Things carried on in much the same vein in the evening. We found a small bar which overlooked the bay and had a couple of cocktails each as we watched the sun setting, which went though a variety of beautiful pinks, oranges and reds. It was stunning, and one of those moments where you sit in silence overawed by the beauty of nature.

Nature was obviously playing one of her cards as it noisily

pissed down all night but at least we weren't camping and the cheap two-bunk cabin kept us dry. Fortunately, the weather cleared enough for us to have a couple of hours on the beach the next morning until we were chased off by the rain. Plodding through the undergrowth towards our cabin we suddenly caught sight of a small, brown slithering snake.

"Bloody hell, Helena" I shrieked "that's just like the snake I saw in the zoo the other day. It can kill you." You should have seen us scarper. I obviously have no idea if it was a baddie, but we weren't taking any chances!

All the excitement, running and rain had quite exhausted us; we had a well-earned two-hour afternoon kip. Well, that's what you're supposed to do when you're on holiday, isn't it. Duly rested we cooked our sausages on the barbecue, took them and our wine over to the restaurant, where we ordered chips and salad – how cool an idea is that! The Australians have got their restaurant system completely sorted; we could certainly learn a few things! Later in the bar we were befriended by some other people, and happily played pool and messed around. There was even some male company that evening in the form of two New Zealanders - they were living in Perth but were on holiday on their boat.

Well, the evening passed as pissed evenings often do, and they invited us to have a latte on board. The bar was shut and the wine had run out so we slowly staggered down to the jetty. Nick (the boat builder) tried to get me to walk out on the jetty, which by then was bathed in the most gorgeous, romantic moonlight. Perfect you'd have thought; but even in my drunkenness I remembered that it was a jetty and there would be gaps, so I told him I was staying put. God, he must have thought I was a complete wombat. However, it can't have been the main thing on his mind, because before long we'd sat down on a wall overlooking the bay, he grabbed hold of me and proved he was an extremely accomplished kisser. Nice! Unfortunately Helena wasn't getting on quite so well, as Dave was proving to be too much of a sleaze. She announced she was going to bed (alone) and my sensible head cut in and I followed her.

What was normally a five-minute walk took considerably longer; as well as being slightly worse for ware, there weren't any paths and because we were walking through the rainforest there was no light. I hate to think how many people we woke up, but the main thing was that we didn't come across any more snakes.

Somebody was obviously thinking kindly of us the next morning as we woke up to the most glorious sunshine. We headed straight for the beach and immediately went for a long swim which significantly contributed to my headache disappearing. I could see the boy's boat clearly now – not what you could call a high-class yacht, in fact it was a huge old thing with black sails, and looked more like a pirate ship! Just then I noticed pirate Nick rowing the dingy towards the shore where Helena was sunbathing. By the time I'd swum back, the morning was arranged and we were invited to go on board - this time for a real coffee. We clambered aboard the rowing boat, and then heaved ourselves up the rope ladder onto the boat. Coffee was indeed served and we were then treated to a sail around the bay. The water was stunning, and was the most intense green colour. We were even treated to some turtles swimming passed. After our sail we all headed back to the bar, where we ordered jugs of beer and whiled away a few hours.

By then I was fine but Helena was still felling very sorry for herself, and was on the water! Before long it was time for me to leave; I said goodbye to Helena and the others, and Nick walked me to the ferry. From the ferry I watched the island slowly disappearing, and Helena waving madly from the beach. The trip back, sitting on the deck and listening to my personal stereo was one of those happy moments, and I felt rested and glad to be alive. It had been a great couple of days – in fact on my pin board I still have a picture of Nick, Helena and myself on the boat, with the island as a backdrop!

I had one job to do when we got to Cairns. Helena had given me some money, as the range and price of booze on the island was ridiculous, and she had another couple of days there. There was a very quick change around for the ferry to return to the island, so I ran like a woman possessed to the nearest bottle shop, scoped up an armful of wine, and then staggered back to the ferry. I'd already spoken to one of the crew members and asked him if he'd deliver the booze to Helena. I duly found him and handed over the loot. I hope she got it. I never did find out!

Chapter 38

Melbourne

It was half past four in the morning and I was hauling myself out of bed. At least I knew that there was an extremely good reason, and that was Melbourne. It seemed to take an age to get there, not helped by a two and a half hour stop in Brisbane. I finally arrived at one-ish, found the bus to the centre and jumped on. I was going to stay with Jen's friend Lisa, who I'd met a couple of times before in Portugal when she'd been on holiday there. She'd told me that when I came to Australia that I must come to Melbourne and stay with her. That day, both she and her boyfriend, Michael, were working, so I got off the airport bus at Spencer Street Station in the central business district and made my way to one of the glass skyscrapers. There I found Michael, who gave me a house key and putting me on a local train, told me where to get off and gave me directions on how to get to their house. The train stopped at stations with familiar names, such as Kew and Richmond, and then suddenly the MCG (the famous cricket ground) appeared on my left. Michael and Lisa lived in an area called Carlton, which was fairly close to the centre of the city and only a tram ride away. As I walked down the main street all the British names and influences had disappeared and I noticed Asian restaurants everywhere; I later found out that it was the main Vietnamese area. Oh bliss! I hadn't had a Vietnamese meal in years.

Seeing Lisa again was great and we practically carried on from where we left off a year and a half earlier in Portugal, for the Millennium celebrations, and Hugo's christening. Getting home from work she poured large vodka and tonics for the three of us, and then we went out for a Thai meal. I'd read that Melbourne was the food city of Australia and somehow I didn't think I was going to be disappointed. After dinner we went to the pub. It was a Friday night, the place was heaving and it was just like being in the UK!

The previous afternoon and evening had been great, but when I woke up on the Saturday morning I was itching to see more of Melbourne itself. Lisa, Michael and myself droved into town where Lisa dropped us off as she was on her way to an interview. Poor thing! It was a Saturday and all she wanted to do was laze about.

Michael and I headed up to Fitzroy which was an artistic area and the home of many Turks and Spaniards. We wandered along Brunswick Street which was lined with interesting junk shops, beautiful furniture shops, bookshops and the most amazing cookshop. Victorian style houses surrounded us, and it was just like being in a town in Britain on a Saturday, milling with shoppers. We then stopped off in one of the many cafés which was full of people who looked as though they were writers or musicians, and watched the world go by. Afterwards, we walked through the park and the view changed considerably as suddenly we were met with glass skyscrapers. There was more diversity yet to come. Lisa picked us up, and we drove down towards the Yarra River and an area called Southgate which was full of shops, bars and restaurants overlooking the river. Digging into delicious pizzas in a beautiful spacious modern restaurant and chatting away amiably, I knew that the cost of the airfare had been worth it and I was in for a good couple of days in Melbourne.

To try and show me as much as possible of the city and the surrounding area in my short time, Lisa and Michael had arranged for us to go away for the weekend. We left the city on the excellently named Batman Avenue, and drove passed the tennis stadium where the Australian Open was held every year. Still on a sporting theme, we then drove for a while on a beautifully surfaced, wide road, which Michael announced was part of the Formula 1 racetrack! After this, we drove west of Melbourne and towards Geelong. Again I was reminded of the UK as I saw signs for Portsea, Sandringham, Brighton and Hastings! It was just so weird. On the way we stopped off in various seaside towns, including Queenscliff. It was a beautiful town full of refurbished grand hotels from the Victorian era. Afterwards we made our way to Torquay. Torquay?! That was where I spent time during the summer when I was a kid. Bizarrely, there seemed to be other similarities. During the summer Torquay was a popular holiday destination but the weather had changed since the morning, and now, in August, in Australia it was cool and damp. The weather wasn't an issue though, as we spent the night at Lisa's parents. They lived in an enormous ranch style bungalow set in a huge field. Lisa's Mum cooked us a lovely meal, we drank loads of wine and had a thoroughly chilled out evening.

The following morning I woke up early and remembered that in the guest bathroom there was a spa bath. I made myself a huge cup of tea and took that and my Rough Guide and sank into the hot bubbles. A couple of hours later and after a hearty breakfast the three of us set off again. Despite the drizzle, Michael and Lisa wanted to take me a short way down the Great Ocean Road. It started at Torquay and wound its way for 285 kilometres west to Warrnambool. Built between 1919 and 1932 as a scenic route to rival California's Pacific Coast Highway, it also acted as a memorial for the soldiers who had died in World War I and provided employment for those who returned. Well, it didn't disappoint and the road twisted and turned giving the most spectacular view of the ocean. Despite the greyness of the sky, the sea was an emerald colour. Our first stop was Angelsea and Michael said we were going to look at the golf course. The golf course?! This one, however, had a difference. And the difference was kangaroos! Bloody loads of them. I imagine it would be pretty disconcerting teeing up, and suddenly having Skippy bonging up in front of you. We then continued on, passing through Lorne, another holiday town, after which the road became really narrow in places where it had been literally gorged out of the rockface. There were wooded hills ascending steeply to our right, and at Kennett River we suddenly left the main road and headed up a small track into the woods. Michael announced that he wanted to see if he could show me koalas in the wild, and that he knew a likely place. The koalas played ball, and there they were; in that familiar pose wedged in the forks of the trees, chilling out, just as you should do on a damp Sunday morning. It was an amazing experience, and although it had been great to see them so close up in the zoo, was infinitely better seeing them from further away in their natural habitat.

This sort of made up for the fact that we didn't have time to continue westwards as far as The Twelve Apostles, the gigantic limestone pillars sticking out of the ocean which I'd seen so many times in photographs. Lisa and Michael had a dinner that evening to attend so we had to turn round. We did have time to stop for a late lunch in Wye River, and suddenly I was transported back to the UK again. We had a tasty lunch in a really British style pub, eating pub grub, but looking out over the expanse of the ocean. We returned to Melbourne a different way by cutting inland though the beautiful Victoria countryside. We headed though the Angakook Lorne State Park, an area of temperate rainforest, and then the woods opened up and there were rolling hills, green fields and sheep, and we were in Wales!

The following day was Monday, and as Lisa and Michael were both working I had to fend for myself. Armed with a tram map and my travel guide I headed off for the centre of Melbourne. I found the right stop, and boarded one of the lovely old, wooden trams which quickly took me to the centre. I was surrounded by beautiful stately buildings, including the magnificent Parliament House, Flinders Railway station and the cathedral. It was all so British, until I walked down Collins Street which was full of expensive, fashionable shops and the skyscrapers and looked like New York. This city was amazing – it was just such a complete mixture of everything. I wondered up to the next road, Bourke Street Mall, lined with trees and seats and full of more shops. I pocked around David Jones, a fabulous department store with a mouth-watering food basement, and then realised I had to eat. Fortunately I was only a few streets away from Little Bourke Street, with Chinatown at one end, which was packed with restaurants, and happily paid for a Chinese buffet where you could choose whatever you wanted.

After crashing out for a couple of hours late afternoon, Lisa and Michael got home, and almost immediately Lisa got the phone call saying that she been offered the job that she'd interviewed for on Saturday. Yippee! Large vodka and tonics all round. We then went to the local bottle shop, bought champagne and red wine, met up with a friend of theirs and went for dinner in a local Vietnamese restaurant. As well as the food being stupendous, (I had my favourite spring rolls), it was a 'bring your own' restaurant so we drank the booze we'd just brought. It makes such a difference to the bill, and you can drink what you want without getting pissed off about paying horrendous prices. It's just such a brilliant idea, and should be made law everywhere! Maybe that could be my mission!

Tuesday was my last day in Melbourne and I'd decided it

was going to be a cultural one, so set off towards Carlton Gardens. It was a beautiful park, and housed the Royal Exhibition Building, built in the late 19th Century in the neoclassical style. However, Melbourne Museum was what I'd come to visit, and that was housed in an enormous, new building next door. It was a huge place and seemed to be an amalgamation of different types of museums. There was the Mind and Body Gallery, the Science and Life Gallery, the Forest Gallery and the Australian Gallery amongst others. I headed off for the areas which I thought would interest me and happily wandered round. It was a fantastic place, full of amazing things to look at. The item that was advertised as the star exhibit was a stuffed horse. Bizzare! Except, apparently, it wasn't any old horse but Phar Lap, a famous racehorse from the 1930's. Of course I went to have a look, but it all seemed a bit spooky to me. I've never really like seeing stuffed animals and a horse was a step too far.

I needed something slightly lighter, so headed for a temporary exhibition, called 'The seductive treasure of gold and civilisation'. It sounded much more up my street, and of course was so closely linked with Melbourne itself. I'd read up a little about the Goldrush which started in earnest when gold was discovered in Ballarat, a small town in Victoria close to where I'd been the Sunday before. Thousands of men arrived looking for their fortunes, including some from Britain, Ireland, China, and also ex-convicts and Australians themselves from neighbouring states. Apparently, large numbers of Australian towns lost their policeman, office and shop workers as gold fever hit. The population of Victoria doubled and Melbourne was, for a while, larger than Sydney.

The exhibition was excellent, and comprised priceless treasures on loan from rulers all over the world. There were gold chalices, gold jewellery, gold swords, gold everything.

Sometimes with themed exhibitions you feel that you don't really get value for money, but despite the fairly hefty 'gold' ticket price, this was worth it. Apart from the many exhibits which were beautifully presented, there was an excellent history of gold.

All museumed out I then wandered back into town, stopping off to have a look at the outside of Parliament House. It had been started in 1856 at the heart of the goldrush and was the home of the Australian Parliament from 1902 to 1927, until it moved to Canberra. It was stunning, with giant columns, and a high set of steps down to street level. Again I thought I'd been transported back to London. I then continued to St Paul's Cathedral, built in 1880 in the Gothic style. I had a quick look inside where I lit a candle for Dad; something I have done in a variety of stunning churches and cathedrals all over the world. Flinders Street Station was next on the tour, not because I wanted to get a train anywhere but to have a look at the façade. Again it was a Victorian building, with an arched entrance and a magnificent dome.

From there I decided to have another look at the muddy Yarra River, so walked across the pedestrian bridge and over to the Southgate Centre where I'd been the previous Saturday. I strolled round the shops, then up the side of the river for a while, before slowly walking back towards the centre, stopping off in a variety of interesting shops, and with aching feet found a tram.

In the evening, so I could see one last part of the city, Michael and Lisa took me to St. Kilda's for dinner. Situated on the coast, it was a strange mixture of sophistication and seediness – full of cafés and wine bars, and then the red-light district. Lisa pointed out a famous nightclub, and told me about a very drunken night she and Jen had had there years before when they were teenagers. Having shown me various spots we then walked up the main restaurant street, and headed for a Malaysian restaurant, which was a favourite of Michael's. As with all the meals I'd had in Melbourne, the food was excellent and we had a thoroughly enjoyable evening. On they way back Michael drove us back through the centre of the city so I could see it at night. Cruising up the wide avenue and looking at the lit up Victorian buildings, and in contrast the skyscrapers, I felt very contented. I'd heard people say that Melbourne couldn't compete with Sydney, with its stunning harbour and sights. They were right that Melbourne didn't have the instantly recognisable skyline that Sydney did, but I hadn't seen it yet, and thought Melbourne was stunning. I loved the mixture of buildings, the different cultures, and the extraordinary range of food – even the weather hadn't been so bad. Granted, it was rather strange suddenly being back in late winter, and wearing boots again, after the hot weather of Cairns and four months of summer in Portugal, but that didn't make any difference to my feelings for the city. I felt that I could quite happily live there if I was ever given the chance.

Chapter 39

Sydney

Everyone's heard all the superlatives used to describe the first glimpse of Sydney Harbour, the bridge and the Opera House. They've seen the pictures, had friends telling them that it's spectacular, but nothing really prepares you for it. I got off the train at Circular Quay, and there it was in front of me – one of the most spectacular, stunning, gob smacking views I had seen, and unbelievably, most of it was manmade. I'd spent all morning waiting to see it, having endured a horribly early start in Melbourne, waiting ages for my suitcase at Sydney airport to discover that it was broken, gone to the luggage place to find out what to do, found the airport bus and finally arrived in the Kings Cross region of the city.

I'd decided to stay in a decent hotel for my few days in Sydney, so had chosen the Gazebo Tower Hotel which was only a quick train ride away from the centre. It was all very swish and I had a large, luxurious room with a good view. The porter whisked away my suitcase to have it mended free of charge, I jumped in the shower and then ventured out. On the plane, to make the most of the time I'd have, I decided what I wanted to do and then mulled over the best travel pass to buy to do it - I settled on one with meant I could use the train, bus and ferries. Armed with my map, I found the station and managed to buy the correct pass. Trust my luck! My pass didn't want to work on the automatic gates but the guard assured me that it sometimes happened and I'd just have to wave it to get through! What a hassle that proved to be! I hopped on a double decker train (how cool) and changed at Town Hall which has to be the weirdest interchange ever. From one platform you could see where you wanted to get to – the platforms are sort of one on top of each other, but on half levels – but when you get there you realise you aren't on the platform you want to be! It was completely bonkers. Being so knackered it was really messing with my head so I asked a guard for help; maybe it wasn't just me, as he grinned and said there were often bemused visitors wandering around the station.

It was a beautiful day, the sun was shining and the sky was so blue. The temperature was considerably warmer than Melbourne and I was a happy girl. I immediately boarded a ferry which took me round the corner to Darling Harbour, from where I got a spectacular view of the Opera House, and then sailed underneath the famous bridge. Coming in towards the ferry stop I noticed a line of restaurants along the bay which I decided needing checking out. It was lunchtime and I was starving. The restaurants were all chic and fairly expensive but I decided to treat myself as it was my first day in Sydney. I sat outside in a beautiful area with well-trained waiters rushing everywhere, ordered a glass of Chardonnay, and waited for my lobster ravioli to arrive. Served with a crisp green salad, and crusty bread it was truly exquisite. I sat there lapping up the view and everything around me - feeling exhausted and unable to move, I did the only sensible thing and ordered another glass of wine.

A while later I got back on the ferry to Circular Quay, and then wandered round to the Opera House. It was just as amazing close up, and it was hard to imagine that the design had been so controversial when it was finished in 1973. Bizarrely enough the pictures that I'd seen of Sydney Harbour as a little girl were ones that Dad had taken in the early sixties when there was no Opera House. I couldn't really imagine it not being there now. I went inside, had a poke around the shop and then looked at the programme for the next few days. The tickets were expensive but I knew that I had to go to a concert, as Dad would have loved to, so queued up and spent $39 to see the Symphony Orchestra on the Friday night.

By then I was completely dead on my feet, so caught the train back to Kings Cross and crashed out for a bit. I had an early dinner in a local restaurant, and wanting to make the most of the following day crawled into bed.

Unbelievably, the next day I woke up at seven o'clock. It was such a beautiful day that I wasted no time in getting out to discover more of Sydney. And discover it I did! I don't think I have ever walked so much around a city as I did that day. I set off through the suburbs around Victoria Street and Darlinghurst Road, admiring the Victorian style houses, which in a way reminded me of pictures I'd seen of houses in New Orleans. From then I made my way down Oxford Street (bizarre!), full of quirky shops and cafés, and people grabbing coffees on the way to work. I walked up Liverpool Street, with Hyde Park!! on my right and then into Chinatown. By then I'd arrived in Darling Harbour, which the previous day had taken me a train and a ferry to get to! Looking at my map I decided to get another ferry but this time stop off at one of the ports on the other side of the water.

Apart from wanting to have a view of the harbour from another perspective which my brother had told me was excellent, I also wanted to get a flavour of residential Sydney.

I got off at McMahon's Point from where I had an excellent view of the city, and I think was often used for shots of Sydney. Before long, coffee was calling so I slogged up Blues Point Road in search of a café. I also wanted to get a flavour of the area where Matthew, my brother, had lived. I couldn't remember which number he'd stayed in, but decided that the location of any of them would have been amazing. I finally found a café cum bar and sank down in a chair where I watched the world go by. It had such a welcoming atmosphere that I struggled to get going again. When I finally caught up with Matthew on my return to Portugal and we were chatting on the phone about my trip, it turned out (I guess not that surprisingly) that that very café had been one of his favourite haunts!

I wandered slowly back to the ferry stop and took a boat that went back to Circular Quay. By then the sun was high in the sky, the water was sparkling and the harbour full of boats of all sizes. It was the perfect weather to be on the water, so I decided to take the ferry to Manly, which was a suburb, seven miles away on the coast. The ferry route which had been in operation since 1854 gave me a different view of Sydney, and then it disappeared and we sailed passed houses dotted on the shores. Docking in Manly Cove it was like being in a British seaside town with a small harbour beach and amusements. The main street was packed full of tourist shops, and a fair amount of tat, but it was the ocean beach that I was after. It was only half a kilometre away and there in front of me was the most beautiful bay, with a strip of perfect white sand. I sat down on the sand, took my boots off and did absolutely nothing for a while. Being right on the coast it only seemed right to have fish again, so I headed for a place I'd read about in my rough guide called the Manly Fish Market. It was a mixture of a fishmonger's with an incredible array of fresh fish and shellfish to buy, and a fish and chip shop. I choose good old traditional cod and chips, and ate them sitting at a table overlooking the ocean. It was divine and so was the view!

Arriving back at Circular Quay, I walked back up to the Opera House and from there to the Botanical Gardens. Established in 1816, it had originally been somewhere where the first settlers had tried to grow vegetables for the new colony. By the time I arrived they were beautiful landscaped gardens with a huge number of plants, trees and lakes. It was all very serene and I spent ages soaking up the atmosphere and the spectacular views of Sydney Harbour. I decided to head back to the hotel, and according to my map if I walked though the rest of the gardens and down to the main road, I'd be able to find a bus. Except I didn't really know which buses went where. There was no choice but to walk, and by then I thought my feet were going to drop off. From where I was I could see the hotel in the distance as it was so tall, and situated high above me. That meant that there was a hill to climb. Looking for a road that I thought would take me in the right direction, I noticed some steps. Oh no, steps! Talk about torture but at least I knew I was on the right track. By the top I was practically crawling, and from there couldn't see the hotel so it was back to trying to figure out where I was.

I made it, of course, but seriously wondered whether I'd be able walk a step again that day. But it was a Thursday, and the information pack in my hotel said it was late night shopping. I decided that if I got the train and headed into the centre of the city where I knew there were a couple of large department stores I'd be able to cope. I discovered a larger version of David Jones, the shop which I'd been to in Melbourne, and then more bizarrely Grace Bros. For ages I couldn't get all those awful lines out of my head and walked around grinning about 'I'm free' and 'Mrs Slocombe's pussy'! I finally managed to concentrate long enough to buy some badly needed jeans, and then all shopped out went in search of dinner. Oh my lord, what I found was a foodie's heaven. Down in the basement there was the most enormous space full of the noises of cutlery and people talking. It was surrounded by a huge choice of food stalls. After my usual indecisiveness when faced with so many choices, I eventually plumped for a curry, which was delicious. However, enough was enough and being horizontal was calling loudly. A quick journey on the train and I was back in my, it has to be said, rather lovely hotel room, lying on my bed and drinking a way too expensive but delicious beer from room service.

There was only one full day left in Sydney so I did the other thing every tourist does and went to Bondi Beach. It was a lovely warm, spring morning and Bondi was a great place to be. It was big and brash, and commercialised, with a string of cafés and restaurants on the beachfront, but the crescent shape of the bay and the view was spectacular. I lay down on the sand for ages and finally got round to writing three weeks worth of my diary. After a while I'd worked up an appetite, so wandered over to one of the cafés and had a delicious sandwich sitting on the grass and then had another little lie down and watched the surfer dudes doing their thing! On the way back to Bondi Junction I jumped off the bus a stop early, as the shops were calling to me again. I just couldn't get over the huge array of things to buy. Good thing I did. I found a food hall. It might not have been as glamorous or as big as Harrods, but it was packed full of beautiful displays of Asian and exotic foods. And what did I end up buying? A pamper pack I saw on the way out for my poor achy feet!

That evening was my bit of culture for the holiday. I arrived at the Opera House, and was greeted by that buzz of excitement you get before a concert. Although I'd seen the outside view hundreds of times, I had no idea what it was like inside. It was modern, compared to many buildings where

I'd seen classical music performed, furnished with light coloured wood, with the seats rising up steeply from the stage area. I had a seat fairly near the back, but the view of the whole concert hall was spectacular, and the music divine. The Sydney Symphony Orchestra played some Strauss, Brahms's 3rd Symphony but best of all Bach's *Brandenburg Concerto* No 1. Apparently when I was little and Mum and Dad played any of the Brandenburg Concertos, I'd leap up, announcing that it was my favourite 'jumping music' and commence to jump up and down. As much as I was enjoying it, I also felt sad. I knew how much Dad would have loved to have gone to a concert in the Opera House, and occasionally had to fight back the tears.

The next afternoon I was due to fly back to Cairns so wanted to spend the time I had left soaking up the atmosphere. To see Sydney from a different perspective I took the bus to Circular Quay and then walked up to The Rocks which is the heart of historic Sydney. It was here that in 1788, Captain Arthur Phillip claimed the establishment of Sydney Town. The area rapidly became a slum; not helped by an outbreak of the bubonic plague in 1900. Apparently in the 1970's, because it was so run-down the whole area was to be razed. After opposition, the traditional cottages and terraces were restored and the area is the busy tourist attraction it is today. Despite this, there were some interesting shops and a great outdoor market situated underneath the start of the bridge. From there I climbed up some steps and got another great view of the harbour. After that there was only time for one last treat in Sydney and that was to have lunch in Doyles. I knew it was a Sydney institution, and Matthew had told me I had to treat myself. There were a number of restaurants bearing the family name but I went to the one there in Circular Quay, with that fantastic view! I sat outside and had a gorgeous king prawn and avocado salad, with garlic bread and wine. It wasn't cheap but who cares?! And that was it. My trip to Sydney was finished, and how fantastic it had been. Of course it would have been even better to have shared it with someone, especially the great food available, but I wasn't complaining at all.

Chapter 40

Cairns revisited

After a fairly intense week of sightseeing it was good to get back to Cairns and chill out. Jen picked me up from the airport, and with Hugo in bed, and Pedro too, with a bad toothache, Jen and I sat on the (amazingly mosquito free) veranda and chilled out until the early hours, helped along with lots of white wine. It was Sunday the next day, so there was a bit more chilling, along with a little bit of shopping.

The following morning I had my auntie hat on, as Jen and Pedro were both working. Not that looking after Hugo was difficult. He was an easy two-year old, and not prone to having hissy fits like some do. In the afternoon, we decided a beach trip was in order, so the four of us set off for Trinity Beach. I hadn't yet been there and was eager to sample another Queensland beach. It was close to the other ones I'd visited, and whilst beautiful it was so windy that it was uncomfortable, and Hugo was literally being blown along. As it happened there was a pub set high above the beach with an open bar overlooking the bay. We sat there sipping cold beers, and watched the sun setting. It was incredible. What a place to live. If I lived there I'm not sure I'd get anything much done apart from sitting around drinking and chatting, and gazing at the spectacular scenery.

The next day Jen suggested taking Hugo for a swim at a local outside pool. Having had little exercise apart from walking, and a lot of drinking and eating, it was an excellent idea. The pool was huge, clean and empty, with absolutely no splashing going on – my idea of how swimming should be. Nothing like the nightmare trips to smelly, dirty, cold pools I'd been to as a child. In the evening we visited the night market so I could buy some souvenirs. Although it was touristy there was a good selection, and I bought the usual soft koalas as pressies, and I have to say one for myself. Worn out with all the shopping and swimming we decided that food was in order so undid all the good we had done at the swimming pool and went and ate pizza. Who cares!

Time was rapidly running out in Australia, so we started to pack things into the last couple of days. On the Wednesday morning Jen and I took Hugo to Kewarra Beach. It was a gorgeous bay and with the tide way out we were able to walk through the pools of water for ages. It was also where Jen's Dad lived and after a couple of hours we saw him walking towards us. He wanted to show me the small bed and breakfast that he ran close to the beach. What a lifestyle! A gorgeous bungalow with a few guest bedrooms, a lovely landscaped pool area, a two minute walk to the deserted beach, and even a resident Green Frog which Hugo was delighted to show me, hiding behind a picture on the wall. That evening Jen's Dad looked after Hugo, and the three of us went out for dinner. We went to eat Clifton Beaches, yet another bay where there was an excellent view, and also one of their favourite Italian restaurants. Going to an Italian restaurant reminded me of the numerous times the three of us, with other friends had gone to *Veranda do Sol*, a pizza restaurant overlooking the sea in Porto, just next to where they had lived.

Except this one was different, and again we were able to take our own wine bought from the excellent Bottle Shop Drive Thru. We had a great meal, including a stunning Seafood Antipasto, chatted for ages and even bumped into the friends of Jen's who owned Birdworld which we had visited for free way back at the start of my visit.

Fortunately the free trips weren't quite over. The next day was a bit of a shock to the system as it was damp and overcast, so we headed to the Tjapujai Cultural Park. Although not really a fan of themed parks of any description Jen had assured me that it was well worth a visit – not least as we paid a reduced rate as some of the original founders were her friends. The park was set up in 1987 and presents Aboriginal culture in the Tjapukai tribal area. Apparently, the local communities have approved and overseen the attractions presented in the park and it certainly had what you can imagine is an authentic feel. The park started with a film, told in the native language, but thankfully with headphones and a translation, and performers on stage interacting with the images. My scepticism disappeared almost immediately and I was intrigued by everything I heard and saw.

Afterwards, we headed outside where we explored a traditional camp. It consisted of a hut, and more interestingly for me, bush foods and medicines. We were also treated to singing and dancing, which was performed in an amphitheatre, with a rainforest backdrop. Unfortunately the boomerang demonstration was called off, as it was still really windy. I guess that had to make sure they didn't take someone's head off.

Fortunately, the next day was sunny and since it was my penultimate one we returned to the lovely Kewarra Beach. After that we had a quick trip to town where I went to Woolworth's (which as in America is a supermarket!) and bought loads of Asian delicacies, which I couldn't get in Portugal; these included dried spices, rice crackers, seaweed etc, etc. Most people leave Australia with koalas and boomerangs - I had those but also half a supermarket!

That evening Jen, Pedro and myself headed for an evening out. We went to a variety of bars and headed up in *The Woolshed*, which had been one of Jen's haunts ten years previously. It was rammed full of people, with some dancing on the tables and reminded me of a skiing bar where I had done just that in St. Anton. Although Jen and I were enjoying ourselves, Pedro wasn't as his tooth was still hurting. He tried to persuade us to go home with him but we were having none of it.

As Jen walked Pedro to the door I had the strangest chat up line I've ever had. A rather cute, tall, blond Aussie approached and asked me if I was English. When I replied that I was he asked what I thought was the best way of cooking roast lamb. I think I said rosemary and garlic, and we chatted until Jen reappeared. She and I had a bit of a dance, drank quite a few more beers and, I have to say enjoyed all the male attention. Although a backpacker's bar it was wasn't just full of teenagers. Mr Roast Lamb tried his luck a few times which was really quite sweet and then Jen and I decided that we ought to leave as we had a really early start the next morning. As we left, Mr Roast Lamb was waiting at the door and I realised that although I'd kissed a Kiwi I hadn't done the same with an Aussie guy. So with nothing to loose I gave him a big smacker on the lips goodnight. Result!

The next morning we struggled out of bed at six thirty - on a Saturday and having only had about five hours sleep and a lot of beer the night before! Fortunately it soon turned into the most glorious day, which was only fitting for my last day in Australia and for a final trip out to the reef. Pedro had managed to get the day off work so the four of us set off for *The Big Cat*, which would take us to Green Island. It was a small, heart-shaped coral cay with perfectly white sand, and despite the superlatives I've already used, the water really was the most amazing turquoise colour I have ever seen. It also seemed to change colour slightly every metre or so as we approached the jetty. The island was more commercial than some of the others I had visited, but this only covered a small area and we were easily able to escape the hoards. One up side was that there were huge beach parasols, which you could hire, and as it was completely baking and we had Hugo with us we did just that.

It was just the most sublime setting. We swan, made sand castles, ate the lovely lunch we'd prepared, washed down with gorgeous white wine and generally lazed around. Jen and I both managed to haul ourselves from our prone positions on the beach and walk around the island, and then as the tide was going out I paddled in the rock pools with Hugo. We were all amazed at how far it had gone, and walking on the jetty were surprised at the numbers of fish, especially the blue parrot fish that were stuck in the pools. Jen and I decided to take the glass bottomed boat tour to see some more fish but we hardly needed it and just looked over the edge. The driver was having problems negotiating the coral as the water was so shallow that in places we were almost touching the bottom - he then announced that it was the furthest out the tide had ever gone! And then, finally what I'd been waiting for - the fin of a reef shark. However, despite cutting the engine the shark wouldn't play ball and didn't come any nearer. That didn't really matter though. Just as we were returning to the jetty I could see Pedro waving his arms and shouting.

"Ha tuberão, ha tuberão", which means 'there's a shark!' And there was! We scrambled off the boat and rushed to where Pedro, and other people were rapidly congregating. Close to the jetty, the shark seemed to be lying on the seabed in the extremely shallow water, ignoring all the other fish near him and all the humans peering over the railings at him. He wasn't that big but I didn't care. I was a couple of feet away from a real, live, wild shark! I hadn't done badly really on the wild animal front, as I'd already seen kangaroos and koalas in the wild, and that scary snake on Fitzroy Island.

Just before we left the island, when on board, the crew threw food to attract more fish; there were two main types and they were huge. One was large and black whose name I can't remember and the other were beautiful blue and yellow batfish, which were tall and upright and the complete opposite of a sole or skate. And that was almost the end of my trip to Australia. We got home early evening and had a final dinner together. Jen had bought some (horrendously expensive) Moreton Bay Bugs, which aren't bugs at all, but similar to cray fish. We ate them, with chips, garlic bread and salad and washed it all down with champagne. Delicious.

And that really was that. The next morning, having said goodbye to Pedro the night before as he had a horribly early get up, Jen and I had a slow get up and then she and Hugo took me to the airport. Hugo was of course excited because he was back at the airport, whereas Jen and I were both feeling rather low. I really wondered if I'd ever see them all again and was struggling to keep control as we said goodbye. Jen promptly burst into tears, which set me off, much to Hugo's confusion.

Australia had been everything I'd hoped it would be and so much more. It was truly an amazing country on so many levels, and I'd only seen a small part of it in the month I'd been there. As I waited to board I was feeling rather glum, both at leaving Australia and Jen, but then remembered that I wasn't just flying straight home. I had a couple of days in Singapore yet to come. Yippee!

Chapter 41

Singapore

I'd already been impressed by Changi airport and was really hoping that the city would be as interesting. It was mainly the food that I was after, and the amazing mixture of cultures. I knew that many people headed for Orchard Road, the area famous for its five-star hotels and expensive shops, but that wasn't for me. I'd booked a hotel in advance which was in the colonial area between Little India and the Arab quarter. It was also described in my guidebook as one for the lazy sightseer.

I found the shuttle bus easily and arrived at the South East Asia Hotel, which was bizarrely located on Waterloo Street. It was seven thirty in the evening when I arrived but still boiling hot and very humid. I dumped my suitcases at the hotel and set off for a wander. Purely by chance I'd arrived on a festival day - namely the Festival of the Hungary Ghosts - which involved feasting and entertainment for the souls of the dead. All the pavements were covered in candles and there were food stalls everywhere. It was a complete feast for the eyes, and not just this but almost next door to my hotel there was both a Hindu and a Buddhist temple, and a food market - hence the reference to the lazy sightseer. I wandered around for a while, had some dinner from one of the stalls but then the hustle and bustle and the stifling heat got the better of me and I headed back to the hotel.

There were some great free maps of the different areas of Singapore in the hotel, and as I had limited time roughly planned what I was going to do the following day. It turned out to be another one of my mammoth walks. It started in Little India, and although Singapore was predominantly a Chinese city, there were minority groups, and this was one I was interested in. Everywhere was full of the lovely smells of spices and cooking, so the first thing was to find some breakfast. I found a local café where after much arm waving from me and giggling from her, an elderly Indian lady served me with sweet potato pasties and tea. I practically spat the tea out. As in my hotel the tea came in ready mixed sachets with milk and sugar and was indescribably sweet! It seemed to be the only way it came so I gulped it down.

Full of sugar I bounced through Little India Arcade; although it had some tourist-orientated shops there was still an authentic flavour and as it was still early was free of bus loads of holiday makers. I happily looked at the beautiful textiles and chatted to a stall holder who sold beautiful incense sticks. Clutching the ones I couldn't resist buying I continued through the area, walking up backstreets with such British names as Hastings, Clive and Campbell.

Having done 'India' it was now 'Arabia's' turn. I headed towards the Arab Street area, which was the heart of the Muslim community. The going became increasingly more difficult and I was clambering up and down different height pavements outside shops. Later, when I read my guidebook there was actually a paragraph about these 'five-foot-ways'. They are roughly five feet wide, and are the walkways in front of traditional shops. The difficulty was that each walkway was higher or lower than the shop next door, and often the pavement was covered in wares meaning you had to dodge the bikes on the road. Having weaved my way through rows of shops selling brightly coloured materials and baskets I came to my goal, which was the Sultan Mosque. It was the biggest in Singapore and was originally built with a grant from Stamford Raffles and the East India Company in 1825. However, a hundred years later the original mosque was replaced by the present, magnificent, gold-doomed building. I approached it from Bussorah Street, which was lined with palm trees and provided a perfect view. I decided to go inside for a look, imagining it would be as beautiful. Naturally, as it was a mosque I was given a full-length robe to cover my bare bits. I was more worried about measuring my length though as the robe was so long I kept tripping over the hem. I have to say that the interior was very bare and there wasn't much to look at so I went back outside to look at it from that view.

So, having visited somewhere which was connected with Raffles, I decided it was time to visit the world famous hotel itself. It was of course completely ostentatious, but still amazing. More then just a hotel it is a Singapore institution, which was built in 1887 and soon became a byword for oriental luxury. I wandered around the areas of the hotel that I could get into, admiring the renovations and extensions that had been made ten years previously. For me, though, the magic of being there was that one of my favourite authors, Somerset Maugham, had been a frequent visitor, and that he wrote many of his short stories in the Palm Court. It was a beautiful area full of wicker chairs and huge palm trees. What I hadn't known before arriving was that there was a small museum hidden away on the third floor. It was only a tiny place but was crammed full of Raffles' memorabilia and history, and also letters and other things to do with Maugham, and Conrad. Fascinating! Leaving there I went to the famous bar but unfortunately I couldn't really justify a famous Singapore Sling and disliking gin I swiped some Raffles' matches instead!

Having 'done' various cultures I decided it was the turn of China. I could have walked over the river and through Chinatown, but it was getting hotter and hotter and my feet were starting to ache. I opted for the MRT, the Mass Rapid Transit. It puts London's underground to shame! It was modern, well run and air-conditioned. As they now have on the new section of the Jubilee Line, the track is screened off whilst you are waiting, the doors only opening when a train arrives. What's more it clearly marks on the ground where you stand to let people off. Of course they've attempted to use marking on the Jubilee line, but people blatantly ignore it, standing right in front of the doors and then wondering why they get trampled by herds of elephants disembarking. Being Singapore this didn't happen and it was a pleasure. I only travelled a few stops to Outram Park, which was on the far side of Chinatown, but the train was a quiet, cool heaven, and I could have easily stayed on for a while more.

The serenity abruptly stopped as I got off. The cultural heart of Singapore, it was full of sights and smells, and despite many redevelopments, a large number of the shop fronts were rebuilt in the original style, which gave a glimpse of how things used to be. It was lunchtime and there were people everywhere, shouting across the streets at each other, waving their arms and most of all, eating from the numerous stalls. I decided to join them. I wasn't especially hungry but needed a 'Scooby snack' so opted for some prawn and fish sticks which came with chilli sauce, and munched on them as I wandered round. After a while my feet had completely had it so next on the agenda was a sit down. I walked over to Neil Road where I found *Tea Chapter*. It was a teahouse where the emphasis is on the art and presentation of tea drinking. On arrival I had to remove my shoes and was escorted through the small, busy shop and upstairs to a serene room, where I was shown to a low table and seated on cushions. The room was beautifully decorated, not in the bright gaudy colours that you often associate with Chinese restaurants, but with natural fabric, beautiful wood, and was full of candles and incense. I was feeling better already. A sweet, demure waitress bought over a tea set, complete with burner and pot of boiling water, and demonstrated the art. It was fascinating watching the attention to detail, and when the lady had finished I was able to sit and make as many cups of tea for myself as I wanted. I was never hassled, and must have sat there for an hour, reading the leaflets I'd picked up on the day, and regenerating. Well, if it was good enough for Queenie who, I'd discovered, had visited some years earlier, it was good enough for me.

Revived, I carried on my exploring of the area and walked up South Bridge Street. It was lined with scores of shops selling pottery, jewellery, lacquer ware, silks, and most interestingly for me, objects made of jade. Even though I'd been spending merrily for a month knew I had to buy something in jade, and armed with my credit card I pocked around until I found them – a pair of jade chopsticks with a little rest in the shape of a fish. The man who sold then to me was obviously delighted and as I left he grinned manically at me. Shopping done, and it was time for another temple and I had one in mind. It was only a couple of blocks away up the same road, and called the Sri Mariamman Temple. It was Singapore's oldest Hindu temple, and probably the best known. Famous for its colourful *gopuram*, or entrance tower, it was highly decorated, colourful and typically south Indian. Along with everyone else I removed my shoes, and left them along with hundreds of other pairs, which made the area look more like a Boxing Day sale than a temple, and joined the mixture of a few tourists and worshippers. The best bits for me were the vibrant ceiling paintings as I have always been a sucker for ceilings, but on the whole the word which jumping into my head was 'gaudy'. I'd never seen anything like it!

Leaving the temple I carried on walking and come to the Chinatown Point. It was a large building, with the main aisle spiralling upwards gently with shops on the outside, which sold a huge variety of crafts including more jade and beautifully crafted mah jong sets. Tempted as I was, it was the need to eat that took me downstairs to one of the famous food centres. The food centres had originally started off as hawker stalls, which were streetside carts with a few tables and chairs. Recently the authorities had moved all the impermanent stalls into permanent hawker centres where there are fixed stalls and tables and chairs. In most there is an enormous choice of foods from a number of regional cuisines. Some have moved into the larger shopping centres, where although some of the atmosphere is lost the food is just as good, and the air-conditioning bliss.

Cool was what I needed and having planned to go to one of the traditional hawker centres the following day, this food court was fine. I choose a Hainanese dish, as it looked tempting and I'd never heard of it before. Originating from Hainan, a large island off the southern coast of China, the mixture of rice and chicken was elegant but simple, and it came with a bowl of soup! Afterwards I decided to walk back to the hotel, have a shower, as I was so hot and yucky and chill out before venturing out for the evening. I walked up a wide road, which was being completely dug up, so there was dust flying around to add to the heat, and feeling more knackered with every step, was then treated to a downpour. It pissed down but at least the rain was warm. I didn't have an umbrella, of course, and had no idea how long the rain would last. Deciding to carry on I was waiting to cross a main road when a kindly Chinese lady insisted I stand underneath her umbrella, and we then walked together until our ways parted. How lovely of her. Can't imagine that happening in London!

Before long the rain stopped but the streets had started steaming. The phenomenon was amazing, and with it the temperature and humidity rose. I don't think I have been hotter or more uncomfortable in my life. I staggered back to the hotel, and stood under the cold shower for ages. The hotel was advertised as having air-conditioning. What this, in fact, meant was that there was an ancient fan on the ceiling, which just circulated the hot air, and although made a slight difference, also made such a racket that there was no way you could leave it on at night. I was only a hundred and thirty seven miles from the equator, so I couldn't expect anything else really. The whole island had once been rainforest and was freely roomed by tigers. After ten minutes of lying like a star on my bed I was dripping again, and ended up having two more cold showers in the space of an hour.

It was going to have to be an air-conditioned complex that I spent the evening in, and after a little research I found just the place. Before that I made the most of the location of my hotel, and went next door to have a look at the Kuan Yin Temple. This was Chinese and one of the liveliest and most frequented, with Kuan Yin being one of the most popular goddesses. It was only built in 1982, but with the flower sellers and fortune tellers outside and joss sticks being burnt inside, it had a real atmosphere. It didn't have the gaudiness of the Hindi temple, and although busy was lovely to experience. A couple of doors away was the Sri Krishnan Temple, which apparently also attracts worshipers from the Kuan Yin Temple who show religious pragmatism in spade loads by burning joss sticks and offering prayers at the Hindu temple!

Finished with temples and already wilting in the heat I walked at a snail's pace toward Bugis Street. In the past it had been an infamous food court where transvestites hung out, but had been demolished when the MRT was built and was now a new complex with shops and bars. Obviously a lot of the character had gone, but it was full of interesting shops, a department store, and some open-air restaurants. I wandered around for ages, and was transfixed when I came to the fountain. Having lived in Portugal for so long I was used to seeing fountains everywhere, but they never did anything interesting. This one was spectacular. It wasn't in an elevated pool as normal, but the water came straight out from the tiled ground, in a variety of formations and with different coloured light projected through the streams of water. I sat there, transfixed for ages.

Food time again, and rather then heading for the food court in the basement I went to one of the little restaurants so I could watch the comings and goings. I had the most delicious deep-fried soft-shelled crabs, washed down with some ice-cold beer. Delicious. I then headed down to the food court. Even when I have just eaten I can still spend ages looking at food, and this place was truly spectacular. There were food stalls from every part of the globe, presenting the food beautifully. They ranged from rows of sushi, high quality chocolates, jellybeans, in fact everything. There was even a supermarket, where I found Marmite and Branson Pickle. I finally settled for a huge Pecan brownie for dessert and ate it looking at the mad fountain.

Sated visually and stomach wise I went back to the hotel through the market stalls. There were imitation watches and clothes everywhere, and also fruit juice stalls. I had a sugar cane juice, which although unbelievably sweet was extremely refreshing. Back at my hotel I had two more cold showers, watched some telly I didn't understand and then tried to sleep in the heat.

The next day was my last in Singapore, so having packed my stuff up and left it in the lobby, I headed out. My first task was a boring one and involved finding out where the bus left for the airport. Apparently the airport shuttle I'd taken, which had dropped me right at the hotel, didn't do the same in reverse, so this meant using a local bus. After ages I finally found the bus stop and got on with discovering Singapore. I continued walking through the old colonial area, and bizarrely, found a *Délifrance*. I stopped and had a delicious *café au lait* and *pain au chocolate* for breakfast. The area was definitely prosperous and had expensive shops and a large shopping centre.

Not far away, set in large grounds was the gothic Anglican Cathedral which had been built in 1863. It was strange seeing something so plain in comparison to the places of worship I'd seen. Opposite the cathedral was the Padang, a large open field symbolising British colonialism. It had been the centre of colonial life and where people had promenaded in the evening. Now it was where members of the Singapore Cricket Club played in the sweltering heat. It was surrounded by more imposing examples of British architecture; these included The Victoria Theatre and Concert Hall, Parliament House, which was Singapore's oldest governmental building, dating from 1827, the Supreme Court and City Hall. The area had a historical past. It was at the Pedang where the beginning of the end of colonisation took place; the invading Japanese herded the European community together, before taking then to Changi prison. And, it was as City Hall that Lord Mountbatten accepted the Japanese surrender in 1945.

In a historical mood I walked down to the river to look at Raffles' Statue, which marked the place where Sir Stamford Raffles first set foot on the island of Singapore. Before this, the island had been used and occupied at various times by the Chinese, the Portuguese and the Dutch amongst others. At the end of the Napoleonic Wars there were many British who were disappointed by the failure of the dream of the British imperialism in South-East Asia. One of these was

Raffles, who was Lieutenant-Governor of Java, and who was given permission to found a station to procure British trade routes. The Dutch beat him to his choice of Riau, an island near Singapore and he was instructed to negotiate with the sultan of nearby Johor for land. He landed in 1819, and at the time the old sultan's younger son had succeeded to power (in a treaty with the Dutch) whilst the older son, Hussein was away. Raffles threw his support behind Hussein, proclaiming him sultan, which helped to legitimatise British claims on the island. In the 1824 Anglo-Dutch treaty, which carved up spheres of interest in Asia, Singapore remained the property of Britain. The colony thrived, and Raffles' town plan embraced the colonial practice still operative in Singapore today. He administered the population according to neat racial categories, which can still be seen. These days Singapore is a modern, bustling city with high skyscrapers, shaped by Lee Kuan Yew who became the first Singaporean to hold the title of prime Minister in 1959.

Across the river from Raffles' statue there was a row of picturesque, colourful shops and restored terraces and bars which were dwarfed by the modern grey skyscrapers. They looked incongruous together. By then it had started to rain so I set off again and walked to the mouth of the river to see the Merlion, Singapore's symbol of tourism - it was a water-spouting half-lion, half-fish statue. From there I walked over the bridge and towards the central business district. Although much of the area was fairly forgettable, the waterfront area was interesting with boats coming and going. Walking a bit further and I came to my destination - the Lau Pa Sat Festival Centre. It was housed in the Telok Ayer Centre, made in the Victorian age from cast iron as a market. Although demolished for the MRT it had been restored and now housed a huge hawker centre. It wasn't upmarket like the food courts inside the shopping malls, there was no air-conditioning as it was open to the elements, but there was the most spectacular range of stalls. What's more there weren't any tourists, just locals who had stopped for lunch.

It was arranged like a wheel, with about eight aisles which met at the hub, where there was a large seating area. Naturally it took me ages to decide what to eat. There were some stalls which didn't figure at all in my choices; although I have tried a variety of suspicious looking foods over the years I wasn't really into ears, feet or heads, and there was a good selection of them. I finally plumped for a Thali. The stall was popular with the locals and the food looked great. For $4 (about £1.50) I had a chicken curry, a portion of curried greens, a poddodum, a naan and a daal, and most interesting of all was that it was served on a sheet of baking parchment on a tray, not a plate in sight. It was absolutely gorgeous, and I scoffed the lot, with admiring looks from some of the locals and the lady I'd bought it from!

Knackered, I jumped on the MRT back towards the hotel. I returned to the market, and having managed to get some cash out with my credit card bought a few bits including a fake Gucci watch for Mum, as she'd always wanted one. Well, not a fake one obviously! Back at the hotel I tried to figure out how I was going to get all my stuff to the bus stop, which was a few blocks away. I'd come out with a suitcase and a hand luggage sized-bag. I still had these which were stuffed full of mementoes; a boomerang, some miniature opals, jade chopsticks, beer coolers, clothes I'd bought, a lovely coffee table book on Australia Jen had given to me, a coffee maker, cuddly toy .... OK, maybe not the coffee maker but I did have the cuddly toys in the form of toy koalas. I also had a Cairns City Council picnic set ruck sack which was full of food I couldn't get in Portugal, and a poster that Phil had asked me to get for him, which was in a very long tube. Coupled with the humidity it took me an age to get the bus stop and it was interspersed with frequent expletives.

Boarding the bus and trying to pay was hysterical, not helped by the driver who had a complete sense of humour bypass. Settling into the bus, we then proceeded to go all over the place before arriving at the airport. I checked all my luggage through, amazed that the check in girl didn't bat an eyelid at all my stuff, and then made the most of the great facilities, before boarding my flight. Going home after a holiday is often really depressing and this was no different. Because the flight had already come from Australia I wasn't able to choose a decent seat and ended up on the aisle next to the crew area. I hardly slept at all and was knackered and in a filthy mood by the time we got back to Heathrow, but of course it wasn't over yet. I had to transfer to Gatwick to get my connection home to Portugal. On that flight it must have been the only time that I have refused any food or drink; I asked to be left alone, and promptly fell asleep as soon as we taxied down the runway. On finally getting to Porto there was one hiccup in that my rucksack, which I picked up from the carrousel wrapped in cling film, had split. I was ushered to a separate room where the customs were interested in the food I had in it, and the luggage staff were arranging to have my bag mended. I was rapidly loosing it, and by the time I finally left, did something I never did from Porto airport and got a taxi home.

It was really weird being back in my modern flat in the middle of Porto after all the different places I'd visited and stayed in. It was, however, great to see my silly cats who hadn't wrecked the place and to find everything as it should be. The cats clambered all over me for hours, being particularly interested in helping me unpack! I sat looking at all the souvenirs I'd bought and thought about the great trip I'd had, until the tiredness took over and I crawled into bed for most of the afternoon.

Part Eleven

A final farewell to Portugal

Chapter 42

A new beginning

The bad, of course always follows the good, and my first day back in Portugal highlighted this. Having had a day of washing and sorting I was delighted when Adam phoned suggesting meeting for dinner. With Steph gone, I knew that Adam would be even more important as a close friend. We had a fun evening, swapping stories about our summers, and fighting the jet lag I was even talked to going on to a couple of bars after dinner. At about half past two in the morning, and very wobbly, we left one of our late night haunts. As ever, picking his moments as we were saying goodnight Adam announced that he was leaving school and Porto, and that he'd be in touch. He didn't say where he was going, and because I was too scared in case it wasn't Portugal I didn't ask. And that was that!

Returning to work after five weeks away kept me busy; there were other friends around, and I spent time with Steph's ex-flat mate Steve. I had my usual birthday weekend in Guimarães with Clare and Russ, and Guy and Ros, and also saw friends who were visiting. One was a teacher, Natasha, from my previous school who was staying with our friend Sabine, and the other was Simone who had given the seminars the previous spring in Berne. She had come over to do some training at work, and as she had looked after me so well, I went to pick her up from the airport. We had various dinners out and I was able to show her around a bit. About the same time I even started seeing one of Steve's new colleagues, Phil, but that was never really going anywhere, and we decided that being friends was the best option.

Having given up on the swimming which I'd been doing regularly I realised that I had to do exercise of some description, and joined a yoga class. It was an instant success and exactly my type of exercise – absolutely no running and lots of stretching. It fitted into my schedule, and I went early in the evenings on Monday and Friday. So, things were chugging along quite nicely; I was busy in my spare time and work was going well. In fact, there was an added impetus to go to work and that was in the form of a Scotsman called Mark.

He was a new teacher at school, and from our first conversation when I'd interviewed him over the phone, I thought he had a lovely sexy voice and he was so easy to talk to. When he arrived in mid-October, although he was an interesting, sociable person I wasn't attracted to him physically in any way - which was probably a good thing as I was his boss. However, slowly things started to change. I don't really know when but I just started being aware of his presence. I also discovered that he'd asked one of the other teachers if I was married or had a partner.

Things warmed up when we all went out for dinner one evening to celebrate the birthday of one the teachers. After a good meal we went to a little bar over the river, which had a great atmosphere, played good music and had a small dance floor. Mark and I spent ages talking, which progressed to him surreptitiously putting his hand on my knee and then asking if he could take me out on a date. What a sweetie. We danced a lot together, causing the other teachers to gossip no end, and finally left at six o'clock in the morning. Although we shared a taxi with one of the other teachers, I was firm, gave him a peck on the cheek and went upstairs to my flat on my own.

We had our date that Tuesday, and it was a beautiful, if cold November day. I skived off work a little early and suggested we head down to Foz to sit by the sea. We went to my favourite bar which had been refurbished, and sat in the lovely new lounge overlooking the sea. Everything was going well so we decided to go out for dinner. We jumped on the bus, headed back into town and went to my local *Churrasqueira* (a traditional Portuguese restaurant with a charcoal grill) and had chicken and chips. Slightly pissed by then I didn't really make a fuss when Mark asked if he could stay, but told him that it was on the condition that he behaved himself. He did, and so did I, but it was lovely snuggling up with someone in bed.

We had our second date that Thursday evening, and I told Mark I felt like cooking. He said he'd go shopping, and arrived laden with stuff for a curry, booze and a chocolate advent calendar. And he washed up! I like men like this. That weekend he wanted to spend time together but I couldn't as I had already made plans. Before I had started seeing Mark I'd finally heard from Adam. He was in Lisbon! We arranged that I'd go down for the weekend, and stay in a B & B in the centre of town, as he had no space at his flat.

Adam and I had a great weekend together. I felt relaxed in his company and wasn't anxious about what might or might not happen, as I was so taken by Mark. We didn't do much apart from eat, drink and talk a lot. We also didn't really feel the need to do anything touristy although we did manage a walk up to the castle, and through the narrow streets of Alfama.

I got back to Porto on Sunday evening and phoned Mark, expecting to carry on our ramblings of the night before when we had spoken in the early hours when both out partying. However, he was desperately upset as his grandmother had just had a stroke and wasn't expected to make it. I felt unable to help, as our relationship was so new, but tried to listen and told him not to worry about his classes and to book a flight home. The next morning in work we went into a classroom to talk privately, I gave him a huge hug and he then told me that his grandmother had died that morning. He had already booked a flight for the next day and would stay until the following Sunday.

I felt so sorry for him, but ridiculously, also for myself, as I just wanted to be with him and carry on where we had left off. He obviously felt the same as he phoned after work and asked if he could come round for a bit. We talked and I gave him loads of cuddles and he said that he felt guilty about looking forward to seeing me, and feeling happy, when he also felt so sad. I guess it's that old ying and yang thing.

So, having had our first potential weekend together, apart, we then had another full week in different countries. We had the silly conversation about me phoning him at his parents, and trying to explain why his boss would be phoning. He took the plunge and said let's make it official, and be girlfriend and boyfriend. I felt like a teenager again - it was great! Fortunately there were lots of things to keep me busy that week, and at the weekend I went to the cinema with Steve, had a day trip to lovely Ponte de Lima with Phil, and then went out for cocktails in the evening with friends from work.

Soon it was Sunday evening and I went to the airport to pick Mark up. It was wonderful to see him, and having dropped off his stuff at his flat we went back to mine for dinner, and started our relationship properly. It was just lovely! We spent practically every evening together until the Christmas holidays; he met some of my non-work related friends for the first time including having dinner at Charlie and

Carina's and going to Guimarães to stay overnight with Russ and Clare. However, we decided that until we knew where things were going it was better not to go public at work. This wasn't the easiest thing as that first evening together various teachers had noticed how well we were getting on. It was also a pain if we all went out together. One evening we went to the cinema, and although Mark and I managed to manufacture it so we sat together, there was very little hand holding, and afterwards we couldn't even say goodnight properly. We even got to the ridiculous situation a couple of times after work Christmas does that we'd get a lift home to our respective flats and then Mark would come back to mine! After the Christmas party we obviously couldn't leave together, and because we were both rather pissed managed to completely confuse each other, with me waiting at my place and him at his!

For Christmas, I went to the UK and Mark to Scotland. I went all over the place seeing friends; to London to see Phil, over to Southampton to see Matthew and his girlfriend Annelies, and then after Christmas to Amanda and Clive's for Georgia's Christening as I was godmother. My last trip went up to Shrewsbury as Steph and her boyfriend Gareth were there from Poland. It was through Gareth, who had been one of the teachers at my school, that I'd first met Steph. We all stayed at Gareth's parents and on New Year's Eve went to a great party at some of his friends. It was great to see Steph again and bizarre meeting up in Shrewsbury! Being busy was great but I missed Mark loads and was happy to get back to Portugal on the 2nd January knowing that Mark would be there the day after.

Chapter 43

A Spanish jaunt

After Christmas, Mark and I fell into an easy, happy routine and spent every weekend and evenings during the week together. We had lots of dinners with friends, and generally enjoyed each other's company. Before long we were talking about having weekends away, and Carnaval seemed to be a good opportunity. After much discussion we decided on Madrid. Neither of us had been there, and with Mark having friends who lived there, and me having the school car, it seemed like an ideal weekend away.

Both being fairly casual travellers, we didn't really worry too much about how long it would take to get there or how to get there. We set off late on the Saturday morning, heading up the scary E1 through the beautiful hills and onto the planes of Spain. Not only had we left the murky weather behind, but suddenly there wasn't a pothole in sight and the drivers actually obeyed the road signs. After ages, we approached Salamanca which was one of the cities we'd thought about visiting. Although only seeing it from the main road, the view of the old city perched on a hill, with buildings of the most amazing pink stone, was incredible. We vowed to make it one of our next weekends away.

Continuing on towards Madrid, we had a few navigating

problems, probably due to the fact that we didn't have a map, and were using the ridiculously undetailed map in our Spanish guide. With Mark driving by then and me navigating, we came into Madrid at five o'clock on a Saturday afternoon at carnaval. Mistake. The traffic was terrible and we had no idea where we were going. That of course made it all the more interesting, and using the city centre map, and armed with the address of Mark's friends we jumped in and out of bus lanes as they kept changing, avoided shoppers and by some amazing bit of map reading found ourselves on the other side of the city. We were in the area where the museums are, and having driven passed the Prado itself found the street we were looking for. The jubilation quickly disappeared though, as we realised that there no parking spaces anywhere. We drove round for a good half hour, finally managing to squeeze into the smallest space ever.

We'd only been in Madrid for a short while, and I could already sense the energetic atmosphere. Mark's friend Will had some things to do, so after we dumped our stuff in his flat, we arranged to meet him a couple of hours later and set off into the late afternoon. The buildings were beautifully bathed in the sunlight, but it was absolutely freezing, like being in a different continent from Portugal. Of course in the summer it's the complete opposite and boiling as it's three hundred kilometres from the coast. Bit of a strange location for a capital city really, and had been chosen because it was precisely in the middle of the country. This was Philip II's decision and he moved the seat of government there in 1561.

We headed straight to the Plaza Mayor, the main square. Although Madrid doesn't have the architectural sights of Salamanca or Seville, it has that famous Spanish flavour and some amazing gems. The main square was one of those. You got to it by narrow stepped passageways, and there in front of you is the most beautiful square surrounded by a sweep of arcaded buildings. The sun was just starting to set and the whole area was bathed in a gorgeous light. Felipe II had obviously been inspired when he planned it in 1619 as a meeting place for his new capital - even if it did take thirty years to build. Many of the buildings had balconies, from which the aristocracy watched festivals, plays and even hangings. By the time we got there it wasn't quite so exciting and instead had expensive shops and cafés. However, preparations for Carnaval were in full swing, and a stage, lights and barricades were being erected.

Weary, after our long drive and craving a beer we walked back out of the square in search of some refreshment. I have long loved *tapas*; it is so civilised. We managed to find a bar in a small alleyway which was empty of tourists but full of locals. There was only a small range of *tapas*, but they all looked excellent. The speciality of the house was *calamares*, so we had those (although not in a baguette as the local were eating them - bit too much starch) and a plate of *patatas bravas*, potatoes in a spicy tomato sauce. Sitting at one of the tables were four old ladies, dressed in their black, chatting away amicably and drinking beer and eating *tapas*. I remember thinking how unlike older women in the UK they were and that when I'm their age that I hoped I'd be doing the same somewhere - preferably hot!

Duly refreshed, we hooked up with Will and other of his friends who Mark knew from when they had all worked together in a summer school some years previously, and in good old Spanish fashion did a substantial pub crawl. Madrid was alive that night, and everywhere was packed with people celebrating. There was a great atmosphere and we all happily chatted away for hours.

The only downside was having to drag ourselves out of bed. Normally on a Sunday at that stage in our relationship there wouldn't have been any rush to get out of bed, but we were in Madrid and had to make the most of it. To add to that, the Prado museum was free!

And what a museum it was. I had wanted to go there for years and I was finally here. Even the outside of the building was stunning. Built as a natural history museum in 1775, it opened to the public in 1819, and now houses one of the greatest collections of works of art in the world. Apparently there are seven thousand paintings in all, with about a thousand and a half on permanent display. You're not joking! I'd never seen so many paintings. It was completely overwhelming, not just the paintings but the setting. Naturally, as we had limited time we had to do the highlights. So, we looked at some of Bosch's work in the Flemish collection and spent ages in the Spanish collection, looking at works by Goya, El Greco and of course, Velázquez, whose *Las Meninas* was the star of the show. In the Italian gallery I was transfixed by Botticello's trio of panels, even though it was rather gruesome, and then with aching feet and throbbing heads from the night before, we couldn't do any more and headed for a café.

After a caffeine hit, it was soon time for lunch, and Will knew a local restaurant round the corner without a tourist in sight, well, apart from us. It was a great lunch, washed down with some wine which soon banished the headaches, and very bizarrely, a slice of lemon meringue pie (my all time favourite), which I spotted on the dessert shelf.

Even though it wasn't the middle of summer, we did what every other Spaniard did and had a much needed siesta in the afternoon. This, of course, set us up nicely for an evening of *tapas*. We started off in a gorgeous *tapas* place, hidden down a narrow alley, which was traditional and cosy, furnished with wood, and walls lined with bottles of wine. What's more the range of food was excellent. Not your run of the mill *tapas*, but goat's cheese, pheasant, crab and other delights. Having spent a while in a classy place we then set off for a major trawl of the local bars, getting in at a horrible time. But hey, when you're in Madrid and all that!

The next day was another beautiful clear and sunny, but freezing one. Mark and I decided to walk towards the cathedral and palace, stopping whenever we discovered anything interesting. The first was a café, where we had the traditional hot chocolate and *churos*, making us feel immeasurable better. For those not fortunate enough to have eaten them, they are long, deep-fried sweet batter. They might be extremely unhealthy but are gorgeous, especially when dipped in hot chocolate. The second stop was for a beautiful little square, the Plaza de la Villa, which I found memorising, and which had examples of three centuries of Spanish architecture. The first and oldest was the 15th Century renovated Torre de los Lujanes, a beautiful tower built by the Moors working under Christian rule; the second the old town hall built in the 17th Century, but remodelled in a Baroque style, and lastly the 16th Century Casa de Cisneros, built in the 16th Century Plateresque (silversmith) style.

From there, having finally found somewhere to cross the main road we approached the cathedral and the Royal Palace. The cathedral wasn't particularly spectacular from the outside, but since I love the vaulted ceilings of churches and always light a candle for Dad in cathedrals, we went in. It wasn't much inside either. Trying to figure out why it seemed so bland the guidebook explained that although it was planned centuries ago, it was bombed out during the Civil War, worked on for ages and finally opened for business by Pope John Paul II in 1993! Maybe that's why it wasn't as ostentatious as other buildings. Who knows!

Immeasurably more spectacular was the Palacio Real, or Royal Palace. The Hapsburg's original palace burned down on Christmas Day 1734, and its replacement was based on drawings made by Bernini for the Louvre. We didn't feel the need to go inside and so contented ourselves with looking through the railings. These days it is only used for state occasions, with the royal family living elsewhere. From the palace we could see a park and some gardens further north so set off for them. The walk was worth it, and the park and gardens a haven from the noise and pollution of the city. It also provided us with a splendid view of the west side of the palace.

For the remainder of the afternoon we wandered round, soaking up the atmosphere, stopping for a gorgeous *paella* lunch, and then later in the afternoon had a few *tapas*. That evening we took the beautifully clean, efficient metro to the outskirts of Madrid where we had dinner with one of Marks' friends at his flat. To be honest I had never met anyone quite like him, and was amazed at his behaviour when we had all gone out a few days previously. He said the most outrageous things, especially to women, although he hadn't got very far with me as I'd been forewarned and wasn't having any of it. I don't really know whether he stood by any of his convictions, but he frequently condoned fascism and even had a t-shirt, which was pro-Franco! Despite all this we had a fun evening, and stayed late, not having to rush as the last tube left at two-ish. Very civilised! So, that was Madrid. The next morning the parking restrictions came back into force, and with everyone back at work, we headed back to Porto. We motored along, admiring Salamanca again as we drove passed, and by mid-afternoon we reached Portugal.

Chapter 44

Lisbon again

The highs of being in Madrid and having a thoroughly wonderful time with Mark were unfortunately soon countered by a low. Charlie and Carina and their family left Portugal. After much discussion, they had decided to move to Britain - for Charlie this was home, for Carina just another country to add to the list (being a mixture of French, Swedish, Italian and French), for the girls something completely different. For me it was having to say goodbye to yet more good friends. I was so glad that I had Mark to ease the loss. Along with Steve, and Phil (which didn't please Mark) we had a final dinner in a lovely restaurant where we ate platters of shellfish, washed down with Vinho Verde.

What was working out well was my relationship with Mark. Everything was perfect and we were having a great time together. We decided to go away for Easter, and choose Lisbon as our destination. Although I'd been there before Mark hadn't, and we also both wanted to go to Évora and Sintra. We drove down from Porto on a beautiful sunny Tuesday before Easter, and stopped off for lunch at one of the picnic areas in the very grandly named Parque Natural das Serras de Aire e Candeeiros. By then the temperature had increased and we were sitting outside in t-shirts. Great!

With Mark driving the last bit and me navigating we managed to get right into the centre of Lisbon and to the Praça dos Restauradoes. However, once we were there we couldn't find the hotel, which was supposed to be on the square. We drove up and down for ages, and finally found the wretched place. Then, of course, was the problem of parking. As we were right in the middle of the city, we didn't bother even trying for a space on the square so drove up the steep roads near the hotel, and eventually found somewhere. The good thing was that although it was a fair trek from the hotel, it was close to one of the funicular railways, the Elevador da Lavra, which meant that we didn't have to struggle with our bags. We did, however, then have to climb four flights of stairs as there wasn't a lift in the hotel. It was bizarrely called the Pensão Imperio, but there really wasn't anything imperial about it. The room was as basic as could be, with a walk down the hall to the bathroom, but it was clean and that was all we needed.

To make the most of the gorgeous weather we headed down to the beautiful Praça do Comércio which I'd so admired on previous visits. From there were took the rickety wooden tram along the water front to Belém. Although I had been there a couple of times previously it was one of those places that you are always happy to revisit, and Mark wanted to go. We wandered around the splendid Mosteiro Jerónimus, and walked over the road to the Torre de Belém, and sat in the sun admiring it. I'd forgotten how beautiful it was, with the lovely Manueline decoration. A beer stop was then called for so we stopped at a small outside café and watched people go by and the sun go down over the water.

In the evening we walked down one of the tiny streets near the hotel, and to a pedestrianised road that had lots of restaurant. Some of them were very touristy, but we managed to find one which seemed more authentic, and were able to sit outside. Naturally, being able to speak Portuguese helped, and the waiter was charm personified. We then found one of the traditional, long, zinc topped bars, and waited for Adam who we had arranged to meet. Naturally, I was somewhat apprehensive as to how the evening would go. I wasn't sure how Adam and Mark would get on, and if it would be at all awkward. I needn't have worried. We headed up to the Bairro Alto, famed for its late night bars and where I had a drunken evening the previous December with Adam, and bar crawled though a variety of watering holes.

It wasn't the easiest thing to get up the next day, but a breakfast of toast and strong coffee did the trick, and we decided that since it was a glorious day we would make use of it and visit Évora. After getting a little lost we finally reached the spectacular suspension bridge which spanned the Tagus and whose grand opening I'd seen on television. The Ponte 25 de Abril (originally named!) was opened in 1996 to commemorate the bloodless revolution of 1974. It looked somewhat like the Golden Gate Bride in San Francisco, and at nearly two and a half kilometres across was the longest suspension bridge in the world. It was amazing driving over it, and with the sun sparkling on the water you felt miles from anywhere. Leaving the bridge we then drove inland toward Évora. It was getting hotter by the minute, and by the time we arrived at the city it was sweltering. We parked easily outside the city walls, and then walked inside. The old city, its whitewashed buildings gleaming in the sun, was perched on a hill. It was incredibly picturesque from a distance, and didn't disappoint closer either.

The narrow, twisty streets led sharply upwards to the main squares and important buildings. Overcome by the heat we made an early pit stop and found some shade underneath a parasol, outside a café in a large square. We hadn't read much about the city beforehand, preferring just to wander and see what we could find. What a find the first thing was! The Templo Romano, otherwise know as the Roman Temple. It was   beautiful, and stood majestically in the centre of a pretty square. There were twelve granite pillars, and a fantastic marble floor. According to the guidebook it was the best-preserved temple in Portugal. I hadn't even known it had existed. Further reading revealed that the Romans had occupied the city for four centuries, and after them the Moors for a similar amount of time. We spent a long time just soaking up the atmosphere - there were a minimal number of tourists, and there was the most amazing feeling of peace and calm.

From there we continued walking, poking around in little squares and following narrow lanes, just enjoying being in such a beautiful city. Of course, the word city, is used way too generously as the place was minute and you could walk across it in about fifteen minutes! Next stop was lunch in a cool café where we had a sandwich and a beer. After that we headed for the church of São Francisco, which was again a haven from the heat. The church itself was interesting, but it was one of the chapels which we had read about that was our destination. Not really for the faint hearted, it was called the Capela dos Ossos, the chapel of bones, and it was exactly that. Every available bit of wall or pillar was decorated with human bones, arranged in intricate patterns. It was cold, and slightly damp, and there was a surreal orange glow to the place. The reason for the bones was that many years previously, building was due to take place in the graveyard where monks were buried. The church decided that the bones had to be re-buried elsewhere, but not having any space hit upon the idea of building a chapel for them. By the time all the walls and pillars were covered, the bones of an estimated five thousand monks were on display. It was one of those places that you don't really want to be in, but at the same time are fascinated by. Emerging into the sunshine and heat was most definitely pleasant, and after a walk round the lovely park, we headed back to Lisbon where we had a leisurely dinner and a few bar stops.

The next day, we decided that we both wanted to go to the Gulbenkian Museum, so jumped on the metro which took us the few stops north of where we were staying and to the gardens which housed the museum. It had been established by an Armenian oil magnate, Calouste Gulbenkian. He had a huge collection of art and wanted it to be displayed under one roof. Although he died in 1955 a foundation was set up the following year, taking his name, and the museum was inaugurated in 1969. There were two main areas – the first held Oriental, Egyptian, Greek, Roman and Islamic arts, and the second European paintings. It was the Japanese and Chinese gallery room that held my attention; full of beautiful porcelains, tapestries and prints and it also had a large collection of jade figures and bowls. I was in heaven. The European art which was on show ranged from the 15th Century, with works by Rubens and Rembrandt, continued into the eighteenth with pictures by Gainsborough, and then ended with some Turner's and finally works from the Impressionist giants, in the form of Manet, Degas and Monet, amongst others. The final gallery was dedicated to jewellery and glasswork, designed in the Art Noveau style by René Lalique, the likes of which I have never seen before. The jewellery was spectacular, and completely over the top. Quite how one person had accumulated so much art, and had the money to buy it was unbelievable. What was great was that it was all on display. Finally leaving, we strolled round the gardens, beautifully landscaped, and admired the building itself which was a landmark in Portuguese museum architecture.

That afternoon I had my fourth visit to the Alfama district of Lisbon. Full of narrow, windy streets it was always an interesting place to poke around. Before that we tracked down a house which Mark had read about and wanted to see; the Casa dos Bicos, or the house of points, which had an amazing prickly façade and dated from the 16th Century. Before climbing the hill we then decided to look for an Indian restaurant which we'd discovered in our guidebook. We easily located it, looked at the fabulous menu and discovered that there was no problem reserving a table. Invigorated by thought of a curry, we stormed up the hill. We did a quick circuit around the castle, and then had a fairly expensive drink in the bar next to the castle, overlooking Lisbon. Just sitting there with Mark, and the lovely view, I remember feeling completely contended at that moment in my life. Having eked out our expensive drinks for as long as possible, there was one more stop on the tourist route that we needed to make. That was the cathedral. Although I'd been inside before I'd never been to the Roman remains, which had been discovered at the back of the cathedral. They were in a large excavated area in the middle of the 6th Century Gothic cloisters. Very few other people seemed to have discovered the remains and we were able to enjoy them in peace.

Then it was time for dinner. And what a dinner it was. Many of the dishes were from Goa and the food was truly exquisite. In true Indian restaurant style we ordered far too much, but not knowing when we would next be able to eat such food, cleared our plates. Both being completely stuffed and extremely tired, we didn't try to fit in another beer so went back to the hotel and crashed out.

The following morning, after a leisurely breakfast, we navigated our way out of Lisbon and headed to Sintra. The drive there was lovely; we wound our way up tree-lined roads and, along with half the world, arrived in Sintra. It was, of course, Good Friday, and a national holiday and it seemed that everyone else had the same idea. We did finally manage to park the car, and then walked into the small town. It was full of tourist shops and restaurants, but was dominated by the Palácio National. The palace had been commissioned by Dom João I (King John I) in the 14th Century, and finished in the reign of Dom Manuel in the 15th Century. This was reflected in the mixture of Gothic and Manueline architecture. We went inside the palace, which wasn't really that big and admired some of the antique tapestries, furnishings, and most interestingly the kitchen with its incredibly high ceiling and hole at the top for the smoke to leave.

As interesting as it was, the other Sintra Palace was what most people came for. Fortified by lunch, we then headed up the steep hill and into the Pena Park. Although able to drive up, there was only so far we could go. Everybody else was frantically trying to park so we had to do the same, and then start walking in the heat. Finally, arriving at the main gates we then had had the horrific task of climbing up the steep path to the palace. But it was worth it and I was convinced I was in the middle of a Disney princess film. The 19th Century palace was a fantasy, complete with domes and turrets and painted in a variety of colours. The royal family had lived there until 1910, and the interior hadn't been changed. As there were thousands of people queuing we abandoned any hope of going inside, and satisfied ourselves by wandering round the outside, squeezing along some of the narrow walkways, and looking at the spectacular views of the surrounding landscape. The whole area had been made a World Heritage site in 1995, and added to that, Byron had a love for Sintra, where he wrote some of his poems.

So, that was our Easter break in Lisbon. It had been great, and arriving back in Porto on the Friday afternoon we still had the weekend before returning to work.

Chapter 45

The last stretch

As always, when everything is going well, things then happen which make you question everything. That was what happened to me a few weeks later. One evening Mark had gone to a party which I hadn't fancied so had stayed in, expecting him to appear at some point later that night. And then the phone rang. It was Will, rambling somewhat incoherently. We had known each other for four years and always spent time together when I was in the UK. Previously I'd wondered whether we could have gone the duration if I'd lived there, but we'd never really talked about it and Will had never suggested the possibility of us making a commitment. I was therefore completely gob smacked when he said that he'd just realised what had been in front of his nose for ages, namely me; that he was in love with me and wanted to commit and come to live in Portugal with me. Stop! What had he just said? I told him that he was drunk and talking rubbish. He did however repeat it all, and asked if he could come out in two days time! I told him that things had been progressing with Mark, that we were very happy and I wasn't going to leave him. I did tell him, that if he wanted a break in Portugal he was more than welcome; however, he said that all he would do was and try and tempt me away from Mark, so a holiday wasn't an option.

After almost an hour on the phone I felt completely exhausted. If he'd told me all that before I'd met Mark, I probably wouldn't have hesitated. Then of course I started thinking about whether Mark and I really had a future. He knew that I was planning on leaving Portugal that summer and following my dream to go and live in France, and I knew that his teaching contract was finishing at the end of June, and that as he had only just started working as an English Language Teacher, he wanted to travel some more. The thing is that we hadn't actually talked about all this. Fortunately, by the time Mark came in he was a bit worse for ware, didn't realise I was so distracted and we both went straight to bed. I knew that I needed to know what his thoughts were, so, on the Sunday evening I broached the subject. As I expected he wasn't ready to settle down in France, and I didn't want to move anywhere different (and go back to living out of a suitcase) so we were at stalemate.

I felt so emotional inside but obviously couldn't tell Mark that Will had phoned declaring his undying love. The other issue was whether Mark and I continued seeing each other, as by July the wrench would be even worse or just stopped there and then. Stopping, we decided would be impossible. So, we continued as we had been, and I tried to put Will out of my head. The fun soon returned, with lots of partying and spending time together, and then I managed to land myself back in casualty.

On one of the fairly frequent Catholic holidays Mark and I had been up to Guimarães to have lunch with my pals. After a good time we got back to Porto and had an afternoon nap! Contrary to what my friends thought, I smashed my head on the headboard as I was getting up from being horizontal. Bloody hell it hurt and I felt incredibly weird. We'd been planning on going round the corner to the Churrasqueira for chicken and chips but I didn't think I'd make the walk.

Mark went anyway and got a takeaway, but I couldn't really eat anything. That was when he started worrying - Rachael not wanting to eat anything!

I struggled in to work the next day, but by lunchtime couldn't cope anymore. I went home to try and sleep but someone was drilling next door. When Mark realised that I wasn't at work, he ordered me to go to casualty, so that was that. It was even worse than the time before.

I was in the same area, waiting for an x-ray as I'd done the previous year. After ages I tried to explain that since there wasn't a cut on my head and that I was feeling sick and faint that I really needed to be seen sooner than later. It worked, in that they put me on a drip for the pain and told me to lie down on a trolley. A long time later and I was still there, with the same amount of pain, and with a drip that didn't appear to be making any difference. I finally persuaded someone to help when blood was going up the tube from my arm; with the nurse saying that it hadn't been turned on properly! Oh good. And then it was time for the x-ray. The technicians told me I'd have to get up and sit on a chair for it. No way. I thought I was going to throw up and faint at the same time. They caught me just as I was about to keel over and then had to do the x-ray with me lying down. Another intolerably long wait and I finally saw the doctor again. By then I was staring to feel a bit better as whatever I was on had kicked in. The doctor told me I was ok, that there was no internal damage, but that I'd had a post-traumatic stress reaction to the bang, and needed to take things easy. I was taken back to a quiet area where I was made to drink some cold tea from a bowl, and promising that someone was at home was allowed to leave after half an hour. I'd been there for hours and would have done anything to get out. Just as I was gathering myself the head honcho or whatever he was called came to check on me. I have absolutely no idea why, but we had to go through everything again. By that point I would have said anything and sworn black was white to get out of the place!

I finally escaped and by then feeling weak with hunger, jumped in a taxi and went home. My knight in shining armour arrived shortly afterwards, and fussed around me. Unfortunately, it was bad timing on my behalf as the next day Marks' friends arrived from Madrid for a couple of days. I managed to make it out for supper the following evening, but then left them to get on with it. I did manage to do the Port tour with them all on the Saturday and true to form Dave (of the extreme views) got us chucked out of a shop selling medals and things when he asked if they had any souvenirs of Salazar, the former Portuguese dictator!!

The following week and feeling back to normal I was on the move - this time to the UK to meet Mum's new fiancé. It had all happened very quickly and she wanted me to meet him before the wedding. It was all rather strange but everyone got on, and we looked forward to the wedding which happened five weeks later in the middle of June.

The other monumentous event was handing in my notice to Alex. He was wonderful about it, and jealous that I was really going to move to France! I hadn't actually got a job but was searching madly on the Internet to get some leads. However, before I became immersed in that, Mark and I had our last two months to be together as a couple. We spent all our time together, not really caring if anyone from school did see us. The weather was gorgeous and we spent long early summer evenings in restaurants and sitting outside bars, by ourselves or with friends.

Towards the end of June was Mark's birthday and we decided to spend the weekend in Salamanca. On the Saturday morning we were both working, so could only set off at 1pm, but the Monday was a holiday so we had two nights away. It was a boiling hot afternoon, and as we climbed up towards the plains of Spain it just got hotter and hotter. By the time we arrived in Salamanca at 7 o'clock it was forty-one degrees. How could it possibly be that temperature at that time in June! We were absolutely dying for a beer, but first of all had to find somewhere to park, and then somewhere to stay. After trudging round for a while we found a cheap and very cheerful *pension* right in the centre but at that time the need for beer was greater than the quality of somewhere to sleep.

We spent the evening walking around the beautiful city, stopping off in a variety of bars. The road parallel to the one where we were staying, the Rua Melendez, was lined with bars and despite being so close to the central street wasn't expensive at all. We spent a while there and then decided to treat ourselves to a drink in the main square. The Plaza Mayor was absolutely stunning, and I thought more beautiful then the Plaza Mayor in Madrid. The eighteenth-century Baroque square consisted of buildings made from the lovely local, golden, pinkish sandstone, were four stories high, and formed a continuous ring around the square. It was the most picturesque, romantic setting for a birthday aperitif.

Having sampled a variety of bars and *tapas* the previous evening we spent the morning on the tourist trail. Walking though the pedestrianised streets it seemed that all the buildings were beautiful, whatever they were. The place just oozed history. Our first stop was the university, and before going in we admired the stunning main door, designed in the Plateresque style, and covered with medallions, emblems and decorations. Inside we ascended the elegant staircase, which took us up to the ancient library. It was crammed full of beautiful books, stuffed onto row after row of wooden shelves which reached to the ceiling, and also littered with antiquated globes. It was a book lover's paradise.

Next on the trail were the two cathedrals. The 'new' cathedral was only a couple of yards away, built in the Gothic style, and finished in 1512. There was another Plateresque entrance, which was dazzling in its detail. There were also elements of the Renaissance and Baroque styles, which meant that the cathedral had a bit of everything. It was certainly stunning, and built of the same beautifully coloured sandstone as the rest of the important buildings in Salamanca. It rather overshadowed the smaller, older cathedral which was Romanesque. Somewhat buildinged out we walked down towards the Roman bridge which spanned the river, and sat down to look back at the beautiful city. It was a perfect summer's day, with the brightest deep blue sky which framed the pink buildings. It was one of those perfectly happy moments, enhanced by being with the man I loved. I made the most of it, as I knew that in little over a week's time we'd be apart.

The time had come for some sustenance so we found a cute backstreet bar and settled in for cold beer and yet more gorgeous *tapas*. And then of course, time for a late afternoon siesta, and a cold shower to try and cool down a bit. That evening we decided to have a proper sit down meal and after rather a lot of bar hopping we found a great Argentinean restaurant, and had a lovely meal.

The following morning we set off for hot chocolate and *churros*. Sustained we ventured out in to the heat of the morning, to do some more sightseeing. We found the Casa de la Conchas, or House of Shells, which was covered in rows of carved scallop shells. As well as being beautiful it was one of the buildings on the pilgrimage route to Santiago. The last stop was the Toure de Clavero, a fifteenth century octagonal tower. It was one of the smallest buildings we'd seen, and very plain compared to the flamboyant Platereseque, but perched among other buildings was my favourite.

Having to get back for work the next day, we set off late morning, and stopped in a small Spanish town to get some supplies for lunch. After crossing the border back into Portugal, we found a fabulous roadside picnic area, with the most amazing views over the valley and munched on fresh bread and cheese - childhood memories suddenly took me back to similar picnics in Switzerland, so many years before, sitting high up in the mountains. After lunch, we happily motored along, despite the stifling heat, when we realised that something fairly serious was happening ahead. The sky had changed colour from bright blue to dark grey and after a while the traffic was being directed off the motorway. We guessed that it was one of the forest fires, which are so prevalent in Portugal during the summer, but this was only June. The deviation took ages, and then when we finally joined the motorway the traffic was horrendous. It took ages to get home and we were both hot and fed up.

After a lovely weekend the reality was sinking in during that last week of June. When we weren't working Mark and I spent every minute together, whether at home or having meals in favourite restaurants. The weekend loomed and that meant it was the last one. On our last day we decided to be touristy, and enjoy the beautiful river so took a cruise on the Douro. It was extremely poignant and we often just sat in companiable silence.

The following morning was horrible and to add to it I had the prospect of a hospital appointment with the rheumotology department to see if they could figure out why I had such bad back pain. Early in the morning we walked to the bus stop together, Mark with all his bags, and said goodbye whilst waiting for the airport bus. And then he was gone, and I caught my bus.

The next couple of hours were a nightmare. I waited for three hours in a crowded, hot waiting area, where having a time for an appointment seemed to mean absolutely nothing! The consultant gave me a diagnosis, which although showed that I didn't have any permanent bone damage, also didn't provide a solution.

As ever, keeping busy was a help to my wows, and I filled my time working, going to yoga and seeing friends. Then, a couple of weeks later my brother phoned me at work to say that our wonderful grandfather had died. I flew back to the UK a week later in time for his funeral. Before that though, was my work leaving party which my boss had organised at his house. He'd provided a fantastic spread in the garden on a sunny afternoon in July, and even better were the bins (new, clean ones!) full of Pimms. All my work colleagues were there, and I received some fantastic presents, and although sad about the reason why I was returning to the UK the following day, I realised that all the people I had worked with for four years had appreciated me.

Granddad's funeral was on the Monday afternoon, and unsurprisingly I was all over the place. He had been a fantastic granddad, and when I was having a terrible time in my teens with Mum, and for years after that had always been so supportive and wise. He also used to tell me fantastic stories of when he was abroad during the war, of his ship being torpedoed off Alexandria and of how it rained frogs in India.

I spent the rest of the week in the UK visiting friends and then flew back to Portugal for my final month there. I had a last holiday planned, and that was to go camping with Clare, Russ and the kids in Spain. On an extremely hot Saturday I drove up to their house outside Guimarães, and we packed the cars full of vital camping gear - inflatable mattresses, pillows, wine; the usual stuff, and headed north.

One little hitch occurred when I couldn't see Clare and

Russ ahead of me on the motorway for a while and had no idea where the campsite was, so couldn't even meet them there. At the same time I was running perilously low on petrol and could see a complete disaster about to happen. Fortunately all was resolved, as I spotted them ahead and then waved madly that I needed to stop. A while later we left the motorway near Padrón and turned inland. Galicia is a beautiful part of Spain and this part of the coastline was no exception. We dove through amazing countryside, often catching glimpses of inviting bays, finally arriving at a lovely campsite situated on a bay on the Ría de Arousa. It was in amongst tall pine trees, and there was a great café overlooking a bay of clear green water. Even better was that there wasn't a Brit in sight.

We had a great four days - not really doing much, apart from sun bathing, swimming, wandering around local towns, and eating and drinking. The idyllic scene changed on the forth night. We had the most amazing summer storm with strong winds and monsoon style rain. Not much sleep was had by anyone in the campsite but the worst was to come when we ventured out of our tents in the morning. The fine orangey dirt had turned to thick, red mud. Ruben, being three, was delighted, and in less than a minute was covered from head to toe, but Clare and I were not impressed. We decided enough was enough, and despite what Russ and the kids wanted to do, we said were going home. Packing up was interesting, and by then everything; clothes, bedding, us were covered in red mud. Lovely! I was able to fling everything in the washing machine although the tent took some serious housing down. Just to add to Clare's wows, there wasn't any mains water at their house because the well had dried up, so she was faced with trying to figure out how to clean everything!

Despite all this we had had a lovely holiday and it was a final chance to spend some time with my best friends. On the way back to Portugal we stopped off in Guarda, a small town on the coast, and had lunch in a local restaurant we'd been to many times before. We stuffed our faces full of delicious *tapas,* including a hot favourite, *Pimentos de Padron,* those delicious small green peppers, baked in the oven with salt. Of course, the catch is that about one in ten is hot enough to blow your head off - a bit like playing Russian roulette with peppers!

And that was nearly it. There was one final chance for me to show off Porto to a visitor as Will arrived a few weeks later. Despite the fact that I'd knocked him back earlier in the year he still wanted to come on holiday and had said that he'd help me move. I realised it was too good an opportunity to miss so we had a touristy, relaxing week together. However, I was still really missing Mark, and when Will started making advances I had to firmly say 'no'. This didn't spoil our week and I took Will to all the usual haunts, and generally ate and drank too much, and lazed around in the sunshine.

I managed a final visit up to Guimarães, and took Will for dinner with Clare and Russ. We had a lovely 'last supper', and made final plans for moving day, which was a couple of days away. Over the last few days I squeezed in a last few beers with other friends and that was that.

On a boiling hot August day, Clare, Russ and the kids arrived and together we loaded up the Mercedes van I'd hired. It took an absolute age, and when we were done rewarded ourselves with a final beer together at the local café at the end of my road. All that was left was to coax Jack and Melton into their cat box, and cram the four of us into the front. Up to then we'd all been too busy to think about the reality of what was happening but then it was time to say goodbye. The first time I'd left Portugal, was at the airport, Ruben hadn't been born and Rosie was only two. That was bad enough. This time was worse. Clare has always hated saying goodbye, and she was in floods of tears, which set Rosie and I off. There was no point in delaying our departure any more, so we left, with me driving to give me something to concentrate on.

I had loved living in Portugal, but knew that it was time to leave - not just because of my burning desire to live in France, but because some of the aspects of Portuguese life were really starting to grate. These included the endless waiting to get anything done at the post office, bank etc, and some of the old fashioned attitudes and intolerance to others. I wanted to remember Portugal in a positive light, so realised the time had come to leave.

Part Twelve

Vive la France

Chapter 46

Early days

About twenty-six hours later Will and I were sitting in a different little bar, overlooking the marina in Palavas-les-Flots, which was my new home. Palavas was a small, Mediterranean, seaside town, straddling a canal, a couple of miles south of Montpellier in the Languedoc. We had taken all my valuables, including Jack and Melton, up to my very small flat and then exhausted, hot and extremely bothered found the nearest bar. It also seemed to be the most expensive bar, at over five euros for a beer! Oh Lord what had I done? I certainly hoped there were cheaper bars, or this would be the end of my bar going evenings in France.

The next morning we woke up late, preparing ourselves for hauling all my belongings in the incredible heat up three flights of stairs and trying to cram them into my bedroom, and lounge cum dining room cum kitchen. Clambering around boxes looking for cups and teabags I realised I could hear a very unfamiliar sound coming from outside. It was absolutely pissing down, monsoon style. How could that possibly be happening after the extreme heat (and no air-con) we'd endured across Spain?

The journey out of Portugal had started well. I knew the route out of Porto well and with only one road up towards

Braganca we made good progress. When we left the motorway to cut through the mountains, Will navigated without any problems. However, driving that way with the spectacular scenery had its downside - it took ages. Will took over the driving and we continued on the motorway through Spain. Soon it was dark and I realised that it was ridiculous to drive through the night, or kip in the van, as there was no space. Quite why I thought it would be ok I have no idea! Outside Burgos I made an executive decision and armed with my credit card we headed towards a motel set back from the motorway.

In my best Spanish I enquired about a room and was delighted to be told they had some vacancies. We managed to back the van into a space right up against the hotel, in the hope of deterring thieves, who I'd knew like nothing better than stealing from vehicles. We took up overnight stuff, my laptop and vital paperwork, and then tried to figure out a way to get the cats inside. I hadn't asked if they accepted pets or not, as we couldn't bear the thought of having to drive further to find anywhere else to stay. So, Will put the cats in his holdall, and whilst walking passed the reception and up the windy staircase we both coughed loudly in case the meowing started. With the cats safely installed and fed although not especially happy, we headed to the restaurant where we were just in time for a late dinner, and some well earned red wine.

I'd like to say we had a good night's sleep, but Melton prowled round all night miaowing, and although Will was immune I wasn't. We set off again in the morning, and drove east from Burgos. Before long we were heading up into the hills, and with the scorching weather of the day before long gone, the clouds came down and it started pissing down. It was slow going over the hills and down toward San Sebastian and Bilbao, and then the traffic started building up. Going into France it crawled along, as people were either returning, or going on holiday. Once into France and going passed Biarritz we hoped it would pick up, but it just got worse. We were stuck in a jam for hours, by which time the sun had broken though and it was becoming stiflingly hot again. Finally getting round Biarritz we joined the A4 that would take us across the bottom of France, and towards Montpellier. I realised then that our estimated arrival time of mid afternoon was way out. We stopped at the next service station, into which half of France were crammed, and searched for a phone. Of course they didn't take coins so we had to join the enormous queue, and swapping from Spanish to French, I negotiated buying a phone card. I finally managed to get through to my Godmother, who gave me the number of her acquaintance whose flat I was renting, and I then had the task of speaking French on the phone. I rearranged a new arrival time with my landlord, and then we set off for a long, hot fractious drive. We went though some lovely scenery around Pau and Tarbes, with many tempting signposts to vineyards, and then up to Toulouse which we navigated around using the slightly bizarre road signs. Then it was another road east passed Carcassone, which looked stunning with the afternoon sun shining on it, and we finally arrived at the coast near Narbonne. We headed north to Beziers, and felt that the end was actually in sight. What was waiting for us was another traffic jam, as we drove up the coast towards Montpellier.

At about seven in the evening, we drove passed the lagoon, full of flamingos which I remember from my childhood, and arrived in Palavas. A really terrible day later and I wondered whether it was an indication of things to come.

The following morning we ventured outside to start unloading the van in the downpour to discover the right hand wing mirror was completely smashed and hanging off.

Oh bugger. Since it was a Sunday there was nothing we could do - the firm we'd hired the van from in Portugal was shut, and there were no garages open in the area. I took it as a bad omen though, and worried about it all day despite Will trying to reassure me we'd sort it out.

What followed was the hardest three hours I think I've ever spent. In the hot downpour, which didn't relent all day, we carried boxes and furniture up the three flights of stairs to my new flat. There was stuff everywhere as the flat was so tiny. From having a fairly large one-bedroomed flat, with a separate kitchen and big balcony, I now had an extremely small home. The lounge and kitchen was combined, with a tiny balcony, and a bedroom which the double bed almost filled. The worse thing though was the most monstrous piece of furniture. It was a large cabinet, made of horrible, old Formica, and dominated the tiny living area. What's more it was full of old fashioned, dodgy, glass crockery. Yuk! We needed to escape the chaos and cramped space, so went in search of some food. We found a cheapish restaurant where we sheltered from the rain and drank lots of beer!

The next morning was blue and hot, but unfortunately we couldn't go to the beach and relax as we had the van to sort out. The first job was to buy another phone card and phone the rental company in Portugal. It turned out that we would have to forfeit quite a chunk of the deposit. Because of this and the fact that Will, who hadn't driven much on the continent, and wasn't happy about driving all the way back without a wing mirror, we decided to try and find a Mercedes dealer. Just what I needed, when I'd envisaged spending a day on the beach with Will before he had to leave.

The tourist office was the first stop, where we found the French equivalent of the yellow pages. Fortunately there was a Mercedes dealer outside Montpellier. We, well I, phoned them up, and managed somehow to explain what had happened. I had no idea what the word in French was for wing mirror but somehow got my point across. Result - they had a right hand side one in stock, and if we went that afternoon they could fit it for us. Something was going right. It was a fairly hairy journey, driving without really being able to see behind, and not having a local map. We made it though, and the mirror was fixed very quickly. It meant that we even had a few hours left of the afternoon, so we headed back to Palavas and crashed out on the beach until late. Will was due to leave the following day, so we treated ourselves to dinner and lots of red wine and had an enjoyable evening together. I even finally relented to Will's advances; I think because I knew I was going to be on my own for a while and had no idea when and where the next bit of closeness was going to come from more than anything else.

After a morning of lazing around, the time for Will to leave had arrived. Rather than just being left at my flat, he dropped me at the supermarket which was on the road out of Palavas, so I had something to do. Saying goodbye was so hard, and the enormity of what I was doing started to sink in. We had a last hug, and then Will drove off in the van, leaving me standing in the heat in the middle of the car park bawling my eyes out. A distraction was what I needed, and it was there in front of me - a French supermarket. I pulled myself together, and retreating from the mid-afternoon heat, made my way inside. It was an instant tonic; wandering up and down the aisles, looking at all the lovely wine, cheese, bread and fresh vegetables. This was one of the reasons I was on my own in a small town in the south of France, and I readily soaked it all up. Having no car I bought what I could carry, and then started the long, hot walk back to my new home.

For the following few days I kept myself busy unpacking all the boxes, and trying to make the flat welcoming and home like. Jack was more than happy to help and clambered in and out of boxes, discovering familiar smells; unlike Melton who was still hiding underneath anything she could find! I also started using my French, and went to the local telecom shop where I bought a mobile and organised for a landline to be installed. I also needed to get a bank account organised so I could transfer the rest of my funds from Portugal. Directly opposite me was a *Societé General* and since that was the bank that Dad had used in Paris, the decision was made. I booked an appointment with the manager, who was very helpful and extremely patient with my French sentences full of Portuguese words, and before long I had an account.

In the mornings I'd make the first cup of tea, and squeeze onto my deckchair on the balcony. If I hung over the edge I could see the boats in the marina and from my chair could watch the locals walk by with their freshly made baguettes. These little things bought a smile to my face, and I realised that being in France seemed so right and the most natural state in the world. Of course I guess it wasn't such a surprise with all the French blood running around in my system. The first link was through Dad's family - apparently Henri De Gournay (a nobleman) had come to Britain with William to help him conquer! The second was a more recent link in that my paternal grandmother's family had been French and come to live in the UK. The final, much more interesting fact was that my great-grandmother's grandmother had been the illegitimate child of the then Lord of a well-know banking and wine family. Unfortunately, her family were paid off and everything was hushed up. I sometimes wonder what a DNA test would show!

On the Friday I discovered that that there was a little food market on the other side of the canal, situated in the narrow street where the shops were. The highlights were a van selling gorgeous quiches and pies, and the ever-present cheese stall. Most of the village was crammed into the tiny area, chatting amiably, and I felt more content than I had done since Will left.

Chapter 47

Montpellier

Whilst it was wonderful looking at all the food stalls and shops in Palavas, if I was to be able to enjoy them then I needed to earn some money. I figured out where the local bus left from, and climbed on board after all the sun worshipers had got out to spend the day at the beach. Although it was the first week of September it was boiling hot still, and I'd much rather have been on the beach with them.

I left the bus on the outskirts of Montpellier and from there crossed over the road to wait for the tram. It was a new system and was quick, clean and efficient. Arriving in the centre of Montpellier it was everything I'd remembered and more. The central square had been completely renovated, and on all sides was edged with cafés. As tempting as they were I had to put my cold calling hat on and get job searching. During that week I went into the city centre three times, left my CV in as many language schools as I could find, talked to as many people in them that were free, and generally acquainted myself with the layout. As much as anything else it kept me busy, rather than sitting alone in a small flat wondering what the future held.

The following week I felt brave enough to battle French bureaucracy, and armed with all the documents I thought I might need, and a few more in case, finally found the social security building in Montpellier. I needed a social security number if I was going to work, and I might as well get that under way. There was a lot of queuing, and form filling, and, of course, lots of practising my French. On the whole it was fine, apart from the fairly regular Portuguese word slipping in when things got complicated. I seemed to be on the right track, and went away with an appointment for the next week, and more documents to bring. That visit took considerably longer and I think I must have spoken to everyone in the enormous area, being moved from one cubicle to another. However, it worked and I had my card within a couple of weeks - unlike my resident's permit, the time spent on trying to get it drove me to drink.

Having gone to the town hall in Montpellier, I was told I had to go to the local mayor in Palavas. Of course, when I went there I was told I had to go to Montpellier, etc, etc, etc. I finally found a sweet lady in the town hall in Montpellier, but even though she said definitively that I had to do it in Palavas, could see that I was close to tears, drink, murdering someone and relented. I don't know why she helped; I think that maybe speaking French had softened her, and she told me she'd put my application through. It still took an age, but at least I was in the system.

The next hurdle, but normally a joy was my birthday. It was the following weekend, and I really didn't want to spend it alone. I talked to my Godmother on the phone, and she said that I would be most welcome to visit them where they lived in a small village in the Cévennes mountains. What she also said that as she and her husband were due to return to the UK in October for the winter, that I could use their second car which they normally parked outside. Oh joy; I was jumping up and down on the spot. What's more all I would have to do was to put petrol in it.

Having opened the cards that arrived on the morning of my birthday, I made sure the cats were ok, and started out on my mammoth journey. It involved getting the local bus into Montpellier, then getting the tram, and then walking to the coach station. I wandered around aimlessly for a while, as you do in coach stations, regardless of which country they are in, trying to figure out which bus stop I needed and finally relented and asked someone. I waited where I'd been told to, and on time a rather dilapidated coach pulled up. I virtually had it to myself, so settled myself in to enjoy the scenery up to Ganges. Leaving the city north of Montpellier we then joined the road up into the mountains. It was quiet and calm until ....now what was happening? We had turned right and appeared to be driving into the middle of nowhere. It had to be the right bus though as I'd asked when boarding. It was of course, just stopping at places which definitely weren't marked on the timetable. We soon joined the main road again and started climbing.

I've always loved mountains and rivers next to each other and soon remembered this particular scenery. The road ran parallel to the dramatic river gorge, and as not driving I could gaze upward at the fantastic views. We soon passed a signpost to Grotte des Demoiselles, a fantastic group of caves and pools of water. Whilst that was beautiful, it was for a tiny restaurant that I remembered it. I'd been there one incredibly hot day years before with Mum, Dad and Matthew. There was only a limited menu, but the food was delicious. I had only been there once but it had always been one of those magical places for Mum and Dad. How different things might have been if Dad had lived and bought a house in the region as they'd been planning?

Before long the coach arrived in Ganges, and stopped in the market square. There, as planned was Jean. It was great to see someone I knew, and on the drive further up into the Cévennes mountains we caught up. She put together a lovely cold lunch of cheeses, bread, salads and fresh figs from their tree and we sat outside in the garden, enjoying the weather. In the afternoon she and I went for a walk in the hills behind the village - not my usual birthday activity, but good nevertheless. What helped was a message from Clare on my mobile.

My strange birthday continued in the evening. Jean had invited my landlord's parents over for a pre-dinner drink. They were obviously curious about their son's tenant, and fired questions at me. Some of the time I had little idea what they were talking about, and nodded politely. Alcohol was what was needed - after all it was my birthday. Being Jean there was homemade booze on the menu - either lemon wine or cherry leaf wine. I went for the latter, which somehow tasted of cherries and not leaves. It was fairly potent, but did the trick. A while late and dinner was produced - an old-fashioned hot pot. I'd obviously not told Jean that I didn't eat red meat, and didn't have the heart to tell her as she'd been so sweet. I ate lots of vegetables, and tried to avoid eating too much meat!

Leaving Jean and Donald's the next afternoon after lunch, I drove down towards Ganges, and back through the dramatic river gorges. With the window down and the warm air blowing I felt happy and positive about the future: I had transport now, a typically French 2CV which would make getting anywhere from Palavas so much easier.

Chapter 48

Sightseeing and work

The following weekend I made use of the car and drove the thirty or so kilometres west towards Sète. I'd read about it in my guide and it seemed the perfect place to spend a lazy hot Sunday. It was a port and was a breading ground for mussels and oysters. I managed to get there without getting lost but then drove round in a circle a couple of times trying to work out which bridge I had to cross to get into the centre. I found somewhere easily enough to park the car for free, and then set off towards the noise and smells. There were canals everywhere, lined with cafés and seafood restaurants. I found an inviting one and plonked myself down, ordered a *café au lait,* and watched the world go by. Sitting there I really couldn't believe how happy just being in France made me - I didn't have a job, knew nobody, but none of that seemed to matter.

After my lovely coffee I had a walk around the small town, ending up in the covered food market which was a delight. Deciding to continue west, I left Sète and headed toward Agde. I'd noticed on the map that a minor road ran right along the edge of the Mediterranean, with a lagoon to the right, so set off to find it. After a few more tours of the outskirts of the town I found it. Wow! What a beautiful drive it was. The road was perched a few metres up from a narrow stretch of beautiful white sand onto which lapped the most incredible turquoise water. I hadn't seen water like that since I'd been in Queensland. There were few cars on the road, and it was an uplifting, tranquil drive.

Agde itself was a sleepy fishing harbour, dominated by the volcanic Mont St. Loup. It was full of narrow lanes and an easy place to amble around. After having a walk round I decided to head just a little further and made for Cap d'Agde, a few kilometres away. It was a new resort, built up around a marina. The restaurants were full of noisy, Sunday lunchtime diners - couples, families and groups of friends. By this time I'd decided I'd had enough as they all looked so inviting and I yearned to be having lunch with someone. To stave away the gathering blues, I decided to head home to enjoy the scenery on the way.

The following week things started to fall into place. I had a successful interview at the Ecole Klesse, run by a man who appeared to know very little about English language teaching. I swallowed my pride and accepted the teaching hours he had on offer, at a ridiculous rate per hour as I needed to pay my rent and eat!

On the Friday, France Telecom were due to install a phone line, but to be honest I doubted whether they would show up, having already been warned about their inefficiency. I was sure that it couldn't be worse then in Portugal but Steph had first hand knowledge and so far hadn't proved me wrong. However, the polite, helpful engineer arrived on time, fiddled around with cables for a while, did some drilling (much to the delight of the cats, who tried to hide in a variety of places) and then announced I had a working line. A result - apart from the fact that I didn't have an actual phone, and hadn't even thought about it.

Having the car meant that it was no problem going to the well-named Jumbo hypermarket. Trying to avoid spending money on all the lovely produce, I headed to one of the little shops near the checkouts, which are such a part of continental supermarkets. I found a helpful assistant, who not only sold me a basic phone, but also advised me on an Internet package, and I went away a happy bunny. Having been talked through the steps needed to activate my email, and armed with a printed off sheet with all the numbers I needed to use, and passwords to enter, I started the task of trying to install it that afternoon. I wasn't at all sure if I'd manage it, with my limited computer skills and the instructions being in French, but I was slow and methodical and it worked. This may be not much to some people, but for me it was a major accomplishment.

I had a phone and a working email address, and they both made a huge difference knowing that I could keep in contact with family and friends so easily. Feeling buoyed up, I decided that I would go to a welcome event, run by the British Cultural Association in Montpellier. I'd read about it somewhere, and although I had no idea what it would be like, and certainly didn't want to get involved with a group of non-French speaking ex-pats, I hoped that it might be a way of meeting people and making some friends.

I drove from Palavas into Montpellier, but deciding that trying to park somewhere in the centre on a Friday would be a nightmare so left the car on the outskirts and hopped on the tram into the centre. Of course it meant that I could only have one drink, but maybe that was better than knocking them back and talking rubbish to people I didn't know. The event was held in a large room of some governmental building, and was a mixture of people who were obviously old hands, and new arrivals. I talked to lots of different people, three of whom became good friends - what's more they weren't all British. The first was an Algerian girl, Insaf, who had moved down from Paris and was also having a hard time making ends meet. The second was Bénédicte; a French girl who I discovered was also a lover of alternative cinema, so we became film-going friends. The last was Bob - we decided a long time after that first meeting that we probably saved each other from madness during the bleak winter which was to follow. Anyway, he was quite a bit older then me, dressed in a beige, linen suit, and looked as though he'd just stepped out of a Somerset Maugham novel. We got on immediately, and what was even better was that he also lived in Palavas. Yippee! I'd found a local partner in crime.

The following week brought my first teaching work at the Ecole Klesse. Since I'd already paid to drive to the tram stop, where I'd be able to park for free, and then paid for the tram, I'd arranged to meet Insaf, the Algerian girl I'd met the previous week. The trip was partly a success – the student didn't turn up but I spent a couple of hours chatting away amiably in French with my new friend. Throughout my time in France Insaf and I used French to communicate, which was great for me, and it was only months later that I discovered she spoke good English! Sometimes I really struggled when talking about complicated subjects, but she made me persist and I'm sure that really helped with my fluency. Apart from having a different language we also had completely different backgrounds. She was a Moslem and that meant she didn't drink. Not that it's the be all and end all, but I'd never had a friend who didn't drink. Sitting in the gorgeous square that first, sunny afternoon, there was only really one to thing to order and that was a beer. The fact that I did and Insaf didn't really wasn't an issue. It was just the way it was. Insaf and I became close friends, although it was a very different type of friendship from others I had had. I discovered many things about Algeria that I knew nothing about, both the politics and the day-to-day life.

Happy with a successful first chat and agreeing to meet again soon, I was also delighted when my phone rang. It was Mum saying that she and Gerald had arrived in Molières for a stay with Jean for a couple of days. I was so looking forward to seeing Mum: not only would it be the first time I'd seen her since Granddad's funeral back in the early summer, but also as she loved the Languedoc so much as well. In fact, some years before she and Dad had thought about buying a house, with Dad actually coming down to view a few properties. Unfortunately his illness put a stop to that.

The following day I drove up to Molières, enjoying the lovely scenery for the second time in as many weeks. Mum and Gerald were staying round the corner from Jean and Donald in the holiday house of friends. We had a pleasant evening, but before that I had a second encounter with the parents of my landlord, as we'd been invited for drinks. They proudly showed us around their somewhat bizarrely furnished house, and then almost bursting with pride showed us the *pièce de resistance* - a plastic trout which squirmed and played odd music. How are you supposed to keep a straight face? Maybe it explained the hideous piece of furniture in my flat - I bet it had come from them!

The following day was Saturday and the three of us went into the local town, Le Vigan. Mum and I then did what we as a family had always loved best and wandered around the food market. I hadn't been to that particular market for years, since I'd taken Mum and Dad up on their offer of a holiday with them and my brother. The market was busy and full of memories; before long the smells proved too much and we went in search of a restaurant. We drove to the other side of the valley, but the restaurant Mum had in mind was closed. Being in France and discussing food, a local recommended somewhere we might like to try. Thinking it was just round the corner we set off, climbing higher and higher up the valley and onto the plain. Convinced we were going wrong we were just about to turn round when we found the restaurant. It was a beautiful place, with a fantastic view of the gardens and countryside. The menu was short, but the food was fantastic!

Having seen Mum and Gerald I felt far happier and settled, and not as alone as I'd felt in the first few weeks. The next evening helped even more. I'd arranged to meet Bob in his local café in Palavas which was on the other side of the canal to me. He knew the owners well, and happily introduced me to everyone, with much kissing and practising of French. I felt very puffed up when they commented on how good my accent was compared to Bob's!

Bob and I sat outside the café swapping basic life stories, and getting to know each other. Unfortunately, he had plans for that evening, so we agreed to meet again soon, and I walked up to the beach for a stroll in the evening sun. On the way back I bumped into him, which resulted in the best, and very drunken evening I had had since arriving in France. We went back to the café as his plans had changed, and had another beer. There were discussions going on about the butcher - it was his birthday and his friends in the café wanted to see him. They phoned him trying to persuade him and his wife to join us as champagne had just been opened. They couldn't be cajoled, as they had family there, including their daughter and her fiancé who was Italian, but did say that after we had finished our bubbles we should go round to their flat to say hello. I obviously felt a bit awkward but was scooped up, and about twelve of us set off for the butcher's. They lived in a large flat, with a huge wall to wall window directly overlooking the sea. I thought we would maybe be offered a birthday drink, but the butcher's wife announced she would cook for us all!

We settled down on the many sofas and chairs, and were

poured large glasses of wine. Although I didn't know a soul there, and had only spent a couple of hours with Bob, the atmosphere was warm and friendly. I spoke loads of French, and was soon accepted as part of the clan. Before long dinner arrived; it wasn't just a bowl of pasta - which is maybe what anyone else would rustle up at the last minute, but a four course meal for sixteen. We had a lovely salad and goat's cheese starter, coated in a gorgeous dressing, a proper Italian Spaghetti Bolognese (or Ragu as the Italians say), followed by a strawberry pudding and then a French cheese board. Oh la la, is all I can say. To finish us off completely we then had coffee and homemade Limoncello.

Completely pissed, Bob and I finally left, thanking and kissing everyone profusely, and staggered into the night. Bob announced that he would walk me home, and as we were walking up his side of the canal he promptly fell over. He was horribly embarrassed but I was too pissed to care, and just stood there laughing uncontrollably. I managed to persuade him not to walk me home as I was worried he would fall into the canal, and we both wobbled to our respective homes.

The following week was the first one when I actually worked. I had classes on Tuesday morning, and Thursday afternoon and evening. Whilst the school was lacking in many areas, the students were fine, and with my teaching experience, they were easy classes.

The first Thursday evening class finished at eight o'clock, and I rushed off to get back to Palavas as Mum and Gerald had arrived that afternoon from Molières. They had successfully installed themselves in the seafront hotel I had booked for them, and we had arranged to meet in a local restaurant for dinner at nine. As I walked round the corner to the tramway, which until then had run like a dream, I was horrified to find most of Montpellier waiting at the stop. It was clear that nothing was going to happen, so I went in search of a taxi. I joined a queue at a rank, and as you do in such situations started talking to the person next to me. A girl was going in the same direction as me so we shared a cab.

Disaster was averted and I met up with Mum and Gerald and we spent a pleasant evening together, especially as I was treated to dinner and ate a huge bowl of *moules frites*. We spent the following three days together, and I was taken to more local restaurants which up until then I had walked passed, looking longingly at the menus and in through the windows. I decided to be brave one evening and cook in my rabbit hutch of a flat. Everything was going fine with my Moroccan chicken dish until the gas canister ran out. I absolutely hated the system, and although had used a heater with a gas canister very recently in Portugal, it had been years ago when I first lived in Portugal that the hot water and cooking relied on the stupid things. It took a couple of days for canisters to be delivered and the garage wasn't open so we had to abandon dinner and go out!

Apart from eating out we also had a couple of trips. One was locally, and a short drive from Palavas along one of the lagoons. It was lovely that so quickly you could leave the bustle of a seaside town, full of people and shops selling tat (even in the south of France this happened) and be transported to a place of quiet and calm. We were visiting the Cathédral de Maguelone, which was built in the 12th Century and stood on an island in the middle of the marshland. I'd never been there before, but Mum and Dad had years before, when Matthew had sung there as part of a choir visit. In the heat of the day, it was somewhere to escape to. The cathedral was surrounded by a ring of pine trees and was cool, quiet and dark. I suddenly felt sad and reflective, and left Mum and Gerald to be on my own. I guess it was knowing that Dad had been there many years before with Mum, and that now she was there with someone else that had got to me.

Another place I hadn't visited before was Arles - most famous as one of Van Gogh's homes. The day before Mum left, we had a lovely drive eastwards towards the Camargue. We passed Aigues-Mortes, which I had visited a few weeks previously. It was built in the 13th Century as a fortress port. It was mainly in tact and the amazingly wide walls still surrounded the town. Whilst the lovely old walls and towers stood imposingly overlooking the plains, inside there were thousands of tourists who had been tipped out of coaches and were fighting to get into the small shops.

From there we continued through the lovely, hot, still day, and into the Carmague. We crossed the Petit Rhóne, and then headed inland away from the lagoons, arriving in Arles. First stop was the Roman Amphitheatre, the Arènes, which was built at the end of the 1st Century. It was a huge place; apparently it had once held two hundred houses and three churches. After the dwellings had been removed it could hold twenty thousand spectators. We sat on the concrete steps and I daydreamed about all that must have happened there, although tried not to linger on the bull fighting which still took place. I could have happily sat there for ages but Gerald was getting twitchy so we left.

We slowly wandered through the lovely town, and came to the cathedral. The doorway was stunning, with the stone carving depicting the Last Judgement. It was a riot of angels, trumpeting the good going upwards and the naughty ones going down to hell. Crickey. In sharp contrast were the beautiful, serene cloisters which we escaped into.

After this it was art time, and the Arles of Van Gogh. Unfortunately, much of the river front and the bars he had depicted were destroyed in World War II, but what remained was the square and café he had painted; the *Café de Nuit*. It was in the Place du Forum, a large square lined with shops and bars, and we sat in the middle admiring the yellow facade which was exactly as it looked in the painting. It seemed only fitting to try and get into the spirit of things, so I ordered the drink of the region, and no doubt a few glasses of what the man himself had drunk, Pastis. This was what France was about - sitting in a traditional square, in the heat of a late summer afternoon, feeling as though you could be part of a painting.

Chapter 49

French friendships

Mum and Gerald left the following day, and for me it was back to my few classes, trying to find more work and building friendships. I met up with Bob frequently and also saw Insaf and Bénédicte. One Wednesday, Bob took me to a bar in Montpellier, wonderfully named the Arceaux, where during Happy Hour a mixture of locals and ex-pats met up to chat. The bar was situated on the outskirts of the town, next to the Viaduct. It was nothing special, very cramped and always full of smoke, but instantly welcoming. That first time I went it was still warm enough to sit outside and when we arrived a number of tables had already been joined together, and there was lots of chatting going on in a variety of languages, and a fair bit of drinking. This was a proper Happy Hour, none of your reduced price drinks, but two for the price of one, and you didn't have to pay, in true continental style until the end of the night. I met a wide range of people there, some who I could easily chat to week after week, and some who became good friends. They were Susanna, from Melbourne, and Deming who was American. There was also a group who regularly went to the cinema, which meant I had more companions for watching films.

After the first week, Bob and I took turns to drive, and it

was a mid-week gathering which I really looked forward to. By the end of October I was starting to make a good group of friends, and even went to a Guy Fawkes Party with Bob. This was all a bit ex-pat for me, but the highlight was when a local must have called the fire brigade seeing a field on fire! The firemen weren't particularly impressed and really couldn't understand why a group of foreigners would want to stand in the middle of a field around a bonfire, on a damp night, eating undercooked sausages and drinking warm white wine - come to think of it neither could I. The best thing was when they tried to leave and the fire engine got stuck in the mud.

By November, work was on the up and I had managed to find some private students, which I could fit in around my school work and was much more lucrative. One girl was the one I shared a taxi with when the tram hadn't worked a month and a half previously, who needed some help with a presentation, and another I had bumped into at the school who was horrified at the price they were trying to charge her for private lessons. And that was where I stepped in. We agreed on a price which suited both of us, and had the lessons in her flat in the new part of town which was easy for me to get to. She was a wonderful student, focussed and interesting. This was in sharp contrast to another one. Susanna, one of the new friends I'd made, had passed him onto me as she didn't need the extra work and had had enough. I could see why.

On a Friday I went to his house, which was enormous and guarded by an equally enormous Alsatian. Fortunately, the dog decided I was his new best friend, and draped himself over me at any opportunity. The lessons lasted for three hours, which is any teacher's nightmare, especially when you're not allowed to have any structure. Basically, Daniel, who was in his sixties, and an interesting character, was very fixed in his views. For the lesson, he would previously have chosen an English broadsheet, highlighted certain articles, and would read them out to me, wanting to know the minutest of details about a particular word or phrase. It was like being a walking dictionary and grammar book. Just to make the three hours even more surreal he had very extreme views on just about everything, and frequently said the most outrageous things! But hey, it was money!

Of course, just when things are settling down, a huge spanner appeared in the works. Having been used to driving to the last stop on the tram, parking for free, and then getting the tram into the centre, I turned up one day to find that the council were now charging for parking. Damn and damn again. I certainly couldn't afford to pay for all day parking, or maybe it was that it meant there would be less money for treats. So, I had to figure out another option. I settled on driving to a tram stop a bit closer into town; there was a road next to some waste ground where I had seen people parking their cars for free. So, I did that for a couple of weeks until one afternoon I returned to the car to find the window had been smashed. Bloody hell, why me, and why on earth smash the window of an old Renault Five. I drove back to Palavas feeling extremely pissed off, reported the incident to the police, and then phoned up Bob, who took me out for a beer to try and cheer me up.

By then it was the middle of November, and Palavas had unfortunately gone the way of other summer seaside towns. Most of the bars and nearly all the canal side shops had shut for the winter, giving that miserable air. There was only really one bar open, which was regularly frequented by a wide range of unsavoury characters, and where it was often impossible to have a quiet drink without being interrupted. But it did for that night, I and drowned my sorrows.

I got the glass replaced in the window, and then came up with the next plan which was to avoid the tramway altogether, and try and park close enough to the centre of town so I could walk. The best place seemed to be near my student, Daniel's house. It meant a twenty minute walk into town, but saved money. Except that there was another little surprise in store. One day I got back to the car to discover a parking ticket - for the love of God......! There were no obvious markings on the road, so I checked with Daniel. For all his annoyances as a student he was very sweet and kind and tried to save me from a hefty fine. He phoned up the relevant department, and checked the markings which despite being almost illegible and invisible were there, so I couldn't avoid it and had to cough up. More money down the drain.

Fortunately a little distraction was on the way. That weekend I had a trip to Paris organised. I'd arranged to meet up with Steph, who by then had moved back to France and was living in her home town of Rennes, so could easily get to the capital. Her brother had a flat overlooking the Arch de Triomphe, so we didn't have to pay for a hotel. So, on the last day of November I caught the early TGV from Montpellier which left on time and swished its way through the countryside.

The trip was due to last about three and a half hours, and with no changes I settled down to enjoy being on a clean, French, on time train, and of course, the scenery. We were doing very well, until charging through a field the train suddenly stopped for half an hour. Bloody hell. However, in sharp contrast to British rail or whatever they call themselves these days, an announcement came over the tannoy to explain what was happening, how long we would be delayed, and then to remind us to go to a booth in the station on arrival where we could collect an envelope and send off our tickets to receive a cheque for compensation. I was convinced my French had let me down; being offered compensation!

I duly found the office, sent off my envelope and a few days later got my cheque. Amazing! Anyway, I wandered around the station for a while, trying to work out where to go, and before long emerged from the Metro at the end of the Champs Élysées facing the Arch de Triomphe. It was a spectacular view, as ever. And then the best thing; there was Steph. It was just so good to see an old friend again. Five minutes later, and I had a different view of Paris; this time looking down from the tiny flat that was squeezed up in the roof of an old government building. Steph and I were staying at one of her brother's flats, along with her other brother who I had met a fair few times in Portugal who had also come with her from Rennes.

Paris was as lovely as ever, despite the rain that fell for the weekend. It was the first time I'd been there and done nothing touristy, but it was great just wandering around, going to cafés and chilling out. On the Saturday night the four of us went to a local restaurant, free of tourists. The food was great, the atmosphere noisy and happy, and after a few bottles of wine I realised that despite not having much of a clue what Steph and her brothers were talking about, because of the slang and family jokes, that I really didn't care. It was just great, being able to really relax with an old friend, and her brothers.

The next day it was still raining, so after a coffee in a lovely (well to me) Parisian café, we drove over to the left bank and did exactly what you should do there, and hung out. Driving back we got caught in a horrendous Sunday afternoon traffic jam, but at least that meant that we could enjoy all the fabulous Christmas windows in the shops, and the lights which had been turned on that day. Knackered from the night before and the wandering in the rain, we bought beer and pizza, and together with the boys all snuggled up to watch a film.

It was all a bit of a shock to get back to the reality of my tiny flat, and the running around Montpellier from one class to a private student to another student. And then, to top it all on one wet night in December I managed to crunch the car. It was my turn to drive Bob and myself to meet our Wednesday group, and it was pissing down. On the way home, rather than dropping Bob at the bridge I drove him to his door. As I continued to the end of the road and drove onto the seafront, the visibility was so bad I turned left into a concrete bollard. O boll.......s! The following day, I inspected the damage. It wasn't good. I'd ripped the black rubber strip completely off, the door and the sill below it were badly buckled, the rain had got in, and to top it all it wasn't my car. It was great having the use of the car, but I seriously wondering whether it was worth it. But if I didn't use it then I wouldn't be able to get into Montpellier easily, and the busses stopped early evening so I wouldn't be able to get back home after finishing teaching late, etc, etc. The doubts started to creep in then, and I first really started thinking that the whole moving to France idea might not have been such a good one.

Fortunately, the rest of December wasn't as problematic, and I spent some happy evenings with my new friends. I'd also decided that regardless of how much it cost I was determined to go back to the UK for Christmas. Apart from that cost, I needed to find Jack and Melton somewhere to stay as there wasn't anyone to look after them. I discovered a local cattery, and went to have a look. Really bizarrely, and unlike anything I'd seen in the UK, all the cats were in together. I felt very sceptical about it, knowing how much some cats hate other cats, and how much of a scaredy cat Melton was. I didn't really feel I had much of a choice as I needed to get away for my sanity, but Melton certainly wasn't impressed when I picked them up after Christmas, and had apparently spent the entire time hiding underneath a blanket in her box. Jack on the other hand decided she was *Top Cat*, had entertained everybody, and made the place her own.

It was fantastic to be back in the UK, and to see family and friends. I stayed at Mum's, which was empty as by then she was living with Gerald. My brother Matthew arrived on the 23rd; and then Will arrived on Christmas Eve. Despite the difficulties we'd had when he'd helped me move, (well to be honest that I had with him because of my relationship with Mark), we'd decided he would have Christmas with us. Christmas Eve was a blur, as the three of us indulged way too much, and were therefore all feeling very un-Christmassy the following morning. Not helped was that fact that Gerald had insisted on having the Christmas meal at his house, so we had to drive the forty-five minutes there.

Christmas Day can be fraught at the best of times, although in recent years we'd managed to have some really good ones. The most memorable being when Granddad was still alive, and Matt had fallen asleep in his trifle. This one was memorable for all the wrong reasons though. It was very regimented, and if we as much suggested that it would be good to have a drink before lunch, got a serious 'Paddington' stare from Gerald. It also meant that we had to toss as to who would drive. It fell to Will, so he was on his starting block as soon as he'd swallowed the last piece of pudding. Can't say I blame him!

The rest of the holiday was great; Will stayed for another couple of days and I then travelled all over the place to see friends. Best of all was seeing Charlie and Carina who I hadn't seen since they'd left Portugal the previous February. Before long my break was over, and it was back to France. It was the first time that I'd ever returned abroad not really knowing what was going to happen. If I was perfectly honest the only thing I was really looking forward to was seeing my two silly feline friends.

Chapter 50

A French farewell

Snowing! It was snowing in the south of France. What on earth was going on? I woke up on the Monday morning, to the familiar stillness, and weird light you get. Of course I didn't really believe it, but there it was as I drew the curtains. Not just a smattering but a foot of the stuff. How had that happened? The previous day was chilly, but the sky was brilliant blue and the sun was shining. I'd wandered round a huge flea market with Susanna, had lunch and I then met other friends at the cinema. I was feeling more positive and had more work lined up starting the Monday morning with a private student.

However, that had to be put on hold. As well as there being a foot of snow, I'd also developed a shocking cold and thought that my head was going to fall off. There was no way I was going anywhere. I curled up on the sofa with the cats and endless cups of tea, and watched French telly.

I tried again the following morning. Unfortunately, as I hadn't cleared the snow the car was covered in half a foot of ice. In the south of France you don't have scrapers and de-icer, so I had to raid the kitchen drawer for something. Hacking away at ice with a table knife is not recommended. It took ages, and the windscreen wipers were well and truly b......d. There was worse to come. I gingerly drove out of Palavas and onto the duel carriageway which led to Montpellier. There had obviously been no gritting or de-icing vehicles, and all of a sudden I was spinning in the car and heading toward a deep ditch at the end of the road. Somehow I came to a stop at the edge of the road, facing in the wrong direction. Amazingly nothing hit me, so very shaken up, I slowly continued. As I approached the next exit I could feel it was about to happen again, and by then thoroughly scared, I left the main road, turned round and went home.

It wasn't the start to the New Year back in France I'd have picked. I was fed up and cold in my pokey flat. I even had to venture out again later in the afternoon as I'd promised to pick Bob up from the airport. Fortunately by then most of the ice had turned to slush and I didn't do any more unplanned spins.

The next hurdle was the flat situation. As well as being outside town, which was really starting to get me down, it had other downsides. There only being one door between the bedroom and the rest of the flat meant that when Jack, my naughty cat, woke up in the early hours and decided to walk over my head and generally stop me from sleeping there was nowhere to put her. If I shut her out of my bedroom she'd just claw at the door. It got so bad that sometimes I'd have to put her in her cat box on the balcony to get some peace and quiet. Not really a solution especially when it rained. The other problem was that the flat next door was occupied by drug takers, and I thought pushers. They'd come and go at all hours of the night and day and because the access to the flats was a walkway past my bedroom I'd wake up every time. I was thoroughly pissed off, so decided to look for a flat to rent in Montpellier itself.

The following week I went into town and started the hunt,

which was completely fruitless. At least I'd arranged to meet up with Insaf for a drink. She didn't really have any advice apart from not paying out for a subscription of a list of places for rent, which when you phoned had already gone. Guess what? I'd just done it.

Something else I'd done was to organise another way to bring more money in. The previous weekend Bob had taken me to a small, traditional French restaurant in the old quarter. We had a lovely meal and afterwards I met the owners, who were also the chef and the manager. Following a brief chat I had a job as Commis Chef and Pot Woman. After a busy work teaching I worked in the restaurant on the Saturday lunchtime and evening service, and the Sunday lunchtime. There were some enjoyable parts, when I plated up tasty starters, but the filling and unloading of the dishwasher, polishing of the glasses and cutlery was hot and boring beyond words. I was also completely knackered!

There was, though, the promise of something a little more exciting. It came in the shape of a tall, gorgeous, green-eyed Frenchman called Guillaume. I'd met him once at the Wednesday night drinks before Christmas and was hoping to see him again. In the middle of January he turned up. Yippee! We chatted away about books and films and food and suddenly Wednesdays were even more appealing. But, there was a huge spanner in the works which jumped out of the toolbox a week later.

It was my second weekend working at the restaurant. I'd done a full week of teaching, and then worked both shifts on the Saturday. On the Sunday morning before going to the restaurant I'd organised to see a flat in town. It was pissing down and the south of France was grey and cold. It took me a while to find the flat, and when I did my heart sank. The front door was hanging off; the whole place looked run down, and the person I'd arranged to meet didn't show up.

Later at work when I was loading the dishwasher, my own grey cloud settled well and truly over me. What on earth was I doing with my life? I hadn't changed career, worked hard, done an MA, to be washing dishes to make ends meet. I struggled through the lunchtime service, fighting back the tears, and just wanting to not be there. As I walked back to the car it starting pissing down, and the flood gates opened. I howled and howled and realised that I really wasn't very happy and that I needed to make some big decisions. The only answer that kept popping into my head that I was going to have to admit defeat and leave France. I phoned Mum when I got home in a tearful state, and said that all I wanted was to be able to talk to Dad. And it was true; I just felt that he was the only one who could make it all better. But he wasn't there, so Mum listened to me rambling on, and told me she'd support me in whatever decision I'd make.

Waking up on the Monday morning I was considerably calmer, but the same solution was still there. I went and did my morning class, and then decided to go to the cinema to try and clear my head. I sat through the second part of *Lord of the Rings*, which completely absorbed me, and forgot all of my troubles. I emerged from the cinema into the daylight, everything was crystal clear and I felt happy and relieved.

My dream of living in France was over. I decided to admit defeat and leave, but at least I'd tried and given it my best shot. With my decision made I then had to figure out what I was going to do, where I was going to go and how I was going to do it. I felt that I really needed some time out to decide what to do next, so when Mum said that I was more than welcome to stay at her house in Chichester, which was empty I was tempted. I pondered it for a while; the plus sides were I'd have a lovely to house to stay in for a while, I'd be in a place which was familiar, and I'd have Lisa, my close friend from school nearby. The downsides were I'd be back in the UK unexpectedly, I'd be in a town, well city, which was small and provincial, somehow I'd have to get all my stuff back, and what on earth was I going to do about my four-legged sillies?!

Familiarity won and I spent the next few days researching international removal companies for all my stuff and a way back for the cats. The stuff wasn't that difficult and I found a good quote but the cats were trickier. Since I'd never had any intention of moving back to the UK, it meant that they would have to go into quarantine for six months. So, I had to find somewhere they could stay which wasn't too far from Chichester, organise all the documentation and book them on a flight. What a bloody nightmare, and a very expensive one.

From making the decision to leave and finally going took a month. I worked at the school until the 12th February, and only did a few more shifts at the restaurant. Making the decision meant that I was much happier and calmer than I had been.

I had lots of teaching work and was busy socially - I even went to a Burn's Night party. Another distraction was Guillaume. I'd seen him each week at our Wednesday evening gatherings in January, and after some fairly full-on flirting we finally arranged to meet on our own in a bar in Montpellier. It was a success and over the following few weeks we spent loads of time together; going out for dinner and talking about music, films, travelling and every subject under the sun, going to the cinema and even salsa dancing. He was a work of genius on the dance floor; unlike myself who kept standing on his toes, and had to stop myself from dribbling as he looked so gorgeous! However, nothing had happened. Not even a kiss. Just lots of companionship and laughing. I was rather confused about it, and even more when my friend Deming figured out who he was. It turned out that a friend of hers was going out with Guillaume's brother, and she gave me all the gossip. Apparently he was arrogant, self-obsessed, a womaniser and had said that he only went out with models. Well!! I certainly wasn't a model, and he certainly hadn't come across like this. Since I was soon to be leaving I decided to try and not think about the strange contrast and just enjoy his company.

Obviously, there wasn't just Guillaume to spend time with. I had all my other friends to see, and of course Bob. I also had a broken and bashed car door to replace and after tearing round all over the place to different scrap yards I finally found a replacement one for the Renault, and got it fitted. I could then take the car back up to my Godmother's house. However, before that it was removal day.

I'd given the company an estimate of the pieces of furniture and the number of boxes. Of course, my stuff seemed to be multiplying in size by the hour. There were some belongings that had to be boxed and sent – my stereo, kitchen equipment, photo albums, books, clothes, nick knacks but other stuff I really didn't want to be parted with. Someone else might not think that piles and piles of back issues of Empire (a movie magazine) I'd hoarded over the years were vital but there was no way I was going to be parted with them. I boxed and re-boxed, and was then left with enough clothes and basics for the remaining week and a half I had in France, and a mountain of other possessions. I got my friends round and they went away loaded with rugs, a cat box, a deckchair, and various other goodies.

I knew that my belongings were a part consignment and would only take up a small area of the van going back to the UK, but had no idea of the size of the lorry which would arrive. I was slightly worried as the streets in Palavas near the canal and sea front were narrow with acute angles. On answering the entry phone the removers were horrified that there were three flights of stirs with no lift, and I was horrified by the size of the van. I had never seen such an enormous one in my entire life. It had taken them ages to get it into my road because of the angles, and then they had to park it. What I was also worried about was how they were going to turn into the road next to the canal and then over the bridge and out of the town. But that wasn't my problem. What I had to do was to try and persuade the two removal men that I had informed the company I was on the third floor and there was no lift. They huffed and puffed and moaned, but finally it was done.

I was right to be worried about them being able to leave. They drove off and five minutes later were ringing on the door to say that they couldn't get round the corner as there was a car in the way. For the love of God! I don't know what they expected me to do - pick up the car and move it out of the way, maybe?

I was left with a very empty, soulless flat, and a few days later was car less as well. I could have driven the car up to Molières on my own but there wasn't any public transport to return so Bob kindly said he'd follow me and then drive me back. What a star! The weather was superb, bright and sunny, and very mild. With Bob behind me I drove the now fairly familiar route up into the Cévennes mountains, passed Le Vigan and up to Molières. I carefully parked the Renault (which I'd all but wrecked and now had a number of new parts, including a brown passenger door - the Renault was red) in the old square near my godmother's house and posted the keys though the letter box. Not wanting to waste the lovely day, we decided that we should do what every respectable French person does on a Sunday and have lunch. We stopped in St-Martin-de-Londres. which was a beautiful little town full of alleyways and intriguing old buildings. We found a little restaurant, and enjoyed one of our final meals together.

Up until then I had been so caught up with working, organising leaving, seeing Guillaume and friends, the reality hadn't really set in. Now I was car less, furniture less, only had one last lesson with Daniel, and that was it. My French dream was over. I'd left Portugal and my good job, flat, friends, entire life to move to France, on what I now recognise was a whim and completely mad. It was all coming to an end, and although I knew that the work I had would never be secure enough long-term, I was having a good time. I'd made friendships which were growing, and was still loving being in France.

The last thing to do was to take the cats to the airport. I'd booked them on a flight five days before me so I'd know they'd arrived safely. It had taken me ages to sort out their flight, collection from the airport and transfer to a cattery where they would go into quarantine. Mum, bless her, had already been to check the cattery out and was happy that it was well run. It would have to be as they were going to be there for six months, the poor things! There was also all the paperwork, but my contact in the UK had assured me everything was in order and that as the cats were going straight into quarantine they didn't need to visit a vet beforehand. However, if I can worry about something then I will. Having delivered the car it was them I was now concerned about.

Clutching all the documents and herding the cats into their new enormous box, I struggled down the three flights of stairs and then Bob and I managed to squeeze them into his car. Fortunately, it was only a short drive to the airport, and we easily found the cargo area where they had to be delivered to. We walked into the office, and I explained where they were going and handed over the documents. One young guy was friendly and helpful, and I started to relax. Mistake! Then a rather officious (not exactly a surprise in France) lady told me that the documents weren't correct and that there should be a certificate from the vet. At that point I was ready to burst into tears but managed to explain (with most of my French vocabulary disserting me) that I had been assured that as they were going into quarantine there was no vet visit necessary. The official ummed and aahed (or whatever they do in French), and then agreed to phone my contact in the UK, who she was clearly used to speaking to. After what seemed like long enough to eat French Sunday lunch she came off the phone and said everything was ok. Praise the Lord for that. With a last stroke though the grills I left my sillies in the care of the ground staff, in readiness for their first flight. I knew Jack would take it all in her stride and be thankful for a long interrupted sleep, but couldn't imagine what Melton would make of it all.

Rather traumatised, it seemed alcohol was needed. As it was Wednesday it meant a last visit to *Les Arceaux* to my friends there. Bob drove so I could drink, and we had an enjoyable, noisy evening followed by dinner at the pizza place around the corner we often went to, and where the restaurant staff were used to us moving the tables round. Towards the end of the evening Guillaume turned up, much to everyone's amusement and whisked me off for a drink. We had a good time but still nothing was happening! Talk about frustrated and confused. Maybe he did only go out with models, but why then were we spending so much time together, and visible to all?

A few days later and it was my last weekend in France. I had a lazy lunch on the Friday with Bénédicte, and then in the evening saw Guillaume again. Still nothing! And then on the Saturday, I think I may have right royally messed things up. We went for a blustery walk by the sea and ended up going for a drink, as the sun was setting, to the converted water tower in Palavas. I'd been there before with Mum and Gerald and we'd had dinner as the restaurant slowly revolved giving us views of Palavas, the marina and sea and finally Montpellier. That Saturday, though, Guillaume and I sat in the bar area chatting easily about what the future might hold for both of us, and how I was feeling about leaving France. Then out of the blue, he looked straight at me and rather seriously said, "Do you want to get married and have children?" I responded, jokingly, by saying that I didn't want that at all. I didn't really know what else to say, and the children part was true. We carried on talking, but there was a weird atmosphere and before long Guillaume left as he had friends to meet. Oh my God! Had he actually been asking me a personal question? I feared that he might have, and I'd practically laughed in his face. Not much I could do about it though. Maybe I'd just have to make a move and see what happened.

The following day Deming and Susanna came round for Sunday lunch - we had a long boozy meal, tying to figure out where Guillaume was coming from, and generally chatted about trivial stuff. Early evening Susanna drove us into Montpellier, and saying a fond farewell to the pair of them and handing over a wad of cash to Susanna, as she was going to pay my outstanding bills, I was dropped off in the centre where I was meeting Guillaume. I'm sure I was still rather pissed so was flirty and silly for most of the evening. We went to a bar for a drink, which I definitely didn't need and then to a traditional restaurant for a lovely meal which Guillaume treated me to. I had a gorgeous plate of monkfish, and in best French tradition he had *Steak Haché* (for the uninitiated, raw chopped mince with an egg on top!) He drove me back to Palavas late in the evening and willingly came up to the flat.

What happened next was certainly weird, but at least it wasn't a normal end to my time in France. Guillaume complained of an aching back, so I told him to lie on my bed and I'd give him a massage. He willingly agreed, so I assumed that finally we'd do what was natural! After a long massage I kissed the back of his neck, to which he jumped up like a startled cat, threw his shirt back on and said he had to leave. Oh! Not quite the reaction I was expecting. Anyway not much I could do so we said goodnight and I crawled into bed on my own.

I'd hoped I'd have the morning to myself to mull things over, and do any final packing in peace before going to the airport, but that wasn't to be. By arrangement, Bob came over to pick up some final things I was donating to his cause, and to say goodbye, as he had a friend staying. Then, then much earlier than planned my landlord and also his parents turned up. I could have really done without the small talk as my head was throbbing with all the booze from the day before and at the same time full of thoughts about the evening before, and I still had too much to do. In the midst of it all, Guillaume turned up, as arranged, to take me to the airport.

It was all rather strange in the car, after the fun of squashing all my stuff in; I apologised if I'd embarrassed him to which he replied that was nothing to be embarrassed about. So, that was that. There was the usual battle with the check-in girl who said I had excess luggage. Well - of course I did. Didn't she know I always did? Although most of my stuff had gone in the removal van, I still needed clothes, essentials and my bedding. Explaining this in my best French, and with help from Guillaume who with one look of his green eyes, and a flash of his smile which could melt the hardest heart, the girl said I didn't need to pay an excess. She did, though, say that the next time I would have to pay. I certainly hoped there would never be a next time, and that if I did live in France again I wouldn't be leaving.

Saying goodbye to Guillaume was weird after everything

that had happened, but not at all emotional. It was saying goodbye to Bob who was dropping his friend off at the airport too, which was harder. He had been my friend round the corner when either of us had needed a beer, taken me to the Wednesday group where I'd made friends and once we'd established the boundaries after he'd made a drunken pass, had been the closet of pals.

Walking into the departure lounge and waving goodbye I didn't know if I'd ever see either of them again, or any of the friends I'd made. I sat on the plane willing the drinks trolley to hurry up, as despite the hangover I desperately needed a drink to stop the tears I'd been fighting for the previous couple of hours.

Epilogue

- Having returned to the UK in 2003, I moved to London in August, together with my cats after their six-month stay in quarantine. I got a job as a Director of Studies at a school in Clapham and since then have stayed in education. I am currently working as an International Contract Manager in a large college - what's more I occasionally get trips abroad.

- On a more personal note, I met the person I thought was the love of my life - because of his concerns about his relationship with his children I also lost him. We struggled for a long time with our feelings.

- On a more positive note I have continued travelling abroad, and have managed to tick off a few places from my list. Nice (for the Matisse museum), Barcelona, Cape Town, Egypt and Petra in Jordan. I even spent two weeks in Colombia!

- I haven't been back to Montpellier but have kept in touch with some of the friends made there, and met up twice with Deming in London.

- I have made many trips back to Portugal - the most important being when Clare and Russ finally got married.

Will I now stay in the UK for ever? Somehow I very much doubt it!

Rachael Gurney

London, 2009

Lightning Source UK Ltd.
Milton Keynes UK
25 June 2010

156100UK00001B/1/P